FOLLOW ME II

Aubrey S. "Red" Newman was immortalized in this poster from the "U.S. Army in Action" series titled "Follow Me!" The artist depicted then Colonel Newman urging soldiers of the 34th Infantry Regiment, which he commanded at the time of the Philippines landings on 20 October 1944, to "Get up and get moving: Follow Me!" Newman hit the beach with the fifth wave of troops to land on Leyte's Red Beach, where Gen. Douglas MacArthur later made his promised "return" to the Philippines. When Newman saw the men of his regiment pinned down by withering Japanese fire, he quickly realized their only hope was to clear the beach immediately and press inland. He says his actual words (subject to a little "genteel censorship") were, "Get the hell off the beach! God damn it, get up and get moving—Follow me!"

FOLLOW ME II

More on the Human Element in Leadership

Maj. Gen. Aubrey S. "Red" Newman, USA (Ret.)

★
PRESIDIO

The text of this book represents a selection of the author's "The Forward Edge" columns originally published in *ARMY* magazine and its predecessors, the *Infantry Journal* and the *Armed Forces Journal*. Return of copyright from the original publisher is gratefully acknowledged.

Library of Congress Cataloging-in-Publication Data

Newman, Aubrey S., 1903-
    Follow me II : more on the human element in leadership / by Aubrey S. "Red" Newman.
       p.   cm.
    "Originally published in Army and its predecessors, the Infantry Journal, and the Armed Forces journal" T.p. verso.
    ISBN 0-89141-472-X
    1. Leadership. 2. United States. Army—Management. 3. United States. Army—Military life. 4. Newman, Aubrey S., 1903-
I. Title.
UB210.N478 1992
355.3'3041—dc20
                                                        92-16711
                                                         CIP

"To the Ultimate Weapon" (Appendix B) copyright ©Anthony L. P. Wermuth. Reprinted by permission.

Typography by ProImage
Printed in the United States of America

To
Sergeant Charles E. Mower
34th Infantry
Medal of Honor
(Posthumous)
3 November 1944

Contents

Preface

This book, *Follow Me II,* and its predecessors, *Follow Me* and *What Are Generals Made of?* are collections of my "Forward Edge" column that ran in *ARMY* magazine for more than twenty-one years—from September 1966 to January 1988. The primary theme concerns the human element in military service.

Like my first two books, *Follow Me II* reflects my life in uniform—centered around my branch, the Infantry. Beginning with my first duty assignment, with school troops at The Infantry School, my infantry career can be summed up as follows:

- Served in eight infantry companies, and commanded three of them for a total of five years.
- Served in eight infantry regiments, and commanded three of them:
    34th Infantry in New Guinea and the Philippines
    511th Airborne Infantry, 11th Airborne Division
    505th Airborne Infantry, 82d Airborne Division
- Ranks held in the infantry:
    10 years as a lieutenant
    5 years as a captain
    10 months as a major (est)
    7 months as a lieutenant colonel (est)
    10 years as a colonel

Of all the assignments an infantry colonel can have, being a regimental commander is the finest—and most testing. At Hollandia in New Guinea, during World War II when I was chief of staff of the 24th Infantry Division there, a sudden crisis developed in my infantry career.

When the Eighth Army was activated in 1944 our I Corps commander, Lt. Gen. Robert L. Eichelberger, was given that command—and the usual "musical chairs" action followed

As the senior major general in I Corps, my division commander moved up and assumed command—taking me along as his chief of staff. This virtually assured me of a brigadier general's star if I could do the job. But, instead of being pleased over that possibility, I was unhappy.

The reason was simple: If that happened I could never become a combat infantryman as a regimental commander in battle (a star could always come later—if that was in the cards). Unfortunately for my division commander, but lucky for me, a new I Corps commander was ordered in a week later—and we returned to our division.

Soon after our return I was honored with a regimental command in New Guinea. Several chapters in Part Three of this book record my combat experience in that proud estate—as commander of the 34th Infantry on Leyte during Gen. Douglas MacArthur's famous "return" to the Philippines in October 1944.

Aubrey S. "Red" Newman
Major General, U.S. Army
Retired

PART I
PRIMARILY COMPANY-LEVEL TOPICS

1

Look Ahead

FIFTY-FOUR YEARS ago a young soldier stood in front of my desk, when I was commander of Company G, 26th Infantry. His uniform was freshly pressed, brass shined, his bearing and manner the picture of a soldier when he reported, "Sir, Specialist McGarvey has permission of the first sergeant to speak to the company commander."

So I said, "What is it, McGarvey?"

"Sir, I request a transfer out of the kitchen. There is no place for me to go there. But if I transfer to a duty platoon, I might make corporal."

I approved his request, and he did "make corporal"—and sergeant, too.

This involved two basic principles of military service: the obligation of every soldier to do his best at his assigned job and the right to strive for promotion—including trying to place himself in the best position to facilitate his advancement.

This promotion angle in our military rank structure exists at all levels in countless ways—from command assignments to selection for our top-level military schools and colleges. There are endless little personal ways this principle operates, but the single most important factor in your future success begins with how you perform your present duties.

There is, however, another basic requirement at all levels—which Specialist McGarvey understood. For officers this begins with newly commissioned lieutenants and is a continuing professional requirement at all levels. It is something that no one else can do for you, yet it is often unrecognized and overlooked.

My first assignment was to the 29th Infantry at Fort Benning, Ga. This was serendipity in action, because at the time there was no better assignment for a new infantry second lieutenant than as a platoon leader with troops supporting The Infantry School.

My primary concern was to do the best I could, from day to day—with the indispensable help and guidance of my veteran platoon sergeant. Rank and the future did not cloud my thinking—or dim my interest in our current routine training schedule.

That system worked fine for more than a year. Then my hard-nosed company commander stopped me in the company street after lunch one day.

"Mistuh Newman," he said in his clipped, abrasive voice, "why are you not down at the post bayonet course, running for record as scheduled?"

"Sir," was my reply, "I planned to get more practice this afternoon, and run for record tomorrow."

"You will run for record today," he said sharply, then continued on his way.

Since I had missed some scheduled bayonet practice while coaching the battalion basketball team, this put me under extra pressure. Nevertheless, I concentrated and managed to make a presentable score. But that "hurry-up" over just one day on the bayonet course started me to thinking—after all, physical skill with the bayonet was hardly a major part of my job. In due course the question began to grow in my mind: Just what was my job as an officer, my special responsibility that was mine alone?

Either the platoon sergeant or the company commander seemed to be responsible for everything. So what was my real job, the job no one else could do for me?

I developed various answers from time to time, but none satisfied me. As a "shavetail" in the 29th Infantry, the importance of a thorough knowledge of drill regulations loomed large. Proper voice inflection in giving commands was a matter of concern, as were other routine duties.

The passing years enlarged my field of view, including tactics and troop leadership. I realized that field maneuvers as preparation for actual war were deadly serious training. But the question still remained, "Why lieutenants?"

Then I heard this story of a cockney noncom's reply to a similar question asked by an American lieutenant who, while on leave in England, was observing British troops at drill.

He saw noncoms giving commands and handling everything while the English lieutenants periodically strolled out and said simply, "Carry on, Sergeant," and disappeared. Inquisitive, the lieutenant cornered a grizzled old Tommy, a World War I veteran wearing ribbons from varied combat service.

"For several days now I have watched your drill," he said, "and always the noncoms are in charge. The lieutenants walk up and say, 'Carry on, Sergeant.' If that is all they do, what are your lieutenants good for, anyway?"

The old fighter considered the question. He appeared to think back to days when the air was full of screaming death, and the ground saturated with the blood of his comrades. Then, with pride and respect in his voice, he answered:

"Sir, when the time comes, they show us 'ow to die."

That Spartan answer did not satisfy me very long. Then, as often happened to me, circumstances made clear answers that should have been obvious—and that were there all the time.

The answer was impressed on me in Hawaii in 1933 when the commander of Company M, 27th Infantry, was hospitalized for an extended period—and I was the only lieutenant in his company. Suddenly, I was the commander of Company M, 27th Infantry.

Of course, *to be ready to step up one level of command had always been a fundamental part of my job*, but I had not thought of it that way before, and had not actively prepared myself to take over command. However, it was a lesson that I remembered—which was surely a factor when World War II came to Hawaii during my second tour there, and I moved from captain in early 1941 to colonel in just seventeen months, becoming the division chief of staff in July 1942.

There are wheels within wheels in preparing yourself for the next higher grade, especially when experience is an important consideration. When, years later, *I* was the assistant chief of staff, G1, (personnel), for U.S. Army, Europe, one of my important responsibilities was to select names of available infantry colonels to recommend for command of our infantry regiments. This was a most important personnel action, and I gave it careful consideration—including coordinating with the chief of Infantry Branch in the Pentagon.

Memory brings back the case of one infantry colonel who came to Europe with an outstanding staff record, and who aspired to be an infantry regimental commander—but who had never commanded an infantry company or a battalion.

I knew this fine officer well, and he became quite agitated when passed over for regimental command, which would have improved his chances of being selected for general officer rank. It was not enough to know *in general* the requirements of the next higher level of authority. If you want a specialized higher level assignment, you have to prepare for that, too—and, often, the right prior experience may be required.

About ten years after beginning my column for *ARMY* magazine, "The Forward Edge," I was the guest speaker at a reserve officers' meeting in the Miami area. Following my talk, a youthful-looking lieutenant colonel came up to me and said, "General, did all those things really happen to you that you write about?"

"They sure as hell did," was my unhesitating reply. "And then some!" I might have added, since I continued to write "The Edge" for another eleven years.

Things always just seemed to happen to me. Maybe serendipity is involved. Anyway, these comments seem in order:

- Frederick the Great said, "The mule that made ten campaigns with Prince Eugene was none the better tactician for it, and to the shame of man it must be admitted, in consequence of his idle stupidity, many old [that is, experienced] officers are not a bit better than the above mentioned animal."

  In other words, to gain from experience you have to recognize, reflect on, and think about the lessons learned so that you can apply them in the future—not necessarily to duplicate them, but to apply the principles to the existing situation.
- Military lessons learned in drill and field maneuvers should be reflected on—not by trying to remember every detail, but by isolating principles and salient features and techniques. For example, on D-plus 2 of the Leyte landings in the Philippines, I requested an artillery preparation on a segment of a ridge line. My request also called for the artillery to mark the flanks of the objective with smoke, to identify it for the aerial bombing

and strafing that would follow—a technique I had seen used in peacetime maneuvers.

It is my hope that those who read the following chapters will find lessons and observations of value that they can apply to advance their own careers—in or out of the military service, since the human element and basic principles are the same everywhere.

2

On the Many Nuances
of Command

SUN TZU, AN ancient Chinese general and one of the earliest military theorists (about 400–320 B.C.), summarizes in his *Art of War* a most perceptive idea:

> The musical notes are only five in number but their melodies are so numerous that one can not hear them all.
>
> The primary colors are only five in number but their combinations are so infinite that one can not visualize them all.
>
> The flavors are only five in number but their blends are so various that one can not taste them all.
>
> In battle there are only the normal and extraordinary forces, but their combinations are so limitless, none can comprehend them all.

This same proliferative thought applies to command and leadership, for no one can know how all the facets, angles, personality factors, and technical considerations are best integrated into countless situations. To understand this fascinating subject we must examine many small but significant sidelights and happenings within our own ken, along with maxims and quotes from others of varied experience and specialized knowledge.

As a place to start, consider this little parable. Everybody knows oats are a favorite food for horses. Also, most people know that when horses are finished with the oats, English sparrows relish the used oats as food.

So it came about one day, after a horse had passed along a country road, that a sparrow flew down to make a meal from the used oats left by the horse in passing. Then, after a satisfying dinner of used oats, the sparrow burst into a song of thanksgiving for the bounty he had enjoyed.

It happened that at this moment a hawk was gliding by overhead looking for his dinner. On hearing the sparrow's sudden song, he flashed down—and no more sparrow.

The moral of this little story is that when you are full of used oats, it is advisable to keep your mouth shut. From a command and leadership angle, used oats include such things as unnecessary orders, bombastic pronouncements, directives to do the obvious, dissertations on half-baked ideas, exhortations about routine matters, and the like.

Using anecdotes and maxims to illuminate command and leadership ideas has long interested me. And so have the pithy comments of others, like those in this "Cerebration" in one of *ARMY*'s predecessors, the *Combat Forces Journal*:

Thoughts on Leadership
[August 1951]

Written in my notebook are these two comments by a fine Japanese officer with whom I was closely associated before World War II:

When commander receives pessimistic report, he should check up and not check out.

To a general, a chin is as important as a brain.

Remarks of Lt. Gen. John R. Hodge at the critique following Exercise SWARMER:

All of us must be on our toes constantly to be as good as the men we command.

Quoted from William James:

Just as a bicycle chain may be too tight, so may one's carefulness and conscientiousness be so tense as to hinder the running of one's mind.

Selected Chinese proverbs:

A man without determination is but an untempered sword.

When the king makes a mistake, all the people suffer.

It is difficult for one man to act a play.
One of Field Marshal Bernard Law Montgomery's rules for success as a general is, in substance:
Get yourself a good chief of staff.
Overheard at a cocktail party:
He gives too many horseback decisions.
On clarity of instructions, or written orders, a West Point English instructor said:
Write your orders not only so they can be understood, but so that they cannot be misunderstood.
A corporal to his squad on maneuvers:
You guys fall out, take off your packs, and relax while I figure out what we are going to do next.
Our commander in chief, President Harry S. Truman, said when he was elected:
As President of the United States, I am guided by a simple formula: to do in all cases, from day to day, without regard to narrow political considerations, what seems to me best for the welfare of our people.
As a military man, I interpret this to mean:
Lead others as you would they should lead you, if your positions were reversed.

> Col. A. S. Newman
> Infantry

Here is another leadership nuance from a small confrontation in Hawaii some forty years ago. I learned about it recently from a friend who served with me there, where it happened during a full field inspection at Schofield Barracks. The senior inspecting officer was a brigadier general sometimes irreverently known as "General Toughey," or more simply as "Tuffy."

The personal field equipment of each man was displayed in front of his pup tent: weapons, mess gear, and folded web equipment, with toilet articles laid out in the prescribed pattern. The general paused and looked at the paraded equipment of Sgt. Hank Cronin, a veteran soldier only a few months away from retirement. Suddenly he lifted an arm and pointed:

"Sergeant," he snapped, "no comb!"

"General," the old soldier said, sweeping off his campaign hat with a flourish and bending forward to show his tanned and leathery skull, "no hair!"

General Tuffy held his gaze a moment, then smiled briefly, nodded, and continued on his way. He thus demonstrated an important angle to command and leadership: Have an observant eye to notice the little things, but keep them in perspective with the overall situation.

Often leaders of genius will express basic thoughts in totally different words. For example, Napoleon said, "The moral is to the physical as three is to one." General George S. Patton put the same idea this way:

"It is not the point of the questing bayonet that breaks the line, but the cold glitter in the attacker's eye."

Napoleon's thought was stated in still another fashion by General of the Army George C. Marshall during World War II. When it was suggested that Maj. Gen. Troy H. Middleton, who suffered from an arthritic knee, should be sent home rather than assigned to command the VIII Corps, General Marshall replied:

"I would rather have a man with arthritis in his knee than one with arthritis in his head. Keep Middleton there."

In ancient Greece, when facing the threat of the Peloponnesian War, Pericles said to an Athenian assembly, "We will resist our enemies in any and every way."

More than 2,300 years later Winston Churchill proclaimed the same principle to the Parliament, when England was threatened with invasion after Dunkirk: "We shall fight them on the seas and oceans. We shall fight them with growing strength in the air. We shall fight them on the beaches. We shall fight them on our landing grounds. We shall never surrender!"

Daniel Defoe (1660–1731), English novelist and political journalist, wrote: "It is better to have a lion at the head of an army of sheep, than a sheep at the head of an army of lions."

Saint Basil (329–379), Bishop of Caesarea and a Greek Church Father, said, "From orders which are improper, springs resistance which is not easily overcome."

Finally, here are two ideas from the memoir of one of our greatest soldiers, General of the Army Omar N. Bradley:

(1) There are few distinguishing characteristics of a successful division commander. Success comes instead from a well-

balanced combination of good judgment, self-confidence, leadership, and boldness.

(2) As signal corps officers like to remind us, Congress can make a general, but it takes communications to make him a commander.

Command and leadership are two quite different functions, yet they are inextricably interrelated—each supplementing and strengthening the other. I think of them as Siamese twins, each essential to the life of the other, joined at the head and the heart, with the head symbolizing command and the heart denoting leadership.

We have looked here at only a tiny fraction of the countless facets, angles, nuances, ideas, and thoughts about command and leadership that occur in military service. Comments are:

- In a recent cartoon panel an overstuffed wife said to her equally overinflated husband, "All you ever do is sit and think. You never do anything we can do together."

  That sit-and-think idea can be overdone, but there is no substitute for it as a periodic exercise—especially when considering the varied aspects of countless influences on leadership. But it is also well to remember the words of Sun Tzu that "none can comprehend them all."

- There is not, nor can there ever be, a finite summary of all you need to know about command and leadership. However, by noting significant little things as we gain experience, by observing other commanders (good and bad), and by reading and studying with a sense of awareness, we can develop an *understanding*. Only with this understanding, based on innumerable small things, can we meet unexpected command and leadership situations (large and small) with confidence and good judgment.

3
The Relationship Between NCOs and Officers

IT WAS MY privilege to participate in the 1985 Organization Day ceremonies of my World War II command, the 34th Infantry, at Fort Stewart, Ga. This included lunch with the officers, where I was expected to talk—but from a new angle. Instead of a prepared speech, the idea was for me to stand at the microphone and answer questions.

As sometimes happens, simple things can become complex without warning. This happened when a young captain asked, "General, will you summarize the relationship between noncommissioned officers and officers?"

That is a fundamental factor in command and leadership, especially at the company level. When I paused to frame a reply, it was clear there was no simple answer. This is an illustration of how, sometimes, it is almost impossible to pass on to others in words what you know and understand from long experience.

Rather than fob off an oversimplified reply, I temporized: "That is such a broad subject that there is no adequate off-the-cuff answer. I will think about it, however, and get something down on paper for you. Next question."

I researched the subject in my files and in the laboratory of my mind and memory. This empirical research, as readers of "The Forward Edge" will recognize, is a recapitulation in condensed form of some things they have read before. This permits these happenings to be viewed as a whole in relation to the young captain's question.

On my first day of active duty (Company B, 29th Infantry, Fort Benning, Ga., in 1925), I sat at my desk in the orderly tent, not knowing what to do. Then a middle-aged soldierly figure came in and reported, "Sir, I am Sergeant Fugate, your platoon sergeant. The third platoon is ready for your inspection."

That took the mystery out of life for me. Especially when, after inspection, Sergeant Fugate stood at meticulous attention and said, "Sir, it is my job to get things done for you. When you want me, pass the word and I'll come running."

After my transfer to Company D, First Sergeant Hildreth stopped me in the company street and said, "Lieutenant, you have Corporal Wiseguy in your platoon, who will step out of line if he thinks he can get away with it. If he gives you trouble, let me know." Actually, the sergeant was giving me a tip: "Wiseguy will be testing you, so the first time he gives you any guff—call his hand." And that is how it worked out.

In 1933, I was assigned to Company M, 27th Infantry, at Schofield Barracks, Hawaii. On one maneuver, I operated a mule pack train in a steep mountain area not reachable by wheeled vehicles. When the mules would not stand quietly to be loaded, Corporal Garrison said, "Lieutenant, you want them mules to stand still—I'll show you."

Then he walked up to a recalcitrant mule, put both hands around one ear, pulled the ear down, and put the tip between his teeth. When he clamped his teeth down on the ear, the mule stood squarely on all four legs—and remained rigidly still.

One day I found myself in temporary command of Company M. As I sat in the orderly room wondering what to do about some problems, 1st Sgt. Doc Dougherty came in—one of those great Old Army soldiers who considered young lieutenants their special responsibility. Bald to the ears, he stood smiling a moment, his gold tooth gleaming. Then he said:

"Lieutenant, things go on like this for days . . . and suddenly get worse. How about a cup of coffee in the kitchen?"

What he was saying was, "Come on, let's get out of this orderly room so I can talk. The problems we are having now are not new— and I'll give you some tips." And he did.

When I assumed command in 1936 of Company G, 26th Infantry, at Plattsburgh Barracks, N.Y. (as a newly promoted captain with nearly eleven years of service), all but one of the nine sergeants had more service. First Sgt. James S. (Big Jim) Redding was one of six who were veterans of World War I, and he had been first sergeant there since before I was commissioned.

I also knew it had been said about my predecessor, "There goes Captain Soandso and the commander of Company G." After assuming command, I invited Big Jim into the office, asked him to have a seat, and said I was aware that he and the other NCOs had made the company the fine outfit it was. Then I added, "So I'll expect you to keep me out of trouble—but remember that I am the company commander."

In due course we had a vacancy for private first class, and Big Jim brought in an order for me to sign promoting Pvt. Joe Blow. Since I had in mind promoting Pvt. Sam Doe, I called for recommendations of three candidates, in order of preference, from each platoon sergeant.

The platoon sergeants seconded the first sergeant's nomination (no surprise), but they also placed Sam Doe in second place—though I had not mentioned his name. I felt strongly that Sam Doe was the best-qualified soldier, so I pulled the private first class promotion order from my hold basket and changed the name from Joe Blow to Sam Doe.

When I assumed command of Company F, 19th Infantry, in Hawaii in December 1939, the situation was radically different from that with Company G, 26th Infantry. Among other things, the supply sergeant was not up to his job, so I replaced him. Also, I soon discovered that the mess sergeant was selling bacon, butter, and coffee from our pantry (via concealment in the outgoing garbage cans). So the second cook became a sergeant, and a good one.

After a detour to the 19th Infantry staff (S2 and athletic officer), I found myself G2 of the Hawaiian Division, as a captain in a lieutenant colonel's slot. I began reading everything I could find about my job: regulations, field manuals, war plans, and office files.

After a couple of days, my chief clerk (a technical sergeant, a two-rocker NCO) said, "Captain, do you know who my best friend is?" When I confessed my ignorance, he continued, "It is Kennard S. Vandergrift. But my next best friend is Captain Newman—as long as he is my boss." His message: "Relax, Captain, I know the score around here and will protect you in the clinches."

Seven months after the start of World War II, I became chief of staff, 24th Infantry Division, as a "bird colonel." One unfortunate aspect of my jump from peacetime captain to wartime colonel was greatly reduced contacts with sergeants. This continued for the rest of my service, but there were brief contacts that I like to remember, including:

- When I assumed command of the 505th Airborne Infantry, 82d Airborne Division, in 1952, at the first opportunity I went out to jump with them. As I rose to my feet with that special feeling jumpers know, a tall trooper approached and held out his hand. "Welcome to the 505, Colonel!" the sergeant said.
- When I was Deputy Commandant, Army, at the Armed Forces Staff College, Norfolk, Va., in 1957, a platoon of the 101st Airborne Division was scheduled to jump nearby in a large Marine Corps amphibious maneuver. Somehow I managed to get myself and Col. Charlie Shettle, a World War II trooper, attached to the 101st Airborne to go along. As we approached our airplane for takeoff—in field dress and parachutes—a weathered Airborne trooper walked up in that direct and confident way old sergeants have. As he halted and saluted, the sergeant said, "We are proud to have you jump with us, General."

I do not recall what I managed to reply, but I know my feeling was, "But not half as proud as I am to jump with you and the famous 101st Airborne Division!" Though I did not know it then, that proved to be my last day in the field with troops.

Now back to that question from the captain about the relationship between officers and noncommissioned officers. Maybe reading between the lines of my back trail will provide some idea of how it was for me yesterday. Then you can decide how that fits you in the Army today—because this personalized relationship varies with individuals, situations, and the climate of the times.

Some comments are:

- Noncommissioned officers help officers command and run the Army, just as officers do for generals—as professional associates, as executives who carry the ball and get things done at their level. The relationship between officers and NCOs is just one facet of this overall operating hierarchy—within established tenets of military courtesy and protocol, as in all command relationships.

- A major factor for success is how you get along with others, and this permeates every rank Armywide. The twenty-year retirement law has lowered age levels within the ranks, since my day of thirty-year retirements. This emphasizes the need for mutual respect, mutual professional competence, and reciprocal good will—and for both sides to take into consideration that the problem requires special efforts when young officers are inexperienced. That is an inherent factor that can be minimized but never eliminated.

4

Employ Lieutenant Years as a Special Time to Learn

RECENTLY ONE OF my friends asked the old question, "You don't look so good, Red. How do you feel?"

That how-you-look and how-you-feel topic is one of the standard amenities of life as a senior citizen. So I gave him my standard reply: "Well, when sitting down and on my second drink I feel fine."

This age syndrome is involved in military life, too, and is referred to obliquely in a letter from a lieutenant who has an APO address. The pertinent extract reads (pardon the commercial, which I am careful not to omit):

> There is a phenomenon developing in the Army now (you have touched this briefly in past articles) on which I would like to read one of your fine pieces. When I entered active duty there was a saying, "Rank among lieutenants is like virtue among whores—nonexistent." The normal promotion time (two years) to captain from second lieutenant no doubt had much to do with this. I have, with almost five years, duty as a lieutenant, noticed that seniors and juniors are again making the distinction between "flavors" of lieutenants. It has become unusual *not* to hear a second lieutenant refer to a first lieutenant as "sir." I believe some discussion of this, from your perspective, would be interesting and instructive.

This change-back toward how things were when I was a shavetail is welcome information. One of the basic factors is age, because distinctions in grade are more easily accepted and recognized if time-in-grade operates to equate advanced rank with added age. Of course age cannot be the controlling factor—nor should it be—but differences in age are a consideration in how you deal with others.

Six years ago, on a visit to the Florida Ranger Camp at Eglin Air Force Base, I discovered that the young captains I talked to had become captains after only twenty-four to thirty months of service. This was a direct result of the Vietnam War, with some political angles that were not clear to me.

After my return from Eglin, during a social function I migrated to the bar. Thus I found myself standing beside one of the Army's most distinguished combat soldiers, a four-star general who had retired several years before.

I mentioned to him my discovery that our Army was promoting officers to captain with two years of service. He and I had spent five years as second lieutenants and five more as first lieutenants before reaching captain. So I asked what he thought about this rank situation.

"You know, Red," he said, "there are many angles to those quickie promotions. The tragedy is they are wonderful young officers, but are promoted to captain before they have the experience to command a company. One of the greatest problems is that, through no fault of their own, they do not have the know-how to manage training.

"Another problem is that lieutenants are virtually the same age as their company commanders. This lack of an age differential adds a psychological handicap to paucity of experience in limiting the young captains' ability to train their lieutenants."

Contrast this with my ten years as a lieutenant. During those years, I was a lieutenant in six companies: two rifle companies and a machine-gun company in the 29th Infantry at Fort Benning, Ga.; a rifle company in the 31st Infantry in Manila; a machine-gun company in the 27th Infantry in Hawaii; and a military police company in the Hawaiian Division.

It was good luck *not* to make captain until I had those ten years of experience and added age. When I took command of Company G, 26th Infantry, at Plattsburgh Barracks, I was ready for the job, including the responsibility to train young lieutenants in my company. In that connection, here is a "Cerebration" from the *Infantry Journal* (March–April 1939):

Give Your Lieutenants a Hand

My thought is this: as a company commander I have a duty to my lieutenant.

That may sound like putting the cart before the horse, but it is a poor horse that cannot, on occasion, back the cart. Your lieutenant has a duty to you, but so have you to him. And a duty often neglected.

A busy company commander owes some of his time to the red-cheeked, perhaps nervous, yet often brash youngster who is beginning the great experience of wearing a Sam Browne belt and giving orders to men old enough to be his father. Sometimes these youngsters need holding back and sometimes they need pushing forward, but all of them need a lot of telling about a lot of things.

In fact, most new lieutenants seem to walk around in a fog wondering what in the name of shoe polish they are supposed to do. The captain is busy; at least he gives that impression, after long years of carefully cultivating a manner calculated to produce that idea. If the captain wants something done, he stops rustling papers on his desk long enough to give the job to a sergeant. It takes time and effort to explain things to green lieutenants, no matter how earnest and eager they may be.

Here are some things for a company commander to include in his duty to his lieutenant:

- Require him to be at the company at least 15 minutes before drill call.
- Correct small personal details, such as wearing his cap at too great an angle, not shining his leather, mannerisms of carriage, voice of command at drill, and the like.
- Teach him the right attitude toward soldiers.
- Assign him instructional responsibilities on the drill ground and monitor his performance to the extent necessary—with particular attention to adequacy of preparation.
- Have him keep dummy duty and guard rosters and a company fund book until he understands them thoroughly.
- See that he learns about service records, clothing settlements, final statements, payrolls, and all the rest.
- Require him to check mess records in detail and initial them. Also to review menus and quality of food served.
- Have him make continuing spot checks of company property.

Also to be familiar with reports of survey, clothing requisitions, statements of charges, and the like.
- Give him a growl when he needs one, and a pat on the back when he deserves one.

Lieutenants are often "put in their place" by ignoring them. Instead, give them missions. And don't tell other company commanders and the battalion commander what a worthless, helpless second lieutenant the government issued you.

His continued worthlessness is a reflection on you.

COMPANY COMMANDER

Of course, many things have changed in the past thirty-seven years, including the centralization of administration and mess arrangements. But the experience principle remains. When I wrote that "Cerebration" I had a new second lieutenant in the company who is now a retired general officer. He also served in the 24th Infantry Division during World War II, so we attended the annual reunion of our "Taro Leaf" Division in Peoria, Ill., this past summer.

One evening, glass in hand, we eddied out of the crowd to swap reminiscences about our shared service in Company G, 26th Infantry, when he was courting the regimental adjutant's daughter (now his wife) and both of us were learning about the Army from 1st Sgt. "Big Jim" Redding. After a while he paused and looked at me.

"Chief," he said (he had been a general staff officer in our division during World War II, when I was chief of staff), "one of the best lessons I learned from you in Company G cost me $9.41. Do you remember?"

When I did not, he reminded me I had him keep the company fund book. At the end of each month he briefed me on the records, then I signed the book. But one month he was short $9.41 and unable to find the error.

When I told him the records were all right, except he had failed to enter $9.41 as "cash on hand," he replied, "but I do not have any cash on hand, Captain."

"Well," my former lieutenant says I told him, "when you write a personal check to the company fund for $9.41—you will have."

"And that," my longtime friend, retired Brig. Gen. Lester L. Wheeler, told me over our next drink, "was a lesson in accountability for official funds that I never forgot."

In summary, here are three comments relevant to the question posed by 1st Lt. Charles E. Kirkpatrick:

- Service as a lieutenant is a special time of learning for which there is no substitute. You are directly in touch with soldiers and the fundamentals of military life—training, supplies, mess arrangements, health and safety requirements, weapons, ammunition, and the like—in a way you will never be again. From this comes knowledge and understanding and a feeling for things as they are that will be invaluable as you progress upward in grade.
- In addition to other considerations, there are only five promotions from second lieutenant to colonel. If you get two of those promotions in the first two years, that leaves only three for the next twenty-eight (unless, of course, stars fall on you). That would be an unhealthy situation.
- Welcome and make the most of your years as a lieutenant and never yearn to cut them short. With apologies to Rudyard Kipling: The things you learn as a lieutenant will help you a lot in the higher ranks.

5

Today's Army Holds on to Old Basics

ONE DAY EARLY in 1975 my phone rang. It was Lt. Col. William O. Child calling from Fort Leonard Wood, Mo. This was a surprise because I did not know him or anyone else at Fort Leonard Wood. But his proposition was even more surprising: They were having a Combat Arms Military Ball there and, based on my writings in these pages, he was inviting me to be the guest speaker.

After fifteen years out to pasture, I felt at home at Fort Leonard Wood. The clock turned back fifty years to my first duty assignment at Fort Benning, Ga.—although there were differences, too. Which suggests the question: How like and how different is the modern Army today from the Army of my time?

Those around me at Wood were younger in all rank levels than in 1925. At Benning we had an all-volunteer Army, too, but needed thirty years to retire, and sixty-four was the mandatory retirement age—as compared to authorized retirement at Wood after twenty years and mandatory retirement for officers after thirty years. But there was no mistaking the same feeling of "belonging" to a special military civilization, within the civilization of our country as a whole. Everybody belonged to the club.

Of course, the time soon approached for me to talk for my dinner and I was worried—not about the substance of what to say, but about the lack of an opening gambit to bridge the lapse of time between us.

When we sat down to dinner, but before being served, the colors were brought in by a color guard and received by the general officer present in a crisply precise ceremony. The four enlisted members of the color guard were immaculately uniformed, brass polished, leather shined, and they marched with the smooth, even rhythm that comes only from disciplined training. Suddenly, I knew how to open my talk.

I started with the grapevine story about what an old sergeant said shortly before my retirement: "First we had the Old Army, then we had the New Army—and now we got This Here Thing today."

This produced a polite but mild audience reaction. Then I continued, "I wish that old sergeant could be here tonight, and see that we have the Old Army back again."

That somehow seemed to bridge the time gap between us; I could become Captain Newman again and talk about memories of company-level service—which was where most of my audience were then serving.

You always wonder how your pearls of wisdom from way-back-when are received by the younger generation, so I was pleased to discover a straw in the wind the next morning when I walked over for a cafeteria-style breakfast in the officers' club.

A young captain preceded me in the line so, tray in hand, I asked permission to join him when he sat alone at a small table. He agreed, but was a bit reluctant to talk at first. Soon, however, we were swapping ideas on our favorite topic: the techniques, tribulations, great privilege, and inspiration of being a company commander.

Finally he said, "General, I don't know if I should tell you this or not; but when the idea of inviting you here came up, I was one of those against it, because I said you would just wave the flag and give us the usual high-level generalities we had all heard before. But you came down and talked to us where we live—so I guess the Army has not changed all that much."

He was agreeing with my premise that the Old Army was back again, so I did not belabor the point by telling him that my real opinion was it had never been away. We just needed to understand the paradox that our Army today is the same but different. For example, supply is more centralized at Fort Leonard Wood than in my day, because there is no supply room at company level.

That was hard for this former company commander to grasp—what, no company supply room? So when there was a chance to talk with a soldier before leaving Wood, I asked if his company had a supply room and received his reply, "No, sir."

"But," I persisted, "doesn't that mean a lot of walking back and forth to central supply?"

He gave me a flat, level look and said, "Well, sir, if others can do it, I can, too."

That put me in my place, telling me in some indefinable way not to worry; his Army didn't need my help. Among other things, he made clear that supply and maintenance are well handled—they just manage it with a different technique.

Five months ago I visited another modern Army post, Fort Stewart, Ga., where the 24th Infantry Division is stationed. The occasion was the annual reunion of the 24th Infantry Division Association, held last year in nearby Savannah. As a result, we were invited to see a live-ammunition firing exercise at Fort Stewart.

It was truly impressive; it was not just the helicopter gun ships, including their rockets and the terrific cyclic rate of fire (Gr-r-r-r-ump!) from Gatling gun–type weapons, and the coordination of other fires as well as troop movements by helicopters, but also the outstanding level of training that existed in order to put on that demonstration of fire and movement.

Here again is clear evidence of the Old Army today in the classic sense: fire and movement, with the high level of training so necessary for success.

One of the most interesting demonstrations was the firing by one soldier of rifle grenades at a point target on the ground. The launcher was different and the fire extremely accurate. Yet, a vital element remained the same: the training and skill of the man behind the weapon.

We also had lunch in troop mess halls, each of us out of the past going to lunch with the unit in which he used to serve. And the modernization of the chow line and the food served was as dramatic in its way as the new developments in weapons. Not only were the variety and quality of edibles better than anything I had ever seen before, but there was a short-order grill for special orders.

Memory brought back mess arrangements in my first duty assignment, the 29th Infantry at Fort Benning, Ga., in 1925. In my company, with an authorized strength of 212 and present-for-duty strength of around 180, we received twenty-six cents per man per day to feed the company, based on the actual number of men present each day.

The mess sergeant (under command supervision) could then buy food from the quartermaster, the post exchange, and on the open market. Mess records were kept to the penny and balanced monthly to keep within that twenty-six-cents-per-man allowance.

This was radically different from the centralized control and issue of food today. Yet, the basic command requirement remains the same: Obtain and serve the best possible food from the resources available—so it is the "same but different" again.

By chance, I obtained an interesting piece of incidental information at lunch that day at Fort Stewart. For the first twenty-five-odd years of my service the food was prepared and served under the supervision of mess sergeants. Some time in the 1950s, that mission was performed by mess stewards. Then I learned that my lunch at Stewart was prepared and served under the supervision of their dining facility manager.

To mix a metaphor, a rose by any other name is still a mess sergeant to me. Also, it was just another illustration of the paradox "the same but different." Added comments are:

- A traditional song at West Point includes the words, "We sons of today salute you, you sons of an earlier day." Speaking for veterans of the 24th Infantry Division Association who visited Fort Stewart last year, I can transpose those words this way: "We sons of yesterday salute you, you sons of a later day." In the current, more difficult and complex situation, what we saw at Fort Stewart typifies the fact that the Old Army lives on in the modern Army—the same but different.

- Sometimes we military old-timers may be inclined to downgrade the military new generations—and vice versa. Daniel Webster, the great senator and orator, once said, "Inconsistencies of opinion, arising from changing circumstances, are often justifiable."

  On the other hand, Noah Webster, our greatest lexicographer, said, "It depends on whose ox is being gored."

  By recognizing that the Old Army, the New Army, and our modern Army are just the "same Army but different," it is clear how pointless it is to gore each other's ox.

- As I was trying to get these thoughts into clearer focus, my wife summoned me to the TV to kibitz on the inauguration of our 39th president of the United States. As I listened to the inauguration address of our new commander in chief I was caught by Mr. Carter's words that all of us must "adjust to changing times and still hold to unchanging principles." In just that way our Old Army remains the same but different in our modern Army.

6

Duty-Honor-Country-Army

ONCE AGAIN THERE is news about the discharge of a West Point cadet for violating the honor system, and the story treats this as unfair, unjust, and unreasonable. The significance of the fact that the violation was a false statement, with no relation to academic studies, is not mentioned. Such incidents have become "news" since the so-called "cheating scandals" at our military academies were publicized by writers who did not understand the nature and purpose of these codes.

This has created a misleading impression by equating military codes of conduct to collegiate academic honor systems when actually they are quite different in purpose, nature, and implementation. These military codes have a direct relation to success in battle and to our national security.

All great nations have a heritage of honor, high sense of duty, patriotism, and military esprit among officers who lead their sons in battle. Thus the honor system at the U.S. Military Academy—the cornerstone of the West Point motto: *Duty-Honor-Country*—is not strange or even new, but is a key fundamental in training for leadership. That is why it permeates all of cadet life, not just academic studies, and guides them as officers in their Army careers. Further, our proud military code applies with equal force to all officers everywhere.

This leadership training has proved remarkably successful for 150 years. Does anyone imagine that great battle captains—like Lee and

Grant, Pershing and MacArthur, Patton and Ridgway—succeeded because they learned tactics and strategy at West Point? It is later in Army service that such military techniques and principles are studied by all officers in schools, drills, and field maneuvers.

More often than not individual violations of honor by cadets (there will always be a few) are non-academic in nature. For example, if a cadet sentry sees another cadet outside of barracks during evening study hours he challenges, "All right, sir?"

The reply, "All right, sir!" means the cadet "is going or has been to an authorized place, and nowhere else, and the purpose of the visit is or was authorized." If, however, the cadet had slipped out of barracks to see a lady friend, that "All right, sir!" was a lie—thus a violation of honor.

If an officer in the military service knowingly renders a false official report, he will (like a cadet who makes a false official statement) be tried. At West Point, the initial action is taken by the honor committee of fellow cadets; in the Army similar action is called a court-martial and is conducted by fellow officers.

It should be made clear, however, that the honor system is limited to matters of honor. The cadet who slips out of barracks to see his girl and gets back unchallenged is home free. His roommates are not expected to report him, unless they learn he lied about it. To overburden the honor code to enforce administrative regulations would be a serious mistake.

Duty obligations are often such that they cannot be covered by so rigid a code as honor, but there are areas where the demands of duty are clearly defined. For example, the cadet officer of the day (on guard duty) is required, quite explicitly, to report all violations of regulations coming to his notice, and he wears a conspicuous over-the-shoulder belt to identify himself.

Sometimes a cadet might make a profane remark in the mess hall, and everybody would laugh—not at what he said, but because the officer of the day was at the table, and would report him for "improper expression." This was not being an "informer," but was a matter of duty—preparation for being an officer, where the duty to enforce regulations and discipline is a basic responsibility.

Cadet officers and noncommissioned officers constantly meet this requirement to exercise control and supervision over their fellows. I witnessed an extreme example of this. A first classman (senior) in my company had completed all academic work and was within a week of graduation, but was close to the line on demerits. When he (call him Tom) was late to breakfast formation, our company commander (his classmate, later a senior general) said: "Tom, I saw you run that late, and will report it. You're near the limit on demerits, but you'll have to get *yourself* through West Point, not expect me to do it for you. Every time you're late I'll skin you for it."

Result: Tom was also reported by a tactical officer for a violation of uniform, skinned again for lates by his classmate, and thus went over the demerit limit and did not graduate.

Nobody blamed our cadet company commander for doing his duty; we expected it of him. We were not there just to get academic grades and a college-type diploma. We were being trained under the Duty-Honor-Country concept to become officers in the U.S. Army.

In World War II, as in all wars, there were countless cases where duty and honor were vital to battle success—like the distinguished three-star general who twice found it necessary, in separate battles, to relieve two-star division commanders of their commands, and both were his West Point classmates. This was difficult to do but essential to victory when the relieved commanders were failing in their missions. The principles involved are the same as those experienced under the Duty-Honor-Country code at the Military Academy.

When a lieutenant heads a reconnaissance patrol his mission is usually to find out if any enemy troops are in an area—where, how armed, and other details. Thus, if he finds no enemy but through overcaution his patrol has not fully covered the area, he has failed in his mission. This raises the insidious temptation to report to his commander that no enemy are present. However, that would be a false report, since he does not know that for sure. If it should prove to be erroneous information the enemy might attack his unit by surprise, thus causing needless loss of life or even defeat.

There are endless variations of how false reports can have serious consequences, at every level and in all phases of military operations. Since the purpose of our military academies is to prepare selected young men and women to be officers, their honor codes are so logical it is hard to understand why there is controversy about them. Compromise these codes and the lowered standards will spread out into our services.

At the time the Air Force Academy expelled a number of cadets for violations of honor, a major national magazine published an editorial headed "The Informer," deploring the fact that the guilty men were reported by fellow cadets. This makes me wonder how that editor would answer these questions:

"You point out that the guilty not only bought and sold information obtained by theft, but also would later be responsible for operating nuclear strike forces on which our national security depends. In the logical extension of your 'informer' thesis, would you have them refuse to report negligence in handling these awesome weapons, or anyone stealing and selling information about them?"

"You say reporting theft and dishonor was wrong. Do you advocate that good citizens everywhere accept the unwilling role of accessories and refuse to testify as witnesses?"

After this brief look at how and why the Duty-Honor-Country concept of training at West Point is founded on standards expected of career officers, these comments seem relevant:

- Now that cadet honor violations have become "news," the stories are usually slanted to indicate that "the system" is at fault, not the guilty cadet—that somehow there should be no violations in a successful honor code. Yet the reverse is true, the difference being that something is done about them. Any honor system must be enforced by those to whom it applies, or be an empty farce.
- The honor codes at our military academies are not moral exercises in an academic vacuum. They are training for careers where there are, on occasion, powerful pressures to compromise integrity both in peace and in war. The accuracy or falsity of reports in battle may be a matter of life or death, even of national survival.
- Guarding against possible injustice is part of it, too. But, as with a woman's virtue, there are no degrees of honor—in spite of heartaches and tragedies involved. Thus, proven honor violations cannot be met with temporizations, at West Point or out in the military service. To do this would compromise our officer's code, that vital intangible so necessary to successful military leadership.
- I believe the "communication gap" that produces misconceptions about the nature and purpose of our honor system at the Military Academy can be narrowed if we adopt and publicize an "Officer's Creed," as a direct extension of the West Point motto. By adding in our active duty principle, "for the good of the military service," this officer's creed (or motto) could be: *Duty-Honor-Country-Army.*

7

Pick the Right Way and Right Man

THE LETTER WAS from Col. Richard T. Firtko, USAR, who had read my book *Follow Me* and thought I might remember his father. I did indeed remember 1st Sgt. John Firtko, one of those great "Old Army" NCOs with whom I had served in the 19th Infantry at Schofield Barracks, Hawaii, before World War II. It was shades of 1st Sgt. John Christopher, senior duty Sergeant Bosco, and others!

In his letter Colonel Firtko reminisced with affection and respect about his old soldier father, and asked if I had heard of this little problem in command and leadership his father had mentioned to him:

As a young lieutenant, you are given a detail of one NCO and several enlisted personnel. Your mission is to erect a flagpole forty-eight feet tall and weighing five hundred pounds. Also available are supplies of cement, sand, and tools. How would you accomplish this mission?

Solution: Sergeant, I want this flagpole erected here. I will return in two hours to see how you are progressing. Any questions?

While I had never heard of that illustration, the principle is clear—but it needs a closer look. How well do you know the sergeant, and are there any special instructions you should give him . . . because *you* remain responsible that the flagpole is erected properly.

A busty movie actress of yesterday is credited with the line, "Diamonds are a girl's best friend." This is patterned after the older saying, "A dog is man's best friend." In my turn let me add, "An experienced sergeant is a novice lieutenant's best friend"—especially when applying the principle, "The best way to get anything done is to tell the right man to do it."

But it is not that simple. So it seems in order to examine in more depth the question of *how* to get things done, beginning at company level.

When I assumed command of Company F, 19th Infantry, at Schofield in late 1939, I noticed the uneven alignment of rifles on the drill field when marching at right shoulder arms. This presented a poor appearance, especially when troops marched in platoon-front lines in retreat parades of that era.

Of course I could just have told the platoon sergeants (I had no lieutenants) to get the rifles properly aligned. But by that time I had more than thirteen years' service and knew it was easier said than done. So I paused before issuing that pass-the-buck order and allowed memory and experience to percolate.

In my first duty assignment with the 29th Infantry, Infantry School Troops, Fort Benning, Ga., close order drill was more emphasized and complex than today. One demonstration for the company officers' class was "Close Order Drill of the Rifle Company" ("Squads Right," "Right Front into Line," "On Right into Line," and so on). And I was a platoon leader in the composite company for that demonstration.

A basic requirement was for everybody in the three platoons (of five squads each) to march with 30-inch steps at 120 steps a minute. So how to train in this? Of course the company commander could have passed that problem to his platoon leaders, but he found a better way.

At a convenient place he had 121 strips of wood 1 inch by 3 inches by 24 inches set in the ground at 30-inch intervals, center to center, with 1/8 inch of each strip above ground. Thus, a soldier could stand with his heels on the first strip and—by *feel*, with his head up—march down this cadence-marching court, against a watch held by a timer. Our captain made it possible, therefore, for us platoon leaders to say:

"Sergeant, have our platoon work on the cadence court for the next hour," and then we just had to check periodically. In that way my Right Guide, 6-foot 2-inch Sergeant Alfred, and Left Guide, 5-foot 4-inch Sergeant Beck—with sized soldiers in the line joining them—all marched with the same length pace to the same cadence, and in unison with the other two platoons. As Sherlock Holmes might say, "Elementary,

Watson—just a little logical thinking *before* you issue orders simplifies life for everybody."

So, from that experience, my solution to the out-of-line rifles in Company F in Hawaii thirteen years later came out this way:

- At a convenient location in each platoon area, paint a thin black line on one wall at shoulder height, and at the proper angle for rifles at shoulder arms.
- Now orders to my platoon sergeants were specific: Have each soldier stand sideways to the wall, with his rifle in place parallel to the line on the wall. When in that position, with his right forearm parallel to the ground, each man will fix in his mind where his right elbow rests against his side, with his rifle at the proper angle alongside the line on the wall.

That solved the problem, without a lot of vocalizing by me and the platoon sergeants.

The point, of course, is that in giving orders to sergeants, and elsewhere in the chain of command, the orders should be as clear and helpful as possible. Nothing causes more ill feeling and needless recrimination than poorly considered orders.

Example: In that flagpole case, arrangements had to be made to get the flagpole to the site—with sand, cement, and tools—before the sergeant could be instructed, "I want this flagpole erected here." Also, the lieutenant must be double-dyed sure that is where the commander wants that flagpole.

Now another case, extracted from my files about Major Threeput, Lieutenant Buckpasser, and Sergeant Hashmarks:

One morning, Major Threeput decided to prepare the rifle range for the chief of infantry's combat squad competition. So he put a bug in Lieutenant Buckpasser's ear, explaining clearly what he wanted. Whereupon Lieutenant Buckpasser passed the word along to Sergeant Hashmarks like this:

"Get the range ready for the chief of infantry's combat problem— you know, the usual thing: seven or eight silhouettes in line, with a surprise target coming up for the automatic rifleman. And get it done this afternoon."

"How does the lieutenant want the targets fixed this year?"

"Just as I said, Sergeant—a line of silhouettes and a surprise target."

So Sergeant Hashmarks arranged an irregular row of silhouettes, and tacked a silhouette on a pole to be raised from the pits as the surprise target. A somewhat GI arrangement, but one the sergeant had seen used before.

The next morning, Major Threeput, who had given his instructions clearly, pinned back Lieutenant Buckpasser's ears and ordered changes. When the major's car drove off, the lieutenant turned to Sergeant Hashmarks.

"Sergeant, I don't think much of your idea of a surprise target. There should be at least two silhouettes in the surprise target, also some prone silhouettes in the line of targets."

A look of surprise crossed Sergeant Hashmark's face, then an expression of resignation. How was he to know . . . ?

Such things result from sloppy thinking, issuing orders without bothering to think them out—then expecting a crystal ball–gazing act to produce an approved solution.

So before you call a good soldier to task for failure to carry out your instructions, be sure the fault is not your own. American soldiers are loyal, willing, and intelligent, but they are not gifted with second sight. If, however, they understand what you want, it will be done that way.

Some comments:

- As you gain in rank and experience, the problems gain in complexity and more people get into the act Also, the actions usually take place further in the future, often remote from your presence—thus requiring the capacity for visualization. But the same principle applies: To get things done, get the right people to do them for you—and give them carefully considered orders.
- There is no finer foundation for a military career than service with troops at company level. It was my great good fortune to be a company-grade officer fifteen years, serving in nine companies, and commanding three of them for a total of five years. At that level you learn to get things done by telling others what to do, and you gain a certain understanding about the process of getting things done from your orders.
- When, in approximately seventeen months, I progressed from captain to eagle colonel as a wartime division chief of staff (1942),

the way to get things done was unchanged. Just tell the right people, of whatever rank, what to do, being careful to direct clearly what you want.

- Finally, it was at company level that I first understood the power and importance of what might be called "The Bulletin Board Principle"—putting papers up on a vertical surface where people can read, study, and be guided accordingly. This principle is an invaluable way to facilitate and control the process of getting things done in complex situations.
- In my view there is no substitute for this technique when coordination is required with many operating agencies; the definitive words are *War Room*. So I became a War Room addict. And, you guessed it—the best way to establish and operate a War Room is to select the right man to do it for you.

8

Coaching Can Help Train Leaders

IT IS INTERESTING, in retrospect, to turn on the TV in your mind of memories from long ago and discover lessons in leadership from this replay of past events. Often, at the time of the action, you did not realize the valuable training you were receiving. Coaching soldier athletic teams was that type of experience for me.

When my best friend and severest critic (BFASC) saw the first draft of this memory replay she said, "The editor won't print that—and if he does, readers won't like it. You make yourself look too good!"

"Listen," I replied with calm reasonableness, "I write it like it was. Can I help it now if I was good then?"

That did not turn out to be the last word in the discussion. But, anyway, my leader-learning experience was supplemented by my first year on active duty coaching the 1st Battalion, 29th Infantry's basketball team in the post league at Fort Benning, Ga.

About a week after I had cut our basketball squad to its final fifteen-man strength, the star forward and team captain came to see me in the orderly room. His request was for the battalion commander to authorize basketball practice on Saturday mornings instead of standing inspection.

"But," I said in some surprise, "we are already excused from drill every weekday at 10:00 A.M. for basketball practice."

"Well, Lieutenant," he replied, "all the other teams are excused from Saturday inspections."

I did not think it justified to be excused from morning drill on weekdays—much less from Saturday inspections. So I said, "I will relay your request. But if the battalion commander asks me if I think it justified, I'll say no."

What Maj. Oscar W. Griswold said was, "Do you think that is necessary?"

When I replied, "No, sir," he said, "I don't either. So we will go to Saturday inspections."

Our star forward and team captain received this news without comment and returned an hour later to say he did not want to play basketball. "All right," I said. "Turn in your uniform to the supply room."

Later that afternoon two more star players arrived with the same deadpan statement. So I assembled all fifteen members of my squad, recited the situation, and concluded with, "I've got to know where I stand. I play basketball on the post team at night because I like to play basketball, not to get excused from anything. Our battalion team will be selected from those who are soldiers first and basketball players second. I hope that includes all of you. But those who are not willing to play basketball—and go to Saturday inspections—please turn in your suits to the supply room."

Twelve of my fifteen players did just that, so I wrote out a notice calling for another tryout for the battalion team and gave it to our company clerk to be typed and circulated to all companies. Soon after my arrival at the company the next morning, our former team captain and star player was in to see me again.

His message was, "The team understands and would like to play for you, Lieutenant."

My reply was, "No, let's have the record straight. You just want to play basketball and go to inspections, too. Please tell the others, practice as usual today, and we'll start from there."

So where does leadership training come in? In no other way could a pristine second lieutenant have experienced such a problem in the control of men. I did not rationalize it then, but, when faced with a direct challenge, did what I thought was right. Long experience later proved to me you seldom go wrong when you do that.

Another leadership principle was involved. General Ichiji Sugita, now a retired Japanese Army chief of staff (who, as a captain, was attached to my company before World War II), expressed it this way in autographing a *Soldiers Handbook* for me: "To a general a chin is as important as a brain."

You sometimes need that chin in a position of authority to reconcile conflicting claims on your loyalty: to those under you, to those over you, and for the good of the military service. More often than not you will face such problems as coach of athletic teams in the Army.

Another and different problem faced me later as coach of our battalion track team for the annual post track championship. I was reminded of this after World War II, more than twenty years later, when a mutual friend introduced me to the deputy post commander at Carlisle Barracks, Pa., by saying, "Colonel Tuttle, do you know Colonel Newman?"

"Know him?" that wonderful "Old Army" officer and gentleman replied, emitting his characteristic explosive and infectious laugh. "I'll never forget him!"

As we shook hands, smiling, both of us remembered a Saturday afternoon those long years ago at Fort Benning. He was the veteran Capt. William "Wild Bill" Tuttle, post athletic officer, and I was the freshman track coach of my battalion team. We met in Doughboy Stadium near the end of the post track meet. If my team lost the last event (the relay—and we did), at least second place in the javelin would be needed to win the post championship.

My ace javelin-heaver reported they would not let him throw his regulation javelin but must use a lighter, whippier type high school javelin. I took the matter to the referee, Captain Tuttle, and got a turndown—even for my man to throw his heavier javelin against the lighter one used by others. So I announced we were competing under protest.

Every time my best man heaved that light and whippy javelin it turned sideways and went nowhere. After the meet, I asked our battalion commander to lodge a written protest, calling for a replay of the javelin event to see who really were post champions.

He did this. So Capt. Wild Bill and a novice, redheaded second lieutenant were the star witnesses before a board of officers. I arrived with both javelins, a rule book, and a scale from the quartermaster butcher shop. By weighing the two javelins, it was demonstrated we had been required to use a nonregulation javelin. But the board decided that, although Wild Bill's decision not to let us use the regulation javelin was debatable, the result of the meet would stand.

What leadership training can be learned from that track meet more than fifty years ago?

For me, it meant independent responsibility for the control of men, *and* obligation to them, that I would not otherwise have experienced. It was a traumatic thing for a brand new second lieutenant of that time to question a decision, bringing a much senior officer before a board of officers to watch javelins be weighed on a meat scale.

My BFASC says I just tell about this to make myself look good. But that is the way it was, and the leadership principle is basic: You stand up for the rights of your military team, whatever its nature. If I had not protested, within proper channels, it would have been a failure on my part.

As with other group endeavors, if you are placed in charge of an athletic team with members who are more knowledgeable in the sport than you are, use their expertise. The technique is simple: Make your best qualified man the player-coach (or recruit an overage former player as coach), and change your title to officer in charge (euphemism for manager)—but with continued daily interest and support in developing the best team possible.

As regimental commander of the 511th Airborne Infantry after World War II, I failed to apply this principle and allowed an earnest young officer to remain as coach of our basketball team when he was not up to the job. I should have called the lieutenant in and told *him* to tell the team he was continuing as officer in charge, then promoted the completely outstanding sergeant on the team as player-coach. (We would have had a far more successful team.)

This just touches the surface of my coaching years and the consequent benefits to me. Other comments are:

- One of the major problems a young coach may face is dealing with a star player who is "over the hill" and refuses to accept the fact. Another difficulty is how to manage a star athlete who makes himself a disruptive influence. In coaching, as in military command and leadership situations, there will always be personnel and personality problems, and each one is different.

    As a coach, I developed a policy of patience and understanding *up to a point*. Then I applied "the apple barrel principle." When the disruptive worm of discontent or just plain progressive cussedness got beyond reasonable limits in one of my athlete apples, I arranged to have him removed from our team barrel. Facing such problems as a young lieutenant was helpful to me later in positions of higher responsibility.

- In 1937 my regiment (26th Infantry) supported the National Marksmanship Matches at Camp Perry, Ohio. While there I heard the saying, "You don't have to have blue eyes and be slightly crazy to qualify as a distinguished marksman—but it helps."

In a similar fashion, you sure don't have to coach or manage an athletic team as a young officer to become a successful leader. But, other facets of your character and abilities being equal, I think it helps a little.

9

Jitters Can Be Hazardous to Your Career

IN THE EARLY 1930s I attended a little everybody-seated, Prohibition-type cocktail hour in Hawaii. One lady present, who had once visited a museum in New York City, was a conversation dominator. So she was holding forth on the dinosaur, the brontosaurus and the like. Finally the host asked, "Have you ever seen a thesaurus?"

When she replied, "No, but I've seen a picture of one," he left the room and returned with a copy of Peter M. Roget's thesaurus (of synonyms and antonyms).

"Well," he said, displaying it, "here is a real one."

Not very polite—perhaps even unkind—but it brings out the principle that in the exchange of ideas it is important to know the meaning of words.

My encyclopedic dictionary defines "the jitters" as: "intense nervousness; nervous fear or apprehension." But to understand the part jitteriness can play in military service we must delve a little deeper for ramification.

In the ongoing Tattoo (last call before Taps) weeding out of my files, two papers surfaced that outline ways in which the jitters can adversely affect a military career. The first was a copy of my "Cerebration" (under a pen name) in the *Combat Forces Journal* (March 1951):

What Gives the Staff the Jitters?

"Jittery staff officers" is a disparaging cliché. It purports to describe staff officers who exist in a constant state of dithers—and implies it is a mystery how such incompetent fingernail-chewers were made staff officers.

No commander in his right mind would select jittery staff officers. So why do some staff officers show strain and tension? There are various reasons, but here are the primary ones:

Staff officers do more work, under various kinds of stress, than officers on straight duty. There are exceptions, of course.

A staff officer must coordinate his work with others, without the power to order coordination. Instead he must secure cooperation. But it places a heavy strain on an action officer to have the responsibility to get something done, without authority to order it done.

There are so many details to be supervised by the average staff officer that he can spend only a reasonable time on each of them. However, when a straight duty officer goes "up to headquarters" he often has a pet project, and picks a place in his own schedule so he will have time to "discuss" it indefinitely.

The staff officer, with other things pressing to be done, finally shows impatience until—eventually—the visitor leaves in a subdued huff to spread word the staff officer is "jittery." Thus, impatience with wasted time is translated into "jitters."

Another situation that produces symptoms of strain develops when a conscientious officer is given a job but is refused the assistants and means needed for the job. The result: a willing but overloaded horse will show signs of wear—and the jittery staff officer syndrome gets another boost.

Then there is the staff officer who runs to the Old Man for minor decisions. It is said he even asks permission to blow his nose. Unless you have been in the position of that staff officer it may be hard to understand, but it is probable his commander operates on the "rule by reversal" principle. That is, if a staff officer makes any decision on his own, the commander will change it if there is another way to do it.

After being reversed a few times, with all the confusion that causes, the staff officer resigns himself to the frustrating role of replying to almost any routine question, "If you will wait, I'll find out the answer."

Usually, the Old Man is busy and the visitor waits, and waits. It is time-wasting and nerve-straining for others—but the commander sits back, comforted by the knowledge he is letting everybody know every day that no staff officer can run his show. And the staff officer is classed as jittery, unable to decide anything —except the private resolve he will never serve on the staff of that commander again if he can help it.

There are variations and additions, but the problem is summed up in three general observations:

- A commander who selects his staff well and gives them the tools to do their work, with reasonable freedom of action within consistent policies, can demand and get their best efforts—without jitters.
- A commander who picks fair-haired boys as staff officers and lets them run the show without his personal check on their actions may have a happy staff family—but he may also have an unhappy command, especially among subordinate commanders.
- Commanders should be alert for indications that members of their staffs show signs of incipient jitteriness. Then take an introspective look at themselves, and decide whether the proper cure is to change staff officers—or to revise their procedures in handling them.

LIEUTENANT LEARNING

The other paper found in the Tattoo weeding out of my files touches a different angle of jitters. It was the retained carbon of my letter to an Army student officer, a lieutenant colonel, on his graduation from the Armed Forces Staff College in Norfolk, Va., when I was that school's Deputy Commandant, Army:

This letter has three purposes: (1) to say you were one of the outstanding students in your class, (2) to enclose a copy of the "Remarks" on your academic efficiency report, (3) to repeat again my advice to you to RELAX.

You are doing fine, but it will stand in your way unless you follow my advice. Actually, I had to choose between writing this letter or making your nervous manner of record on your efficiency report.

My thoughts and observations are:

- Your tenseness may be only in the presence of senior officers, since your faculty advisor did not mention it.
- You "snapped to" like a recruit around me, even on two occasions after I had discussed the matter with you. This is not an attitude appropriate for your rank.
- Such tenseness can be overcome—*but you must work at it*. You cannot relax in the presence of seniors if you do not relax in your daily living, and you must practice that.
- In conversations with others, let a silence fall when someone asks you a question—for a few seconds anyway. Nothing will tense you more than the compulsion to answer questions instantly; further, an instant answer means beginning to talk before you think. That results in needless tension, as you struggle mentally to keep up with what you are saying.
- This is not just a theoretical matter, because it affected your official record here. Specifically, I would have included the phrase "potential general officer" in your report if it had not been for the fact that *after I had talked to you on the subject* you were still as jumpy as ever.
- In my view this nervous reaction is a matter that can be cured, at least in large measure. I ought to know, because I had the same trouble. For an airborne trooper to overcome fear of heights he must practice looking down from heights—which is why they have practice jump towers. It is hard at first, but when you practice looking down you set your mind to overcome the involuntary reactions to instinctive fear.

  Similarly, you must put yourself in positions which you have found cause an involuntary nervous reaction—and *practice* not letting your nerves get the best of you.
- I may be wrong, but I think the crux of the matter is that you have an overly intense desire to become a general officer. You must not let that matter too much, because it really should not.

You may not believe this, but as an infantryman I would not swap my Combat Infantryman Badge for a star—and you already have the Combat Infantryman Badge and battle decorations to go with it.

You may feel I've overstated what I've tried to say. But it is just that you have a bright potential and I want to be sure I do not fail in my obligation to point out this correction that is so important to your future career.

It was a pleasure to know you, and I wish you every success.

The quoted documents cover only two angles of how the jitters can affect military careers. These comments seem relevant:

- My *Reader's Digest* "word finder" gives twenty-five synonyms for nervousness. If you add them up, stir well, and divide by two, the answer might approximate a definition of jitters. It is the antithesis of "cool, calm, and collected."
- On the other hand, jitters is not a proper term for dynamic and driving personalities, because they have self-confidence and are in control of themselves. They do not have the shaky element of involuntary indecisiveness that characterizes the jittery gentry.
- The nervous tension back of the jitters can, if brought under control, be transformed into the kind of driving force that gets things done—in command and staff, and in leadership. Elbert Hubbard (1856–1915), whose wonderful "A Message to Garcia" was about a soldier who was not jittery, once said, "I thank whatever gods there may be for my indomitable will."

  You can bet old Elbert did not have the jitters, because he would not let that happen to him.

10

A Good Man
Is a Good Soldier

I ONCE RECEIVED a fine letter from a Sgt. Maj. Vaughan D. Herrick, saying he was a "Forward Edge" reader. Sergeant Major Herrick felt, however, that these little essays were written primarily for officer readers and suggested I slant some toward enlisted men.

Having had no enlisted service—unfortunately, since this would have made me a better officer—I cannot speak from personal experience of the man in the ranks. I have tried to write "The Forward Edge" in a manner that would be readable to enlisted men as well as officers, with the hope they would thus gain a better overall understanding of our Army. But Sergeant Major Herrick had a sound point. So here are some thoughts I would give any young man leaving to join the Army.

Son (I would say), if I were entering military life as you are about to do—knowing what I know now after a lifetime in uniform, including more than fifteen years at company level—the following ideas, factors, opinions, and considerations would guide me:

- The first thing to get straight is that you are entering a profession. Why this viewpoint is missed by so many recruits has always puzzled me. As in any other profession, good-time Charlies and deadbeats travel a bumpy road.
- To go from high school to college is from one young society to another; it's a much greater transition to go from high school

or college to the Army. Suddenly you are in a man's world, dealing with serious responsibilities to others. Equally vital to understand, you no longer work alone (as in taking academic tests), but must work in concert with others—which is much harder.

- A good businessman enjoys his work and it's the same way in the Army. For a poor businessman life is a burden and it's like that in the military profession, too.
- Life in uniform is what you make it, just as it is "on the outside."
- The armed services rest on a foundation of discipline—which is not the disagreeable thing many civilians visualize, nor is it hard to understand. Discipline is the willing obedience to all orders and, in the absence of orders, to what you think those orders would have been.
- Don't be too quick to get "chummy" with new acquaintances; they may be the wrong chums. If you run with the wrong crowd something happens inside your heart and to your attitude as a man and a soldier—and *that's* a real misfortune.
- Reserve your ideas on how to reform the Army until such time as you have won that right by experience, increased rank, knowledge, and understanding.
- Many things that seem senseless and useless to recruits have been proved by long experience to be the best way to serve the overall good. Young men new to the service should be slow to decide they know more overnight than all others who have preceded them. First learn to swim with the tide—there will be plenty of time to swim against the tide later.
- Nothing is beneath your dignity that others must do—whether it be cleaning latrines, sweeping barracks, or any of the many fatigue details that *somebody* must do.
- To say "sir" demeans no man. It's a custom that helps military men at all levels bridge the rank gap—recognizing its existence while talking man to man.
- Similarly, saluting is a distinction reserved for military men— a friendly and professional greeting between soldiers in good standing (guardhouse prisoners are not allowed to salute). Take the salute out of military life and everybody would miss it.

- The more you know about anything, the more interesting it becomes. Don't wait to be force-fed information—ask questions, study manuals, and practice techniques with weapons and equipment. You will soon be an expert in many skills and fields if every day at every opportunity you seek to know.
- Save part of your service pay each month; there is something intangible about this that makes you a better soldier. A man with empty pockets finds it harder to hold his head up with the pride of a fighting man.
- Develop the habit not only of being on time, but of so regulating your days that you are on time without scrambling. Also, the best way to get ready for inspections in ranks, in barracks, or in the field—with weapons serviceable and equipment complete—is to stay ready. It's so much easier that way.
- Nothing is more unsmart than to go AWOL—unless it's getting into whiskey or drug trouble. The price paid is beyond calculating: in money, loss of soldierly reputation, reduced chance for promotion, and to your self-esteem.
- Don't have your feelings stuck out to be bruised, or they will be. When dealing with thousands of people, it's not possible to rub everybody's fur the right way all the time when issuing orders. Just do what the man says—and forget it.
- Observe those who have been in the service for years; watch how they meet problems and perform their duties. Emulate things you admire in good soldiers; avoid errors made by poor ones.
- Just as "ignorance of the law is no excuse" in civilian life, it's the same way with military regulations. Study those that affect you personally: uniform and barracks regulations, guard orders and vehicular regulations, fire regulations and alert instructions, weapons control regulations, and others.
- This may sound overly "regimented," but it's not: You live under all sorts of restrictions in civilian life you never think of because you are used to them. (No litterbugging or public nuisances, punch the time clock, do what the boss says, and so on.) Get that way in uniform, too.
- Don't drift; aim for advancement. Whether or not you plan to make the Army a career, study promotion patterns, pick a road

upward, and start climbing. Like many others in the past, you may change your mind and stay in. Military service is a worthwhile and satisfying profession, an interesting and rewarding way of life for good soldiers.

- The same things that make fine soldiers make successful civilians, including good character and good habits, sense of responsibility, getting along with others, good judgment, and the continuing will to strive. Military service has an intangible something to offer any man—regardless of what career he may later follow—but you have to reach for it.

- The Army has no quick and easy method to make a man out of a bum. An interesting comment on one case was made by a senior general in reply to a soldier's father who had written a letter berating the Army for not instilling discipline in his son. The general said, tactfully, it was hardly reasonable to expect the Army to do in six months what the father had failed to accomplish in eighteen years.

- For some reason not clear to me, most civilians take the attitude that as soon as a civilian screwball puts on a uniform, the Army made him what he is. Yet each of them remains the same kind of pig's ear in uniform he was in civilian clothes in his own hometown. So don't let these few misfits disconcert you—they seldom last long in uniform anyway.

- The gripers are the unhappy ones and they always distort facts. Look closely and you'll see they are really kicking themselves, trying to alibi their own failures and weaknesses.

- The measure of a man and a soldier is the ability to take it when the going is rough. To "blow your top" does not make you a tough cookie; it's just lack of self-control. Any dope can lose his temper.

- All successful men need human understanding—the ability to understand people and what makes them do what they do. Military service offers an unparalleled opportunity to cultivate this quality and to learn to get along with others, as important in civilian life as in the Army.

- Finally, don't get the idea the above applies only to enlisted men. Officers are soldiers, too, and before any man can be a good officer he must first be a good soldier.

Sergeant Major Herrick agreed with these guidelines for enlisted soldiers and joined with me in this final thought, which we both feel is particularly important for recruits to understand:

- Military service is nothing to worry about or sweat out. A good man will be a good soldier. You can't be passive, however; to stand still is to fall behind—*you must strive*. And to strive does not take the pleasure from life, but is the sauce that makes the enjoyment keener. It's the best way to live in uniform and like it.

11

Haste Now Can Cost Later

THE FAMOUS SAGE François Duc de La Rochefoucauld once said: "Everyone complains of the badness of his memory; nobody of his judgment." In this sense "judgment" concerns skill in making decisions.

We have discussed before some general principles of decision-making, but there are also supplementary angles that involve small actions taken by individuals for their current convenience.

Like other military lessons from my younger years, the importance of considering possible boomerang effects from some small day-to-day action was illuminated for me by 1st Sgt. "Big Jim" Redding of Company G, 26th Infantry. When one of our soldiers wanted to go to the U.S. Military Academy Prep School run by the Army, Big Jim said, "He is a fine boy, Captain." Then he laughed and added, "The company will take no chance in sending him."

That cryptic remark puzzled me, so Big Jim explained it. He had been first sergeant of that company on that post for eleven years before I joined, and one year they got a trouble-making recruit who was a high school graduate. So when notice came around about candidates for the prep school, Big Jim suggested the young wise guy be nominated.

"That was a mistake," Big Jim said, "because five years later I got him back as a lieutenant."

This illustrates the principle that actions taken for a short-term gain may end as a long-term loss. An example of this is the soldier or officer

52

who, after investing several years in the military service, decides to resign (or not reenlist) because he does not like his current station or his present boss. In retirement I have met civilians who did that and now call it their biggest mistake.

When such actions are taken, they are not viewed in the light of major decisions. Rather, the idea is to do what you want at the time, without the evaluating process of asking yourself, "Are there any good long-term reasons not to do this?"

After nearly fifteen years' service, and as a junior captain and grass bachelor in Hawaii, I was enjoying two privileges: commanding a company in the 19th Infantry at Schofield Barracks, and living off post in a small cottage. Then the grapevine reported I was scheduled to be the regimental S2 and would have to live on post in the bachelor officers' quarters with a gaggle of newly minted lieutenants.

It happened that at this time I received a phone call about transferring to Honolulu for command duty in the military police there. That sounded more interesting than convoying papers from a staff "in" basket to an "out" basket, while riding herd on those lieutenants in the BOQ.

So I called Honolulu and said, "Yes." But several days later a phone message reported that Hawaiian Division headquarters had nixed the idea. When I went up there to discuss the matter with G1, the rough and tough old chief of staff, Col. Eugene Santschi, Jr., intercepted me in the hallway.

"Captain Newman," he said directly, "you are not going to military police duty in Honolulu. As a career infantry officer you are where you belong. You will not thank me for this now, but some day you will."

He was right. The hovering clouds of World War II were clearly visible, and when Pearl Harbor came I was where I belonged: in a combat infantry division. And every time I think about it, I thank Colonel Santschi for that.

There is a little footnote to this footnote to history, as reported to me via the ubiquitous Schofield Barracks scuttlebutt system. It concerned a young officer in division headquarters who noticed there was a cushion in the chair where the chief of staff sat during staff conferences.

The young officer remembered this when he visited a novelty shop in Honolulu one day, and noticed a thin, inflatable rubber cushion for sale. This cushion had a special air-release valve on one edge, so that if anyone sat on the cushion the escape of air produced a realistic sound.

Upon reflection, the young officer recalled that it was the custom of the old chief of staff to arrive at staff conferences on the minute, after all others were there, and take his seat ceremoniously at the head of the conference table. So the young officer bought the cushion.

Everything worked as planned, to the great amusement of the assembled staff officers—also to the red-eyed anger of the rough and tough old chief of staff after he sat down, then investigated the resulting unseemly sound and found the inflatable cushion under his regular one. Fortunately, he never discovered the perpetrator of this lèse-majesté gambit.

The point here is that the young staff officer got the laugh he planned for—but risked a written reprimand that would have remained in and damaged his personnel file for the rest of his career. Was the small, one-time gain of a belly-laugh prank worth the long-range risk?

Any discussion of a small gain at the risk of big trouble later must consider the results that can and often have stemmed from "just one more drink." It would be nice to say that even in my salad days (when "green in judgment") I was careful never to take "one too many." But that would falsify the record because, as a second lieutenant in the Philippines in the late 1920s, it never seemed to occur to me that another drink or two might involve a decision that could affect the rest of my personal and professional life.

One night in Manila in 1929 was an unforgettable lesson in the school of experience. I was just out of the hospital, where I had been immobilized six weeks with a broken hip from playing on a soldier basketball team. There was no Prohibition in Manila, so I resumed my empiric endeavors to discover what my alcoholic limits were.

Thus, I was happy to attend an official regimental cocktail supper at the Elks' Club with another second lieutenant named John, a fellow investigator into alcoholic parameters. It was a fine party, with cocktails relaxing the formal mess-jacket atmosphere. But John and I thought the evening needed a little livening up. That's when we got the idea to unstuff the stuffed shirts of a couple of married first lieutenants who were too young to be taking themselves seriously.

So we picked one out, descended on him, expressed real interest in his views on things, and invited him out to the stag bar. We knew our patsy would not stay long, because his wife had him on a pretty good leash. So we used a little quick-drink method we knew about.

This involved a somewhat bawdy little song, whose lyrics ended with "bottoms up!"—at which point we "down the hatched" our drinks. So he just kind of automatically followed suit.

Of course, we had him between us for better control and maybe double-teamed him a few times on drinks. We soon had him well-organized, then took him back and presented him to his wife.

After giving him a long and pointed once-over, she gave us a dirty look and said, "Thanks a lot!"

That worked so well we tried another one, with maybe John doing most of the singing and me most of the "bottoms up!"

The next thing I remember was the next morning, with no knowledge whatever of how I got home. There I had been, walking around under my own steam and could have been guilty of murder and not known about it. The obvious question is: How could a dope like that end up wearing stars? Part of the answer is that I did not remain a dope like that, because I learned never to underestimate the dangers inherent in alcohol.

Some comments are:

- Immaturity is taking the place of judgment when dislike of your current post or antipathy toward your present commander is allowed to sucker you into a decision to your future disadvantage—like quitting the Army in a pout and a huff. There will be other assignments and more commanders in the future, but this is the only Army we have.
- Properly controlled, a social drink or two with friends is one of the pleasant amenities of life. But there is no more universal or more dangerous "small" action than the question of whether or not it is safe to have another drink. Publius Syrus, Roman slave and poet of the first century B.C., said it this way: "Wine has drowned more than the sea."
- I do not recommend frequent "taking counsel of your fears," thus reducing your life and career to a continuing series of vacillations over minor matters. But judgment, like memory, can be sharpened with practice. So when a warning bell rings in your mind over some small temporary convenience today, let judgment consider what the future consequences might be.

12

The Importance of Pursuing a Hobby

IN THE FALL of 1923, on the day before the Army-Navy game, my West Point class attended a lecture by the professor of chemistry, Col. Wirt Robinson, a much loved and respected officer. It did not occur to me then that the fine old gentleman—bald and portly, nearing the sixty-four-year retirement age—would, in one hour, have a far-reaching effect on my life.

As we settled in our seats, we knew this would be no stereotyped lecture, for he was an imaginative speaker—like the time he explained how modern gunpowder was invented in the fourteenth century by some old European monks "monkeying around" in a laboratory. This day he began by stating his scheduled topic.

"Now," he added, "if I talked on that subject you young gentlemen would sit there thinking about the Navy game tomorrow, letting my words enter one ear and exit the other without a trace. Therefore, I've changed it to one I hope you'll listen to: 'The Importance of a Hobby to an Army Officer.'"

That radical switch from an academic lecture to a bootleg subject captured our attention. He explained that an officer needs some way to broaden a strictly military life, and that a selected hobby was one method of doing this. Also, if properly chosen, it would be an always available means of relaxing the stresses and strains of official duties, thus making us more effective officers.

He emphasized that each man must select his own hobby; like choosing a wife or trying on a hat, no one else can do it for you. The choices are endless: from photography or stamp collecting to golf; from woodworking or historical reading to painting and sculpture; from mountain climbing or gardening to fishing—whatever best suits your needs, interests, and aptitudes.

This led to discussion of *his* hobby, which was nature study. He outlined its many aspects, from bird watching to bug collecting, from study of plants on land to marine life in fresh or salt water, with many types of possible specializations under each heading. Further, how serious or technical you want to be need not be decided in advance. He had started with nature walks, but ended by writing books on what he observed.

"Now," the old gentleman concluded, "there are often ways knowledge gained in your hobby can accomplish something useful. For example, if you know that hawks have exceptional telescopic vision, and that they hate and will attack owls on sight, it's easy to clear an area of hawks. Just put a stuffed owl in a dead tree on a hilltop, and wait in a concealed blind nearby with a shotgun."

He then reached under the lecture counter for a large wicker basket, which was full of hawks he had killed the preceding day on nearby Storm King Mountain. He next showed several action photo slides of hawks attacking a stuffed owl—and being shot down. But it was the basket of dead hawks that changed words to reality, a visual aid that fixed his lecture in our memories to stay.

Eight years later, in 1931, I was back at West Point, this time as an Army lieutenant on an athletic detail trying (unsuccessfully) to repeat my 1928 membership on the American Olympic team. It was my athletic swan song, bringing with it the realization, athletically speaking, that I would increasingly resemble the "old gray mare." Not what I used to be.

It was then I recalled Col. Wirt Robinson's memorable lecture and understood that competitive athletics had been my hobby for years. Now, with reflexes failing and the old legs going downhill, it was apparent that what had been a stimulating challenge would gradually grow less satisfying, and even become increasingly frustrating. So, while I would continue recreational sports, there was need for a lifetime hobby to be phased in—which posed the question: What?

Remembering that he had said each person must choose his own hobby, I decided to make an estimate of the hobby situation. So I sat down with paper and pencil, listing the requirements this hobby must have:

- One to follow the rest of my life.
- Independence from geographical location or climate.
- One I could exercise in sickness and old age.
- Involve no excessive impedimenta or cost.
- Conversely, should bring some financial return—even offer opportunity for considerable income if I decided to make it my retirement avocation.
- Should, if possible, be of value professionally while on active duty.
- Also, should be one I could work at as little or as much as I wanted to.

Next I made a list of potential hobby interests, including those mentioned above, and added all others I could think of: from free-lance writing to watch repairing, silversmithing to cooking, astronomy to lapidary, antique china or coin collecting to furniture refinishing—even such things as archaeology, taxidermy, and cartooning.

Finally came the logical step of matching and weighing each hobby mentally against the requirements. Instead of being a laborious procedure, this was easy, because free-lance writing seemed, for me, to stand alone as best meeting all my demands.

I set the project aside for a couple of weeks to let it cool. But the answer still came out the same: free-lance writing.

So I bought a portable typewriter, subscribed to *Writer's Digest,* and taught myself touch-typing. My first article—titled "Carpentry on Commutation," illustrated with photos and sketches of furniture I had made from packing boxes—was published in the *Infantry Journal.* The check was eight dollars for a completely "off trail" piece.

In the years that followed I received countless rejection slips from all directions, took correspondence courses with *Writer's Digest,* and, finally, began to make progress in writing short pieces for the *Infantry Journal,* then *Combat Forces Journal* and *ARMY* magazine, often under pen names.

There were years when I wrote nothing for publication, especially during World War II and the late 1950s. But writing became an increasingly fascinating hobby the more I learned, and on occasion I wrote for local newspapers, including a weekly column.

There was, however, one unfortunate side effect: My writing was probably a factor in getting me assigned to staff duty for most of the last half of my service. But that is over now, and writing keeps me busy, able to afford a better brand of bourbon, and happy in retirement.

Many of our most successful men had hobbies. The best known, perhaps, were President Franklin Roosevelt's stamp collecting and the oil painting of Sir Winston Churchill and President Dwight Eisenhower.

Over the years, I noticed a surprising number of senior officers had hobbies, often so unobtrusively exercised most people were unaware of them. One top general in Hawaii before World War II was a woodwork hobbyist, and a multistarred general still on active duty is a skilled cabinetmaker. An internationally known four-star admiral designed animated clocks and other intricate tinkering projects, while one of our most important four-star commanders today is a radio "ham."

In Florida, where I live, the happiest older people are those who earlier developed a hobby or avocation. One of my retired officer friends and his wife became orchid fanciers, an interest they shared for years and developed into a remunerative business. Now, for the widow, this provides an added income—and an absorbing interest.

A distinguished senior general was asked on the eve of his retirement, "Are you taking a job or do you have a hobby?"

"Neither one," he said. "I'll just be retired—hunt, fish, play golf, and work in the yard."

Actually, that's a comprehensive hobby program—and it worked fine for him.

If you don't have one now, should there be a hobby in your future and, if so, what? Only you can decide. Here are several pertinent considerations:

- Some say, "The military profession is my hobby." That is true if you are a good officer—but you can also lay the groundwork for another from which you will never retire.
- The word "hobby" shouldn't be applied too restrictively; perhaps "interests" is a better word. This includes such varied activities as music appreciation or playing bridge, reading and collecting whodunits, or growing roses.

- No matter what extracurricular activity you adopt on active duty, one basic principle should be clear: Never permit it to interfere with or reduce your interest in your professional career and duties. Rather, if your hobby is kept in perspective, you will become a better officer, for all work and no play will make any Jack dull.
- Finally, never let any interest or hobby become a monkey on your back, no matter how absorbing it may become. Ride your hobby; don't let it ride you.

13

ROTC Graduates: Good as Ever If Not Better

"IT IS A pleasure and privilege to speak at this, your commissioning ceremony," was my opening sentence as guest speaker in addressing the Army and Air Force Reserve Officers' Training Corps (ROTC) graduates and guests at Syracuse University on 2 June 1972.

Guest speakers are entitled to open with a story, so I told them about old Uncle Bill Greenlee. Uncle Bill owned a mule and a plow, and plowed spring gardens for professors at Clemson College (now Clemson University) in South Carolina, where my father was a professor.

One spring Professor Johnson, who taught mathematics and lived across the street, asked Uncle Bill to plow his garden.

"No, sir, Perfesser," Uncle Bill replied, "it ain't the right time of the moon yet."

"But, Uncle Bill," Professor Johnson protested, "Professor Newman is professor of agriculture, and he says it is the right time."

Uncle Bill pulled off his sweat-stained old felt hat, held it over his chest with one hand and scratched his head with the other before he said, "Well, it is this way: Perfesser Newman is just gettin' his education, but I done got mine."

So I said to the ROTC graduates, "I feel a lot like old Uncle Bill Greenlee. You are just starting your experience as officers, but I have done got mine—and learned some lessons the long, hard way."

Of course, the question was: After twelve years in retirement, what could I say of value to new second lieutenants as they faced the varied challenges and responsibilities of officers?

The answer was easy when I asked myself: What can I say now—looking back on thirty-five years of active duty—that would have helped me most, if somebody had told me early in my own military career?

Some of my thoughts on command and leadership for neophyte Syracuse University ROTC shavetails may be helpful to other lieutenants elsewhere. Instead of dealing in generalities, here are several selected happenings cited—along with guidelines adduced from them—beginning with a lesson I learned fifty-two years ago as an ROTC cadet at Clemson College. It comes readily to mind today, because it deals with haircuts.

It was the custom at Clemson for upperclassmen to clip the hair of freshmen right down to the skull on 1 April, to celebrate April Fools' Day. So when students assembled for the usual half-hour in our general assembly hall—for a prayer, news summary, and administrative announcements—hundreds of skinheads were scattered among the seated cadets. The faculty, in chairs on the rostrum, would keep straight faces, ignoring the naked heads.

During my freshman year the commandant of cadets, an Army colonel, decided to put a stop to April Fools' hair-clipping. Since the college was then a fully uniformed cadet corps of twelve hundred, he issued a flat order that the practice would stop.

But when the day came there was the usual scattering of skinheads in the assembly hall—and faculty members had more trouble than usual trying to keep straight faces. Because before the commandant (the Army colonel) could take his seat he had to step over a ring of hair nearly a foot high around his chair on the rostrum.

Guideline: Do not issue flat, arbitrary orders that you cannot enforce.

As a company commander I sent my new lieutenant down to be briefed in the supply room—not just for a conducted tour, but a planned schedule of instruction by the supply sergeant. Next came a similar schedule in the mess hall with the mess sergeant, and after that by the first sergeant and company clerk in orderly room administration.

Company commanders today are not much older than their lieutenants, and some may not do this. But any young lieutenant can, after touching base with the captain, initiate his own orientation:

- Ask the first sergeant to assemble copies of standing orders and manuals you ought to read—then read them carefully.
- Study regulations about any duty assignment you are given. We have wonderful manuals, and if you read up on your job you will be surprised how soon you are recognized as professionally qualified in your field.
- Go to the supply room and ask the supply sergeant to set up an instructional schedule for you there. There is a lot to learn about supplies. Be sure to find out how weapons are safeguarded and accounted for, inquire about ammunition storage, and read safety regulations.
- After you have the picture in the supply room, ask the mess sergeant to explain all the records he keeps. Also ask him to tell you how he draws rations, organizes his work shifts, and anything else about the way he runs his kitchen and handles his men.
- Ask the first sergeant to explain the duty roster, sick book, and other working procedures in the orderly room. Learn how personnel records are handled and study regulations about them.

Guideline: The sergeants in your unit can be a new lieutenant's best professional friends—while both you and they observe proper military courtesy, with mutual respect for each other.

Two principles are involved: (1) An officer should never be too proud or stiff-necked to learn from anybody who knows more about any particular subject; (2) this does not apply only to newly commissioned second lieutenants but continues throughout an officer's career. When you reach senior rank it is called a "briefing" but is still the same thing: You seek information from those who can give it to you.

Before closing my talk at Syracuse, one cornerstone fundamental had to be covered. All too often I have heard young officers complain, "They don't give me enough to do, not enough responsibility." These young officers never seem to realize that in saying this they have confessed their failure to meet the one responsibility of an officer that cannot be delegated: the responsibility to be a self-starter!

If you find yourself with nothing to do—and you will on occasion—start thinking: "What, among all the things I can do, should I do now that I have the time?" Read regulations, prepare instruction for drill, design better training aids, spot inventory sensitive items of supply—the list is endless, and the choice is yours.

When you do this a most interesting change takes place in your professional life. The more you know, the more you want to know. The better officer you become, the more exacting duty assignments will come your way. And the more pressing demands on you as an officer, the happier you will be.

So I urged the ROTC graduates, wearing their shining new gold bars: "If you remember nothing else I've said here today, remember this guideline: Be a self-starter! Don't expect somebody else to program the computer that is your brain—program it yourself!"

Of course, I discussed other things important to new officers in their command and leadership careers—like judgment and common sense, human understanding, and others. But it is time to include here some things I learned from the Army ROTC graduates at Syracuse University.

On the morning before my talk at 3:00 P.M. I was privileged to meet with five Distinguished Military Graduates of the ROTC who received Regular Army commissions: Larry S. Flatau, Brian J. Klaiber, Patrick J. Walsh, William A. Wiley, and David F. Witchi. These were outstanding young officers, and we spent three hours walking over their beautiful and impressive campus.

There were chairs and tables spotted around for homecoming guests, so we stopped for several roundtable seminars. Those informal discussions are the basis for five comments:

- These young officers met every standard of my day. Further, they surpassed us in at least these interesting qualities: relaxed self-assurance and self-confidence.
- All were proud and happy they joined the ROTC, and that they followed through to earn commissions. Further, they told me, many of their university classmates now regretted they had dropped out of ROTC or had not enrolled initially.
- They all had neat haircuts, with the fine clean-cut appearance that—during my thirty-five years of active service—typified good officers. In answer to my question they agreed, with amused tolerance, that their abbreviated haircuts marked them as "squares" in the eyes of the university long-haired element. But that is nothing new, because there were both squares and free-wheelers in my time, too.

- Two of the five were going on to another year of advanced study before beginning their active-duty careers. This underlines the heavier emphasis on academic training in our modern Army— among other changes to meet the more complex technical demands of this electronic-nuclear-space age.
- I looked for evidence of the much publicized "generation gap" during our campus chair seminars, but we had no trouble communicating. Their standards, hopes, goals, and ideals were at least as high as in my era. These were the top men of their group; but, later in the day, when shaking hands with the other neatly uniformed young officers at the commissioning ceremony, this satisfying feeling was reinforced: We are getting top-quality officers from the ROTC—as good if not better than ever before.

14

Intemperance Can Become a Tyrant

MY MORNING NEWSPAPER had a dispatch reporting that the Pentagon has announced establishment of a rehabilitation program to treat an estimated 150,000 alcoholics in the armed services. The General Accounting Office (GAO) is cited as authority that 5 percent, or one out of every twenty men, are alcoholics. This makes me wonder what standard the GAO used to classify an "alcoholic." There were not that many in my day.

Curiously enough, this report comes at a time when the current all-volunteer Army program is in full swing with its permissive policy of no reveille, more hair, no KP, and beer in the barracks. Since beer is alcoholic, one program appears designed to cure hangovers from the other. My experience with alcoholic beverages for more than forty-seven years—as a social-hour drinker, and observer of drinkers of all kinds and degrees—qualifies me to comment on alcohol and its effects on those who tipple.

Some may say a study of what alcohol can do for you, and to you, is not fitting to a military journal. But the record shows that from the dawn of history soldiers have been no strangers to wine, women, and song.

Since I can't carry a tune in a tuba, others will have to comment on the beneficial effects of song on a soldier's psyche. As to the part women play in military life, I am not without some knowledge and experience, but editors hold the rigid view that an author should understand the subject about which he writes. So that brings us back to alcohol.

When I reported to Fort Benning in 1925, Prohibition was in force. But some on the post, like thousands of civilians across the nation, circumvented the law in spite of possible penalties.

One incident, involving a lieutenant who later lost his commission from drinking, reflects an intriguing facet of how alcohol can affect a man. It was reported to me by a classmate named Wayne, who witnessed the event.

On this Sunday morning the lieutenant woke up in what is known as a hungover condition. Since you could not get a drink on the post, and bringing a bottle on the military reservation was risky, he had brought the hangover back from the nearby town. So he had to return to town for some hair of the dog that bit him—but his car conked out on a sandy road before he got off the post.

That's where Wayne found him, and stopped to offer help. To Wayne's amazement, the hungover lieutenant seized a tree limb from the ditch and dealt the hood of his car a clanging blow.

"Say, what the hell did you do that for?" Wayne asked.

"Because this damned thing has run out of gas again," the bleary-eyed sufferer said, and belted the hood of his car another furious clout.

This highlights a basic fact: When alcohol reaches your brain and mine—there are no exceptions—*we become changed men*. How much changed and in what fashion varies with individuals and the amount of alcohol consumed. If you are one of those unfortunates whom alcohol runs off his rocker, there is only one way to escape going to hell in a bottle: Don't touch the stuff again, ever—not even one teeny-weeny sip.

Another incident from those Benning days concerns my first "client" when I was defense counsel of a special court-martial. He started in the Army as a good soldier, became a private first class, and was on the way to becoming a squad leader. Then he discovered alcohol, and invested his extra Pfc. money in the local liquid dynamite known as Georgia corn—at bargain bootleg prices.

My client was one of those good soldiers, when sober, whom alcohol transmutes into disagreeable belligerent troublemakers. One morning he arrived on the rifle range in the transition stage between under the influence and hungover.

As a result, he tangled orally with a sergeant and ended by taking a poke at him. So the court found him guilty as charged, and sentenced him to four months in the local gaol.

Whereupon my client said to me, "Lieutenant, can I speak to the court?"

"No," I answered.

But he turned to them anyway and began, "You bloody bastards . . ."

When the president of the court, a short-fuse type, older captain, leaped to his feet, I jumped forward and—with the help of the guard—hustled my client out of the room. That was the most effective legal act of my courtroom career, because it saved him from another trial.

Within days the former good soldier was in solitary confinement on bread and water, still fighting the world in the prolonged mental hangover that can be worse than the temporary physical kind. Like the lieutenant whose car ran out of gas, his only hope for the future was to swear off alcohol, completely and for good.

But there is also another side to the use of alcohol.

One of my Old Army friends at Benning was a veteran captain, who rose from the ranks in World War I after years as an enlisted soldier. Before leaving the post I stopped by his quarters to pay my respects and to thank him for his helpful advice.

To my surprise he was having an end-of-day drink of Coca-Cola (it wasn't Coke then) and Georgia corn. He didn't offer me one, but did offer some advice and admonitions.

His final caution was, holding up the Georgia corn, "Look at that bottle and get this straight: A bottle can be your friend or your enemy, and if it's not your friend, it is your enemy. So leave it alone—but I hope you do not have to endure that fate."

Some of my more mellow bottle experiences are of record in articles like "Forge of Experience" (ARMY, October 1967), "Memory of the Past Renews the Joy" (January 1969), "What are Generals Made Of?" (July and August 1969), and others. In addition, I learned some things the hard way—including when and where and how much it is safe for me to drink.

Also, in many and varied troop duty assignments—including a memorable tour as a lieutenant in the Hawaiian Division's military police—I witnessed the tragedy, heartbreak, and stupidity that too much alcohol can bring. Here are selected recollections:

- Young soldiers, officer and enlisted, who let the tropics and a plethora of cheap alcohol wreck their lives in the Philippines; lost commissions, injuries in accidents, black marks on efficiency reports, and—worst of all—the Sad Sack souls who became alcoholics because they had not the sense to see that, for them, alcohol was an addictive, deadly poison.
- Broken and mutilated bodies, as well as the severely injured and scarred who lived, that resulted from automobile wrecks I investigated as an MP lieutenant. Often, especially at night, at the scene of the accident there would be the sick sour smell of vomit and alcohol. And more often than not the driver of at least one of the cars had been drinking. Unfortunately, death and injuries were not limited to the drinking drivers themselves.
- The lieutenant in my company, a once great athlete, whose former superiors failed to "lower the boom" on his drinking before it was too late. When I arrived, he was a hopeless alcoholic, and it became my painful duty to prefer the charges that eliminated him from the Army.

There were other instances over the years, from privates to master sergeants to general officers—and in some cases their wives—whose personal lives and military careers were irretrievably damaged by too much drinking. The following comments seem pertinent:

- Spare me those who use alcohol as an alibi, claiming they were "tight, so not really responsible." Drunk or sober, every man and woman is responsible for what he or she does.
- Many young people put a blight on their lives while inebriated, before they discover their alcoholic limitations: like a liquor-induced automobile wreck for a man, or a liquor-induced seduction for a woman. Only luck saved me from trouble in my early bottle initiation, for which I am grateful to fate. But Lady Luck is a fickle floozy—so don't depend on her.
- As to why people drink, there is a whole complex of interwoven motives, including: for excitement, to be sociable, to relax, for a nightcap, to think, to remember, to forget, and others. But to drink as a substitute for solving your personal problems is the sure road to disaster.

- I do not believe one of every twenty men in uniform is an alcoholic. Nor do I believe in treating officers like irresponsible children, such as the proposal a few years ago in certain official and unofficial circles to outlaw the traditional Airborne Prop Blast ceremony. But I am of two minds about the idea of beer in barracks. This may aggravate the alcohol problem; but, on the other hand, perhaps easy availability of a quiet beer or two in barracks will keep some people out of off-post beer joints. We'll have to wait and see how it works out.

- In summary, alcohol can be a boon to human companionship, a relaxing balm for the body—or turn your life into a hell on earth. It all depends on your ability to handle it.

15

A Volunteer Army Is More Fun, but . . .

LIKE OLD GEN. WINFIELD SCOTT of Mexican War fame, I have a "fixed opinion." My fixed opinion is that, in the present and fore-seeable world situation, the all-volunteer Army proposal ignores the lessons of our history for the past two hundred years. The record shows we cannot hope to buy enough volunteers, thus the effort to do so is financial folly. This does not mean, however, that I am against an all-volunteer Army as such. Far from it, because I served in one for fifteen years, and it was a lot more fun.

From privates to generals, members of that little army of the 1920s and 1930s were all Regular Army volunteers. Its professional competence made possible the tremendous military expansion for World War II, but we knew how to laugh and enjoy life, too—which included practical jokes.

Consider, for example, the little diversion organized between halves of one of our post league football games in the late 1920s at Fort Benning, when the 2d Battalion of the 29th Infantry played the tank battalion in Doughboy Stadium. The capacity crowd, including many wives and families, rustled with mild interest as a plywood tank "float" rolled onto the field. Many in the stands guessed that the 2d Battalion planned to pull the oldie of blowing up that symbol of the tankers.

This was good prognosticating, for smoke soon boiled from the tank as its crew scrambled out and deserted it on the run. There was scattered applause mixed with boos, interrupted by an explosion on top of the tank. Then a brief silence, followed by laughter and some high-pitched feminine screams. The explosion was just a large firecracker but, in addition to the sound effect, it caused one side of the plywood tank to fall off—and out popped some fifteen to twenty cats of all colors and descriptions.

The feminine squeals came from the owners of some of the cats, and several of them, cheered on by the crowd, tried to rescue their felines on the spot.

Among aggrieved pet owners there was talk about tarring and feathering the brash young lieutenant who put on that halftime show. Then, just when it seemed things would blow over with no official notice taken of the affair, the lieutenant got a formal "You will reply by endorsement hereon" letter from regimental headquarters.

The complaint letter, written in a feminine hand and attached as an enclosure, called for disciplinary action against the "heartless perpetrator" who had kidnapped her little Fifi. Especially since innocent, pristine little Fifi had been confined with all those uncouth boy alley cats, who had ruined her virtue. Not only that, it happened at a critical time for Fifi, who soon was expecting unplanned offspring—which meant she could never have pedigreed kittens (it seems that, pedigreewise, the melody lingers on). This entailed considerable loss in money value, so the lieutenant should also pay sizable damages.

Let the record show, however, that the imaginative lieutenant who thought up the catnapping caper was not taken in by the fake letter. He endorsed it back to the effect that he had reliable information that little Fifi was in need of a shotgun wedding before she met the boys in the tank.

More dynamic extracurricular exercises were conducted during the annual student encampment of The Infantry School. These included such traps for fall guys as "snipe hunts" and "badger fights." My favorite was the "enraged husband" gambit.

A prime organizer of such off-duty mummery was Capt. Russell Skinner. He was also a star participant in quite a different enterprise. The occasion was the annual baseball game between a team from the student officer classes and one from the school's staff and faculty.

From my seat in the stands at Gowdy Field I was watching the staff and faculty warm up, when a motorcycle and sidecar rolled slowly through the gate on the first-base side and proceeded toward home plate. Spectators tittered, then laughed when they got the idea.

The passenger in the sidecar was Captain Skinner, dressed in blouse and garrison cap, with large cardboard cutout eagles on his shoulders. The whole left breast of his blouse was covered with oversize ribbons and decorations. He bowed and smiled to the crowd, then heaved up his chest and flicked imaginary dust off the ribbons. A second student trotted behind the sidecar holding up another blouse on a hanger, also covered with an exaggerated display of ribbons. It was marked "ANNEX."

Among those witnessing this charade was the second baseman on the staff and faculty team, a dynamic eagle colonel and former all-around athlete. He did not say a word, though he knew this burlesque was pointed at him, because he habitually wore by far the biggest display of ribbons on the post, many of them foreign decorations awarded by European nations after World War I.

When the slow-moving sidecar was halfway to home plate, Captain Skinner executed a double take toward a man with a camera (planted of course), and ordered his sidecar over to pose for a picture, being sure to get the "ANNEX" in the picture, too. He then noticed a stage-prop movie camera being set up near home plate, so he directed his driver over there where he preened around for more pictures. Finally, he left, to continued laughing applause from the stands, again ostentatiously flicking imaginary dust from his ribbons.

It was a devastating spoof, and a lesser man would have had a hard time playing his best after that. But Col. Waite C. Johnson, whom I was privileged to know quite well on the tennis courts, was no man to fold under pressure. Though he was then over fifty years old, in my book he had the last laugh—because he not only played errorless ball in the field but banged out a line-drive double the first time he came to bat, and followed that with a sharply hit single.

More vignettes from those days come to mind, but these are enough for our purpose here. What have they got to do with an all-volunteer Army? Space is not available to summarize my visualization of the whole picture, but four comments seem relevant:

• Those of us in uniform then loved the Army, were in it because we wanted to be, and we had the kind of good time that money can't buy. Certainly money didn't buy it on the 1922–41 pay scale; the pay of an eight-man squad was $216 a month, while a second lieutenant drew $125 for more than five years and a first lieutenant $175 for another five to ten years.

- In the past twenty-five-year effort to buy volunteers, the rank structure of soldiers and commissioned officers has been distorted as a means of raising pay over and above frequently raised pay by grade. This ill-considered jump upward so fast in rank, and then no place to go, is (only my opinion, of course) in large measure self-defeating. It places early undue emphasis on promotions, then closes the door on them. The result is a different atmosphere from that in which the old lightheartedness bubbled to the surface in that all-volunteer time.
- Let me add that, in my view, it is not the tensions in the world situation today that make the fundamental difference. It is the great expansion in numbers of men required in the armed forces, and the unsound concept of trying to meet this need at the same time we attempt to do away with the basic obligation of every citizen to help defend his home on call.
- No one dislikes the draft more than I do, especially when I remember how much fun we had during my years in the all-volunteer Army of the 1920–40 period. But our national security is the first consideration. Even the great Roman Empire disintegrated when it tried to buy enough soldiers to defend it. Money never has and never can replace the obligation to answer the call to arms when needed to supplement volunteers. This is as vital to national survival in presenting a resolute face to deter would-be aggressors as it is to fight any war forced upon us.

16
Our Fighting Fiber

YOU HEAR AND read questions like these about how soldiers of yesterday compare to those we have now: Were they tougher then? How was it possible to develop so many fighting soldiers for World War II from civilians? Are Americans losing their fighting fiber?

In many ways soldiers in the ranks are different today and their place in the general order of things is changed. Many factors go into this. Curiously enough, comparing the marriage of a private in 1925 with another private's marriage in 1967—forty-two years apart—reflects some interesting facets of these changes.

Soon after I joined my first company the middle-aged leather-faced latrine orderly, with a long foreign name, came in and asked our captain's permission to get married. He would lose certain fringe benefits if he married without permission.

"As a private first class you can't support a wife," the captain admonished.

"She has a job, too, Captain."

"But you may have children, and she couldn't work then. Have you thought of that?"

"Well, Captain," the soldier said, "I've been going with her for three years, and ain't nothing happened yet."

He got permission.

Not long ago there was a newspaper item about a nineteen-year-old Army recruit on the West Coast who planned to get married while on a three-day pass over the weekend. When his pass was withdrawn, that stopped the wedding plans. But not for long, because the prospective mother-in-law wrote to the President of the United States. After a telephone call from the White House the three-day pass was on again. And so they were married.

What has happened to the Army between the weddings of those two privates? Especially since I never heard of a congressional letter about a soldier in my first twenty years in the Army, much less a White House phone call.

To begin with, in those Old Army days every man was a volunteer—thus there by his own choice.

By contrast, a major percentage of those in uniform today are draftees, or serving in some kind of "obligated service" short tour. The average soldier is much younger, and the turnover rate far higher. There are other differences, too, for their educational level is higher—often including college. Further, their pay has been radically improved, and many have private means, and their ranks include young men from influential and wealthy families—unheard of in the all-volunteer Army. A natural result is more married enlisted men.

Before World War II the number of men in uniform—Army, Navy, and Marines (there was no separate Air Force)—was a small fraction of what it is now. Today there is hardly a family in the United States without one or more members who are in, have been in, or may be in one of the services.

Because of this new situation—especially the far greater size and enormously increased military costs—the armed forces hold a place in our national life they never had before.

This has its frustrating effects on commanders, but there are other sides to it, too. Amazing advances in technology place proportionately greater demands on soldiers for more skills, higher education, and increased intelligence—which the Old Army soldier would have been hard-pressed to cope with.

Did the wartime soldier of World War II fight as well as the Old Army type? Even more to the point, are Americans losing their fighting fiber?

One of the best ways to see courage in action is to watch scouts out front in combat (see "Lonely Lead Scouts," *ARMY,* February 1967).

These are almost without exception "wartime soldiers"—two anonymous men in each infantry squad who answer the call "scouts out!" They were—and are today in Vietnam—average Americans. Trained and toughened by professionals, yet still "citizen soldiers." But they measure up in the guts department; the fighting fiber was and remains there.

Only two men in my regiment won the nation's highest battle accolade: the Medal of Honor. Neither was a prewar professional.

Consider Pvt. Harold Moon, Company G, 34th Infantry, a devil-may-care youngster and about as far as you can get from the weathered, long-service soldier of the Old Army. The first night of our landing on Leyte he was at the point where the Japanese counterattack struck the flank of our regiment—and his battle performance in the dark hours between midnight and dawn simply defies description.

No, the Army did not give Harold Moon—or thousands of others—what it takes. The Army had to organize, train, and equip the units. Skilled commanders and staffs prepared campaign and battle plans, and there were competent leaders all the way down to the front lines. But in those final hours, that invisible something Private Moon needed was there in his heart the day he entered the Army. He brought it with him from civilian life, as have so many other Americans. Professional know-how and leadership cannot create it in a few weeks or months of wartime training. It can, however, be heightened and aroused when it's there.

Another facet of our modern Army was brought out at my last station. In one staff section a veteran sergeant was doing his best to instill what he considered proper soldierly discipline in the drafted and obligated-service men under him. With their higher education and quick facility with papers, and more independence resulting from the nature of staff work—plus the freewheeling attitude of this new uniformed generation—the old field soldier was making heavy work of it. With both sides a bit frustrated, perhaps.

But one day he was pleased to receive a picture postcard from a young soldier home on leave. The sergeant felt he was making some headway at last, for on the card was a hand-written message: "Wish you were here."

But his satisfaction was short-lived, because the central feature of that picture postcard was a small island in San Francisco Bay, and the only installation on it was Alcatraz prison.

A point to note is that highly educated private had imagination, and would probably have made a fine officer. This highlights one of the big changes in our modern Army: Not only are a high percentage of enlisted men potential officers, but officer candidate schools have commissioned thousands from the ranks, which was not possible in the Old Army.

In summary:

- The most basic reason we were able to develop our great fighting Army so quickly for World War II was that civilians who entered our training camps—many of whom became officers—already had an inner toughness of heart, a dormant will to fight, of which they themselves seemed unaware.
- This was true because we have a national fighting heritage, though we don't think of ourselves as a martial people. From earliest childhood, however, we learn of Gen. George Washington and the Revolutionary War. Then there were the War of 1812, the war with Mexico, the Civil War, the Indian wars, the Spanish-American War, and, finally, World War I—which played a far-reaching part in developing our national posture to face up to the world situation. So our Regular Army did not have to convince those vast raw levies of men for World War II that Americans were fighting men. They already understood that, knew their relatives and friends expected them to meet the test, and each man's pride demanded he not fail.
- Let no man underestimate this intangible factor, to which now have been added World War II, Korea, and Vietnam to further strengthen the fighting fabric woven into our national heritage.
- The character of the American people has not changed—though the average recruit may need more physical conditioning in basic training. Don't let the few so-called hippies, draft-card burners, and various misfits, and special pleading psychos, fool you— no matter how much the news may feature and blow up "stories" about them. Look at the true index: the battle performance of our soldiers in Vietnam.
- Finally, it's a well-recognized military fact that the fighting heart of a people is a national resource and a basic element of national power. It's not something you lose overnight. And, when

you get right down to it, that's what soldiers are made of. Organize, train, equip, and lead them—then those lonely lead scouts and their frontline buddies will face eternity in the future as they have in the past. There are things to worry about, but that's not one of them.

17

We Must Match the Man with the Job

EVERYBODY—WELL, ALMOST everybody—laughs at Lonely Hearts Clubs. Some of them are run by gyp artists, but some are business enterprises designed to perform a service: match a suitable lonely man with a compatible and equally lonely woman. These organizations are founded on a universal problem of personnel management the we in the Army face, too: the continuing need to fit every man and woman in uniform into the niche for which he or she is best suited.

I doubt if any problem causes more unhappiness than the kind of job each soldier is assigned, especially among drafted men and obligated tour officers. Many come into the Army feeling they must be given duty that uses their civilian skills, so their training and talents will not be wasted. But the needs of the Army come first, so we must get as many soldiers as possible into jobs where they can contribute most to the Army's mission.

Recently I was guest speaker at a civilian luncheon club. Afterwards, a fine-looking elderly gentleman asked me why his son, who had been trained in reconnaissance units, after arriving in Vietnam, had been transferred to the infantry. The father blamed the Army for his son's battle wound because he had not been assigned duties for which he had been trained. Why did the Army do that?

"Well," I said, as kindly as possible, "everywhere I go that kind of question comes up. It would take miracles in personnel management

80

to train hundreds of thousands of men in all the varied skills needed, in exactly the right numbers, so that every man could be kept in those duties in Vietnam, especially when vacancies created by battle casualties can never be known in advance. If 500 men trained as replacements for reconnaissance units arrive in Vietnam, and only 400 are needed, the extra 100 must be assigned other duties. When the infantry is short—which it often is—and those trained for reconnaissance units also had basic training in infantry, that is where they go.

"The Army would like to assign every man to duties he wants, but clearly that is not possible because somebody must do the tough jobs, too. The law of supply and demand—the needs of the service—is as unbending in the military as in civilian life. Without knowing the details in your son's case, that's the best answer I can give."

Unfortunately, those who ask such questions are seldom satisfied with this obvious answer.

Assigning a man to duties for which he is trained can cut two ways. Consider my experience, after becoming a general staff officer of the old Hawaiian Division in 1941. Then my problem was to avoid the staff duty for which I had become qualified. In this I was unsuccessful; for nearly all of my remaining service I was condemned to staff duty.

By nature I was a commander, so I constantly requested command assignments and, briefly, commanded three regiments. From the first regiment I was relieved of command by a piece of Japanese steel on Leyte; from the third I was promoted out of the job; and from the middle one I was prematurely shanghaied to staff duty again—thus enabling me to fully understand that saying sometimes attributed to Voltaire: "May God defend me from my friends; I can defend myself from my enemies." (The saying is, of course, much older.)

However, the point remains that often the decision is based not on how well or how little you are trained for a job nor on your desires, whether fair or unfair, but on the needs of the service as determined by those who do the assigning.

Before World War II things were simpler. The Army was small and the skills required were less varied. With the great expansion of men in uniform, beginning in World War II—and the tremendously varied skills needed—new methods and systems were necessary. So the MOS (military occupational specialty) system was a logical development. But the law of supply and demand remained, so we meet that new word, "reclassification."

Of course, the MOS system cannot remain static. As time passes new refinements are added, like changes and additions to code numbers, automatic data processing and computers. As G1 in Europe I visited the repple-depple there and witnessed the interview system that matched incoming replacements with the needs of requisitioning units. When things didn't come out even—and they never did—the only possible solution was to reclassify overages in some skills into the shortages in others, to fit available skills to existing vacancies.

Before leaving Heidelberg, I saw the initiation of automatic data processing, where punch cards filled out for our needs were electronically transmitted to punch cards in New Jersey. There assignments were made directly to units in Europe, thus short-circuiting the repple-depple and shortening the pipeline. Still, no machine can spew out electronic assignments that make everybody happy.

This search for better ways and methods to match the man to the job continues. The fine article by Lt. Col. Richard J. Bean in the June 1970 *ARMY* tells about the new "Referral Program, a DOD-sponsored computerized man-job matching system for retirees seeking second careers," which is designed to meet the need that results from the retirement of 65,000 to 70,000 men each year (more than 50,000 of them in enlisted grades). So they need a new "assignment" in retirement.

It's that Lonely Hearts Club principle all over again; in this case the need to "marry" the right man to the right job in industry. Business needs mature, disciplined, adaptable, trained men in a wide assortment of skills and experience that these retired people have. So the Department of Defense is stepping in to do for industry and retired servicemen what they cannot do for themselves.

Higher on the active-duty career ladder there is a directly competitive slant to the selection process. These two brief sidelights tell their own story:

Recently I learned how Gen. Dwight D. Eisenhower finished No. 1 in his class at the Command and General Staff College. In those days, one of the most prized professional goals was not only selection for Leavenworth, but to be designated a distinguished graduate. One of his classmates told me that General Eisenhower did more than just "want" that distinction. He enrolled in correspondence courses from Leavenworth before he was selected to go there. So luck had nothing to do with his outstanding No. 1 rating, or with the top assignments that followed because of that fine record.

Several ambitious colonels who had spent most of their service in cushy staff jobs arrived in Europe when I was G1 of USAREUR. They wanted regimental command to better their chances for selection to star rank, but over the years they had avoided troop duty, so division and corps commanders and Seventh Army headquarters did not want them for the simplest of all reasons: They were not the best qualified regimental commanders available. It still puzzles me that those colonels ended up disgruntled, blaming G1 for not somehow getting them these key jobs for which they had not prepared themselves.

We have taken a quick look at only a few pieces of the jigsaw puzzle of assignments, but here are several general comments:

- Many skills in civilian life are valuable in the armed forces, too, but there are also many military skills for which there is no counterpart. So it is inevitable that a high percentage of men entering military service must be trained for jobs in which they have little or no experience, and the nature of which is objectionable to them.
- In job hunting for retirement there is no substitute for "Seek and ye shall find." Further, there is no better place to start seeking than through this new Department of Defense Referral Program, beginning in your local personnel office. All career servicemen—especially those nearing retirement—should read that article by Lieutenant Colonel Bean in the June 1970 *ARMY*.
- The right job wants the right man, just as much as the other way around. To get the duty you want, make yourself the best qualified man for it.
- Troop needs are never static, for the law of supply and demand is constantly changing to meet new situations. Further, there is no featherbedding in military service, so "reclassification" and "retraining" are inevitable. When you look at them as opportunities, things will start working out better.
- Few if any men have served a full military career without being led down some garden paths they didn't want to travel. It may not make you happy to remember what Confucius said, but the smart man and good soldier will take his advice, and relax. It's easy to damage your tomorrow by futile struggles today. This is the Voice of Experience speaking.

18

Gone Are the Days . . .

IT IS SOP (Standard Operating Procedure) for young squirts to feel that old goats clutter the landscape of progress. This is the way most active-duty soldiers view relics of the horsey days: failing to realize they may have missed something special in never having hefted a saber or straddled a gelding.

Some of the swank went out of being a soldier when the jingle of spurs and the smell of horse sweat gave way to the mutter of motors and the reek of exhaust fumes. And not only in the cavalry. An infantry corporal showed me how to make mules stand still when loading a pack train of those four-legged trucks: One man bit down on the tip of a mule's ear while another adjusted the pack load.

Fort Riley, Kan.—home of the Cavalry School—was a name to reckon with before mechanized vehicles, paratroopers, and guided missiles. To take the troop officer's equitation course at Riley was a rare privilege for an infantryman, not unmixed with physical hazard. My presence in the school year 1930–31 was designed to make a silk purse out of an equestrian sow's ear: a finished rider out of an infantryman.

My name was soon prominently inscribed in the horsey archives at post headquarters, for I was the first man in the class to sign the "police book." If you and a horse parted company involuntarily you were policed, and custom required you to sign the book—with date, place, name of horse, and your alibi.

One day early in the course the class went out for a morning cross-country ride. My troubles began at the first jump, but the hard-boiled instructor—an outstanding cavalryman named Gus—was not impressed. I had had similar problems before.

Then we headed for a rock fence, so I gave my steed a spur goose and crop wallop. At the last second he slammed on the brakes, slid into the fence on his butt, and bounced me off. Only a desperate grip on the reins saved a long walk home.

The horse and I were still tagging along, well lathered, when we arrived at the hippodrome, an enclosed area with a wide assortment of jumps. Here I was policed again.

Eventually we headed for home, and faced the last jump half a mile from the stables. It was a solid one, made of revetted earth with a telephone pole mounted horizontally a foot above the revetment.

Having qualified to sign the police book twice that day, I was in a mood characterized more by determination than by good judgment. My basic plan for that final jump was simple: Accelerate my mount to such a speed that he would not be able to stop.

This was done, but he was also going too fast to get off the ground and clear the jump. The result was the damnedest crash—the horse and I cartwheeling in a somersault to a scrambled-egg landing.

Gus was there to see it. He sat on his horse, speechless, watching my fallen charger regain its feet—no bones broken, fortunately—and trot briskly for the stables, empty stirrups flapping. When I struggled to my feet, Gus wheeled his horse and headed for the stables, too.

It's a desolate feeling when no one loves you. But when you add to this the requirement, on a cavalry post, to walk home from a ride and sign the police book three times in one day, it's a low point in your military orbit.

This was not the only time Gus was without words to express his cavalry view of my infantry riding. On at least one of these occasions I did not even have to sign the book.

It happened in the East Riding Hall. I was on William Tell, a bob-tailed jumper of considerable ability who had a tendency to hump his forehand and tuck his forefeet when he got in trouble on a jump. We weren't strangers, having once come down a cliff-like canyon slide together a bit too fast and done some freewheel tumbling at the bottom.

One of the jumps this day was a four-foot single bar, set the narrow way in the hall to give a short-run approach. An experienced rider will tell you that a four-foot single bar, with all that empty space under it, will buffalo some horses.

Gus was sitting his mount in the middle of the riding hall, watching. I brought William Tell around in a tight turn. He saw the bar and tried to run out, but I had him locked on target so there was nothing to do but jump.

William was slightly out of step when he took off in a prodigious leap—humping his shoulders and tucking his forefeet. Both of us sailed over the jump—but not as a unit. In a split second I saw we were parallel in mid-air with William out from under me to the right, but it appeared that if I extended my arms I could grab him around the neck on landing. There wasn't time to realize that this would cause my body to swing forward and be trampled underfoot as William continued on, or become the underneath man in a sudden pile-up.

I did get an arm around William's neck, my body did swing forward—and, miraculously, William managed to land with a slight crowhop and stand still. Thus, by tucking my feet I found myself hanging like a locket from a necklace of my own arms around William's neck. But I was not yet policed, because I wasn't on the ground.

Gus sat motionless. All other jumping stopped and the class closed in a semi-circle around a tableau without precedent in the history of the Cavalry School.

Of course, I could let my feet down a few inches and stand up—but then I would be policed. It seemed possible that, if I could get one toe in a stirrup, I might make it back on the horse. This took time, sweat, and struggle, while pop-eyed cavalrymen offered advice—though none of them would have been caught dead in such an endeavor. But I did make it back into the saddle.

Gus heaved a sigh and reined his horse away. Sometimes, even for cavalrymen, words are inadequate.

There are many things about that course to remember for those who love horses. Like our end-of-year riding competition, "The Standard Stakes." This was not limited to Cavalry School students, but open to all officers on the post. A real wing-ding contest.

So I entered, with about a hundred others. As advised by an officer who should have known better, I wore riding boots. The competition began with a quarter-mile run on foot to a picket line of horses—first come, first choice to mount up. Running in riding boots soon cramped the calves of my legs so that I could hardly walk, much less run. Thus,

I started the half-mile ride to a pistol range at the tail end of the long line of riders. I dismounted at the pistol range, ran to my firing point, picked up the pistol, and fired at a Coca-Cola bottle on a stake at twenty-five yards. Not an easy target to hit after running a quarter mile and riding a half mile under stress. Further, you had to keep shooting until you broke the bottle, going back for more ammunition when the five rounds at the firing point were used up.

I got my bottle with the second shot and mounted another horse, having gained on the field. I rode about a mile over jumps to a saber course, was handed a saber, and rode that course. On a fresh horse, it was a quarter mile to the foot of a rimrock formation where you dismounted and led the horse up the rocky incline. On top, you mounted and rode another half mile on a dogleg course to a rifle range. With one or two others I cut across the dogleg "rough," doing some broken-field riding through a ravine between scattered large rocks, and gained on the field.

At the rifle range you fired at a ginger ale bottle dangling from a stake at one hundred yards. Once again it was shoot until you broke it (several never did). By hitting on the first shot I moved up some more, and took off on my final horse to the top of the steep rimrock. Here I dismounted and led the horse down on foot.

The easiest path was clogged with horses and riders. So I broke a virgin trail, jumping over the ledge in front of the horse and plunging down through brush, accompanied by a shower of rolling rocks, followed by the thundering horse at the end of the reins a few feet behind—to arrive at the bottom still right side up, ahead of everybody on the easy trail.

Climbing aboard the nag again, I set course for the finish, some half dozen others still ahead of me. It was soon evident I was not gaining on them, in spite of vigorous use of conventional means to accelerate a horse. So I yanked off my wide-brimmed Stetson campaign hat, swung it in a flapping wallop against the horse's rump—and turned loose some Indian-style war whoops. Apparently no cavalryman had ever done that to the plug, for suddenly he came to life. In rodeo style I continued to fan the air and the nag's rump with my Stetson, keeping up Comanche war whoops—and passed all but two of the leaders.

There was a distinct lack of applause from the crowd at the finish as I came, hat-swinging and whooping, over the line to capture third place. That was not the way the Cavalry School taught riding. However, third place won a silver goblet. Applause, or no applause, that trophy is now on display in my study, where it assuages memories of signing the police book so many times—and certain other painful scenes, such as my struggle to get back on William Tell.

You young fellows will retire to the shadows in your turn, though that may be hard to visualize now. As you sip your sunset toddies I hope your memories of the spark, clank, and swoosh in your active-duty days will be as satisfying as are my recollections of the years when hell-for-leather gave the Army its special swank of the oat-burner era.

While your memories will not have the same tone and tine as mine, still it's well for both of us to realize that, for success, the different challenges each faces in his day require the same qualities of mind and heart.

PART II
PRINCIPLES FOR ALL LEVELS OF COMMAND

19

Military Service Cornerstone—Obey Orders

WHEN I WAS at the U.S. Military Academy (1921–25), the baseball coach was Hans Lobert, who had been a well-known big league baseball player (and a character) under John McGraw, the famous manager of the New York Giants.

The word was that as a player Hans became a minor legend when, with a man on first base, he came to bat with orders to bunt and thus advance the runner without risking a double play. Hans got a pitch he liked, however, hit a home run—and manager McGraw fined him one hundred dollars for disobeying orders.

This leads to the basic definition of discipline: the instant and willing obedience to all orders and, in the absence of orders, to what you think those orders would have been.

Applying that principle in battle has never been more spectacularly demonstrated than by the famous "Charge of the Light Brigade" in the Crimean War at Balaklava on 25 October 1854. Because of a misunderstanding of orders, some six hundred cavalrymen rode headlong against the Russian Army.

That spectacular battle action was memorialized in Alfred Lord Tennyson's famous poem, including these words—not quoted verbatim, but as they have hummed in my memory since I read them long years ago:

Cannon to the right of them,
Cannon to the left of them,
  Volleyed and thundered.
Onward rode the six hundred,
  Someone had blundered.
Honor the great charge they made,
Honor the Light Brigade,
  The noble six hundred.
Theirs not to reason why,
Theirs but to do and die.

But it is not that simple. History records exceptions where orders were disobeyed—and with far-reaching, favorable results. Usually it was because the junior was closer to the action and was thus in a better position to make the right judgment. Sometimes, however, the junior officer had a finer mind and the resolution to act on his judgment. The following two violations of orders in battle, both by the great British admiral Lord Horatio Nelson, resulted in major victories.

In the Battle of Cape St. Vincent on 14 February 1797, Nelson was a commodore aboard the British ship *Captain* in the Mediterranean fleet under Adm. Sir John Jervis. One major mission of the British fleet was to destroy the Spanish fleet, which would weaken the naval strength available to Napoleon.

When the Spanish fleet was sighted, it attempted to avoid battle. So Admiral Jervis ordered a change of course and by flag signal ordered each ship to change direction in succession, which called for all ships to continue in file and make the turn at the point where the leading ship changed course.

In wind-powered ships, depending on visual communications, this facilitated control and was a strict requirement when ordered. Nelson, however, saw that this change in succession instead of together (all ships turning simultaneously) would allow the Spanish fleet to escape without a battle. Nelson simply disobeyed the order and turned his ship toward the place necessary to intercept the Spanish fleet.

To his credit, Admiral Jervis realized Nelson was taking the only route to bring the Spanish fleet to battle, and Admiral Jervis signaled the other ships to conform to Nelson's lead. This resulted in a major British victory.

Four years later, on 2 April 1801, Admiral Nelson was second in command to Adm. Sir Hyde Parker of the British fleet in the Baltic, facing the fleets of Denmark, Sweden, and Russia. Admiral Parker wanted to wait for a fleet action in open water, but Nelson wanted to take the initiative by attacking the Danish fleet in the harbor at Copenhagen. Admiral Parker would not agree to this but gave Nelson permission to take part of the fleet under his command and attack the Danish fleet anchored in the harbor at Copenhagen.

This was a daring operation and, after the battle was well under way, Admiral Parker lost his nerve and flew the flag signal "Discontinue the action."

When Admiral Nelson gave no indication he had seen the message, his signal lieutenant called his attention to the order. Admiral Nelson replied, "Acknowledge it."

After a time of pacing the deck, Admiral Nelson asked if his own order for "Closer action" was still flying and added, "Mind, you keep it so."

Then he said to the ship's captain, "Leave off action? Now damn me if I do! You know, Foley, I have only one eye [he had lost the other in a prior battle action] and have a right to be blind sometimes." Then, putting the glass to his blind eye, he announced, "I do not see the signal. . . . . Keep my signal for 'Closer action' flying."

It was a violent battle, with the British taking heavy damage. The result, however, was a great victory for England and acclaim for Admiral Nelson.

But if he had lost the battle with disastrous results for England, what would have happened to Lord Nelson, in spite of his great name and prior battle record?

The above two footnotes to history were at a high level nearly two hundred years ago. Now we will consider one at a lower level within my personal knowledge. It happened in World War II during the Hollandia operation in New Guinea in the Humboldt Bay area. I learned about it after the fact (my landing was in the Tanahmerah Bay area) and came to know the fine young officer involved.

There was both strategic and tactical surprise with little opposition to the landings. The U.S. forces soon had a considerable tonnage of supplies and ammunition ashore, including explosives, on the Humboldt Bay side. Then a single plane came over one night and dropped a bomb in the supply dumps and ammunition storage areas, starting a fire that spread, setting off explosions.

To counter this, a major from one of the support units called on an infantry company commander nearby to take his company in and get the fire under control. The captain demurred because the tactical situation was completely under control, and he felt this would unnecessarily risk the lives and limbs of his soldiers. So he refused to obey the order.

The major then preferred charges for refusing to obey a lawful order. While the court-martial convicted the captain, in view of the circumstances the only sentence was a Letter of Admonition (okay this time, but don't do it again).

The question might be asked, "Have you ever disobeyed an order?" The answer is, "Yes, in Germany in 1954 when I was assistant commander of the 5th Infantry Division."

I was temporarily in command of the division on maneuvers and returned to my command post one day to find the corps commander there. He was unhappy about the situation he found in one company. After briefly stating the reasons for his unhappiness, he added, "I want that company commander relieved!"

When I replied, "Yes, sir, I will investigate the situation," he stared hard at me and repeated, "I want that company commander relieved!"

So I replied again, "Sir, I will investigate it." He then gave me a long, hard look, turned on his heel, and left the command post. So I looked into the matter.

For complicated reasons too detailed to outline here, there had been a misunderstanding, and the corps commander had not talked to the company commander.

Then I made a second mistake. My first mistake was in failing to reply, "Yes, sir." This would leave it to be *assumed* I would look into the matter before taking action.

My second mistake was failure to report in writing that I had not relieved the captain, with a summary of my reasons. This would also have given the corps commander the chance to state reasons I may have overlooked and to repeat his order.

In retrospect, I did owe my company commander the loyalty of checking first before relieving him, but my failure to follow proper procedure later did not enhance my professional future.

This leads me to make these comments:

- In this "obey orders" principle, there is no limit to the complexity and variety of situations, from the lowest levels of authority to national levels. In addition, there is a wide assortment of procedures, including giving lip service to orders on the surface but failing to carry them out with the professional effort and good judgment necessary for success. This is a form of disloyalty.
- Another method of getting around an order is to analyze it, looking for ways to reduce its scope. For example, higher authority may limit offensive actions to battalion or regimental level without prior approval. Under such orders, a reconnaissance in force can be launched. If this is successful, authority can be requested to exploit success. This method was used in World War II.
- There are times when a lack of current information on the changing situation may bring into play part of that definition of discipline, "and, in the absence of orders, do what you think those orders would have been." This is the ultimate test of discipline, professionalism, and judgment.

If the existing situation calls for you to fail to comply with an order, the first requirement is professional good judgment in the changes you make. Further, if the time element permits, the best solution is to recommend or request necessary changes. If the time factor demands immediate action, however, it is of high importance to inform your commander as soon as possible of your actions vis-à-vis his orders. Among other reasons, it is always possible he may have information you do not.

20

How and When to Pass the Buck

THERE ARE TWO kinds of situations that revolve around the question of who is going to occupy the hot seat. One concerns who gets the blame when things go wrong, and we always have with us some who try to blame others for their own failures. But these wiggle-warts never go very high in the Army. The other kind concerns decision-making, and involves that gentle art known as "passing the buck." My observation is that buck-passers, unlike blame-passers, sometimes reach high rank—if they are clever at avoiding the onus in sticky issues.

As I have mentioned before (*ARMY,* November 1963), when I commanded Company G, 26th Infantry, at Plattsburgh Barracks, 1st Sgt. Big Jim Redding had a sign on his desk facing the orderly room door: THE BUCK STOPS HERE. One of my favorite memories is of seeing that sign in action. It was the day after payday, and I started out for lunch. This gave me a passing view through the connecting door into Big Jim's office.

A soldier we'll call Private Hungover arrived at the orderly room door and raised his hand to knock. Big Jim looked up, noted the bloodshot eyes and suffering look, and thus realized Hungover was there to request permission to see me about a three-day recuperative pass. Without hesitation Big Jim pointed his pencil at the sign on his desk and said with quiet finality, "No."

The question of who is to say "Yes" or "No" is relatively simple, compared to some damned-if-you-do and condemned-if-you-don't situations. So we'll look at two case histories with a high buck-passing factor, and no precedent or policy for guidance.

I was still commanding Company G when Capt. Ichiji Sugita of the Imperial Japanese General Staff was attached to us for six months, under an exchange program. (See "Friendship: Great Cohesive Force," *ARMY*, August 1965.) When our regiment was ordered to Camp Perry, Ohio, to provide logistical support for the National Rifle Matches, I was in daily association with this wonderful officer and gentleman for several months.

Everybody in our company and regiment knew that Captain Sugita was an official guest, and both liked and respected him. But at Perry he would be among strangers, in a strange uniform, and so would be almost sure to meet unpleasant incidents, including lack of normal military courtesy. To avoid this I decided to put him in a U.S. drill uniform like the rest of us: leggings, ice-cream breeches, OD shirt, and campaign hat, with all insignia, except no U.S. on his shirt collar but an extra set of captain's bars instead. Captain Sugita understood my purpose and liked the idea, so we did it that way, without asking permission from anybody.

There was no precedent, regulation, or policy covering this, so I could have written a letter requesting permission to do it. But that letter would have been an engraved invitation for buck-passing from battalion to regiment to corps area (no army commands then) to Washington—where it would be "coordinated" in the War Department (no Pentagon then). Thus some minor G2 type, without personal knowledge or understanding of the related circumstances, would be horrified—so back would come the answer: "No!"

The month at Perry passed without incident, but some weeks after our return to Plattsburgh a letter arrived from corps area, demanding to know why a foreign officer had been allowed to wear the U.S. Army uniform. It was bucked down to me.

I replied that our visitor had been assigned to me with no instructions, except that he was an official guest and observer attached to my company; thus he was my direct responsibility. After stating reasons for the action, my indorsement pointed out that he was always under my immediate supervision and, further, there was nothing classified at Perry, anyway. Also, that I considered that my decision, based on detailed personal knowledge, was right and proper. That was the last I heard of it.

Apparently my immediate superiors appreciated the fact I had not passed the buck to them, for no one at battalion or regiment suggested I be less independent in the future. [Incidentally, Captain Sugita remains my lifetime friend and, more than twenty years later, he became chief of staff of the Japanese Army (Self Defense Force) in the early 1960s.]

The phrase "jittery staff officer" is not very flattering, but that is what I was in one buck-passing jam I faced as G1 of U.S. Army Europe in the mid-1950s. The situation centered around the fact that I exercised general staff supervision over the school system for military dependents.

Congress raised Civil Service pay, under which our teachers were paid, forcing us to cut the school year by several days. Of course "accreditation" for our students by civilian academic associations was vitally important, so anything that endangered this was a serious matter. To forestall any doubt about this point, we sent a news release to *Stars and Stripes,* which was distributed theater-wide.

After lunch some days later my secretary said I had a phone call from a reporter of a civilian-owned weekly that, like *Stars and Stripes,* was on theater-wide distribution—and which had a penchant for giving the military a hotfoot. I said, "All right. I'll take it."

Then a little alarm bell rang inside my thick skull. So I stopped my secretary before she could put the call through to me. "Tell the reporter I'm available for an interview any time, but I don't talk on the phone for publication to anyone I don't know about an unnamed subject or purpose."

It seemed odd that no request for an appointment resulted, so I sent for my experts in grapevine information. Through channels unknown to me they scouted around and returned with this combat intelligence:

(1) The civilian-owned newspaper went to press an hour after the phone call to me, with a "scare" news feature that implied that shortening the school year was endangering our school accreditation. My intelligence experts thought that phone call might have been to ask a when-did-you-stop-beating-your-wife question, with a possible unwary answer from me

providing an added fillip to the story. (Unfounded suspicion? Maybe. But hotfooted staff officers fear another hotfoot.)

(2) The release we sent to *Stars and Stripes* had been buried on the inside pages of the paper when printed—and the sentence saying accreditation would not be affected had somehow been omitted! (I never did solve that one.)

(3) There was still time to make a hold-the-press call to *Stars and Stripes* and to rush over another release with a clear and positive statement that accreditation was not endangered. Since *S&S* would hit the newsstands before the other newspaper, that would prevent any false flap among our students and their parents.

I could have double-timed over to the command building to the chief of staff or commander in chief for a decision on whether to try to get the civilian paper's press run stopped and the story corrected (which I was certain could not be done), or to run our publicity—and thus do it to them before they did it to us. Unfavorable publicity is a primary command interest, but all of my information was scuttlebutt, and time was crucial. So I kept the buck and sent out the news item, calling on *Stars and Stripes* to print it front page center. This left my bosses above the battle when the feathers hit the fan, if the two news stories conflicted.

The stories did conflict. The civilian-owned newspaper was thus hoist on its own petard, and mad about it. It didn't make me happy, either, but it was the lesser of two evils, and it illustrates a vital element in deciding whether or not to pass the buck: Consider the time element!

A book could not cover all the twists, turns, and intricacies of when, how, or whether to pass the buck. But certain principles seem clear:

- The three widely different incidents—Private Hungover, the Camp Perry uniform business, and school accreditation—have one basic element in common. The first man to have all the facts, who was certain he knew the proper action—and who had authority to act—made the decision.
- However, as in so many facets of our professional lives, personalities must be taken into account. In considering whether to decide or to pass the buck up, it is important to know your superior. It is not enough to ask yourself, "From the facts and

the situation, should I decide, or pass the buck?" You should also ask, "Will my boss want to carry this ball, or will he want me to keep him off the hook and make the decision?"

- Finally, always remember the one unforgivable sin: Never hold the buck so long that when you do pass it, the time element will have your boss in a hole before he gets the ball.

21

To Command Requires Control

IT IS A popularly accepted idea that the toothache of a mouse hurts as much as the toothache of an elephant. When applied to command problems in our military hierarchy, however, that analogy is strained by the complex intangibles required to exercise command of elephant-sized organizations; but the principle remains unchanged: At all levels, *to command you must control.*

Memory trips in "The Forward Edge" have touched on this principle tangentially. Further, the idea was addressed directly at company level in peacetime (*ARMY,* July 1975). Military judgment, common sense, and human understanding were involved at that level—but there was no requirement to work through others remote from the commander's presence. Further, there was little need for visualization of special situations that required command action in advance of the need.

One of my early company commanders not only commanded our company, he controlled it in his fashion. For example, the day the company formed in our company street in readiness for a battalion parade, with troops marching by the reviewing stand in column of platoon-front lines, Captain Hardnose received the first sergeant's report, then walked over to the first platoon—ignoring the platoon leader—and moved some soldiers right and left in the platoon front to more accurately "size" the line by height, so that the heads sloped down evenly from the tall right guide to the shorter left guide. He repeated this for the second and third platoons.

This sizing problem exists at regimental level, too. Obviously, however, Colonel Eagle cannot physically do the job himself, nor can he wait until parade time to solve it. He must use the chain of command—in advance. I like the method used by one Colonel Eagle known to me. Since it was a minor matter, he used the informal phone message technique, giving this oral order to his regimental operations officer: "At our last regimental parade, the sizing by height of men in our platoon front lines was ragged. Put out the word by phone to all units that I want that corrected for the organization day review on Friday."

This not only exercised the chain of command, but recognized the equally important principle: It is not enough to let your subordinates do their jobs—it is your duty to make them play their parts. Thus, Captain Hardnose should have solved the problem at his level by issuing the oral order: "Platoon leaders, size your platoons."

So what about the "hurt" of the problem to Colonel Eagle vis-à-vis Captain Hardnose? There is no pain meter for such measurements. In my opinion, however, the stress from problems becomes more variegated with increased rank levels.

Since the battle is the payoff, it is worth examining what history reveals about how two successful commanders controlled their units—how Gen. Douglas MacArthur and Gen. George S. Patton, Jr., handled two specialized but radically different battle situations.

In the North African amphibious landings during World War II, General Patton was the commander in the Fedala area in Morocco. Things went slowly, and on the second day the issue was far from decided when he went down to the beach where vitally needed supplies were coming in by landing craft, under shellfire and periodic strafing by Vichy French planes. He later wrote:

> The situation we found was very bad. Boats were coming in and not being pushed off after unloading. There was shellfire, and French aviators were strafing the beach. Although they missed it by a considerable distance whenever they strafed, our men would take cover and delay unloading operations, and particularly the unloading of ammunition, which was vitally necessary, as we were fighting a major engagement not more than 1,500 yards to the south.

Patton remained on the beach for eighteen hours, thoroughly wet, knocking himself out to speed the unloading—personally pushing off boats and trying by his example to keep men working when French planes came over.

In commenting on this procedure, Patton wrote: "People say that Army commanders should not indulge in such practices. My theory is an Army commander does what is necessary to accomplish his mission."

After much reading about how General Patton operated, I think his action that day was largely influenced by a plan to create a certain mystique about himself as a commander that would give him an intangible control over his command that orders would not produce. Two more incidents come to mind in this connection.

On one occasion in France, he came upon a truck stuck in a muddy road, with some soldiers sitting quietly in the truck. He promptly and profanely demanded they get out and push. When they did this, they suddenly discovered their immaculately uniformed Army commander right there in the mud pushing along with them.

In another case, he came upon a tank immobilized by some mechanical failure, with members of the crew standing around, who were amazed to see their three-star general get down on the ground and crawl under the tank to see for himself. What he learned, if anything, does not matter—he had created a message that would be broadcast on the scuttlebutt communications system.

These and countless other flamboyant incidents, including that boat-pushing effort in the North Africa amphibious landing, created an aura about General Patton in the minds and hearts of his men that gave him a control over his troops in battle that was an irreplaceable part of his genius for battle command.

On the other side of the world from Africa, a radically different critical situation developed in New Guinea, which was solved by out-of-routine command action. By the time I arrived in Australia with the 24th Infantry Division, assigned to I Corps (Lt. Gen. Robert L. Eichelberger commanding), the story about the capture of Buna was the big subject of postmortem professional conversation.

General Douglas MacArthur's strategic decision to "defend Australia in New Guinea" eventually led to the division-level drive (without artillery) over the Owen Stanley Mountains to capture Buna on the northeast coast of New Guinea. This was successful—but not until the issue was in severe doubt, with much travail for the troops involved.

When the Buna operation was prolonged and in serious trouble, General MacArthur flew from Australia to Port Moresby in New Guinea to be briefed; he then sent for General Eichelberger and key members of his I Corps staff.

On their arrival in that pleasant room in the frame house on the hilltop at Moresby, General MacArthur briefed them on the situation, striding up and down, giving high intensity to his instructions, which ended with these words to General Eichelberger:

"Go up and assume command at Buna." He then added, "Bob, I want you to take Buna, or leave your body there!" He then turned to the I Corps chief of staff, Brig. Gen. Clovis E. Byers, to add, "And that goes for you too, General!"

In due course, with added troop assistance and increased logistical support, Buna was captured—a strategic defeat from which the Japanese never recovered. This footnote to history must be added: In the fighting at Buna, General Eichelberger's fine young aide, then-Capt. Daniel K. Edwards, was shot down beside him at close range and seriously wounded; General Byers was also wounded.

Two great commanders, generals MacArthur and Patton, followed procedures so out of routine as to defy any effort at classification, yet each contained one primary element that was central to their successful control: resolution.

Several writers have asked why General MacArthur did not go up and take command at Buna himself. The location and situation at Buna were too complex for discussion here, but this much is clear: For General MacArthur to have bypassed his aggressive and combat-experienced corps commander, General Eichelberger, would have been the same basic error made by Captain Hardnose: failure to use the chain of command as the best means to exercise control within his command.

Two comments are:

- The fundamental means of command control will always be issuance of proper orders and use of the chain of command. Recently a dedicated young active-duty captain told me of a new addition being considered to make our existing field order form more effective in the control of operations. The possible change is to add a paragraph for "The Commander's Intent," which seems a fine idea to me.

    I issued only one formal written field order, after our amphibious landing on Leyte, in my all too short time as a combat regimental commander. In retrospect, however, I believe such a paragraph in that field order would have given me better control of my command because they would have better understood the purpose of my follow-up fragmentary orders.

- Sun Tzu, an ancient Chinese general and military writer, said, "In battle there are only the normal and extraordinary forces, but their combinations are limitless; none can comprehend them all."

The same principle applies to the means of exercising control as a commander. Thus, successful leaders not only study and use all normal means of exercising control, but they also are constantly alert for opportunities to use extraordinary means. These will vary with the situation and the personalities involved and within the limits of the commander's capabilities and his judgment. This will always include decisions as to when, where, and for what purpose the commander exerts his personal efforts.

22

Developing the "Cold Glitter"

GENERAL GEORGE S. PATTON, JR., said, "It is not the point of the questing bayonet but the cold glitter in the attacker's eye that breaks the line." In other words, the bayonet is not going anywhere unless the soldier takes it there. Thus, the problem becomes how to get that "cold glitter" into the soldier's eye.

General Creighton W. Abrams, another great battle commander, pointed the way to one requirement when he said, "Pride—build on it; never demean it!" As General Abe knew from experience, personal pride is an essential element of that cold glitter of determination in battle.

We have no simple rule on which to base building martial pride, but *leadership* and *training* are fundamental; however, many auxiliary factors are involved, varying from patriotism and unit esprit de corps to the local tactical situation. Among other influences, I believe the formalities of various military ceremonies may have a greater cumulative effect than is generally recognized.

The graduation parade of my West Point class of 1925 followed the routine of other parades and reviews—full-dress uniforms, marching lines, band playing, guidons and flags flying. This pattern of parades and reviews was followed during my active-duty years. The uniforms were different in the Army, and the weapons combat ready—but the inspirational effect and feeling were the same.

How could any soldier go through these ceremonies without martial pride building within him! I served in eight infantry regiments,
one special troops regiment, and seven divisions, and ceremonies were
the icing on the cake of training, drills, and military service.

There were other types of ceremonies, too, including honor guards
for visiting VIPs, formal guard mounts, military social receptions . . . even
some cocktail parties were ceremonies in their fashion. The unique
"Prop Blasts" of airborne units were ceremonies to "socially qualify"
newly jump-qualified officers.

To remove these ceremonial aspects from military service and training would turn military life from the prideful profession that it is into
a dreary routine. In my fixed opinion, this would produce less effective soldiers and units for battle—especially for peacetime-trained units
when war comes unexpectedly.

Consider two ceremonies developed since my day, ones that I have
been privileged to share in recent months. First, the dining-in of the
2d Battalion (Mechanized), 34th Infantry "Dragons" at Fort Stewart,
Ga., in February 1986. (This was a stag affair—when ladies are present,
it is called a dining-out.)

We were seated for dinner in a rectangular arrangement of tables,
with all seats facing inward. The head table—for the commander, two
guests, and two staff officers—was at one narrow end of the rectangle.
The junior lieutenant present sat alone at an individual table at the
opposite end from the commander and facing toward him.

This general pattern, with the modus operandi now followed, was
adopted from the British after World War II.

Two staff officers masterminded the ritual of mixing the dragon punch
in a large bowl on a small table in front of the commander. After the
adjutant read an extract from the regimental history, another staff officer
presented for the commander's approval a bottle containing an appropriate
liquid to commemorate that action. The bottle was then poured into
the bowl.

Here are the ingredients that went into that dragon punch:

Tequila—for service on the Mexican border in 1915.
White wine—for combat service in France during World War I.
Moonshine whiskey and 30-W motor oil—for service as the first
motorized regiment in the Army, Georgia and South Carolina area.

Pineapple juice and Australian beer—for service in Hawaii and Australia during World War II.

Philippine beer—for service during World War II, from New Guinea into Leyte and subsequent recapture of the Philippines.

Plum wine—for occupation duty in Japan after World War II.

Rice wine—for early and extended service in the Korean War.

Schnapps—for service in Germany, 1963–1968.

Dust—for service at Fort Riley, Kan., 1968–1970.

Canooche swamp water—for service in southeast Georgia; now part of the Army element of the rapid deploying U.S. Central Command.

After this mixture was sampled by the commander, he declared it to be official dragon punch—and everybody had a cup. How did it taste? That is hard to describe, but it had a kind of beige historical alcoholic flavor . . . and I liked it.

When these preliminaries were complete, the colors were posted by an immaculately uniformed and meticulously trained color guard. The symbolism and dignity of this ceremony never grows old.

Now we come to the part that is hard to describe: the interplay between the commander and "Mister Vice" (vice commander), the junior lieutenant present at his table opposite the commander . . . who put in his two cents at every opportunity.

"Fines" were imposed by the commander of one (or more) cups of dragon punch (publicly consumed) and one (or more) "pieces of silver" (quarters) for mistakes reported by anybody present—like a misplaced ribbon or other miscue, including recalled derelictions from the recent past. You will have to attend a dining-in to understand how it works.

During this specialized byplay of fines and penance, dinner was served. After I performed my function of summarizing a few memories, the commander made his closing remarks, and the colors were formally retired by the color guard. The ceremonial part of the dining-in was now over, leaving us more closely integrated with shared pride in our unit.

In May 1986 I was the guest speaker at a banquet of the 1st Battalion, 29th Infantry—sixty-one years after I had reported to that unit in 1925 at Fort Benning, Ga., as my first active-duty assignment.

This was an innovation since my time, a formal dinner in a large civilian facility in nearby Columbus. All members of the battalion were invited, with their wives.

Officers and men were in uniform, with wives in long evening dresses. The ceremonial evening opened with a receiving line, and my conservative estimate is that my wife and I shook hands with five to six hundred in that line.

We had an excellent dinner, with wine. This was followed by a fine military-related play, put on by members of the battalion, designed to memorialize our unit's combat casualties.

The commander then made an inspirational "command talk." My turn followed as guest speaker, in which I discussed our historical heritage as infantrymen; and the chaplain's benediction closed the formalities.

Another type of ceremony that fosters unit esprit is the celebration of unit Organization Days—like the one for the 34th Infantry that I attended in 1985. These vary in scope from unit to unit and year to year, often including a parade, review, or other ceremonial formation.

In my view, the most effective are at separate battalion, regimental, and division levels. Fundamental to these ceremonies is a review of the unit's history and, often, recognition of a Soldier of the Year and other matters of current interest.

As with the 34th Infantry dining-in, I do not see how any military man could fail to be a better combat soldier after accumulating a background of varied military ceremonies.

Not to be overlooked are ceremonies incident to veterans' organizations. In July 1986 I attended the Annual Meeting of the Legion of Valor, in Asheville, N.C.

Its general meeting was opened with that simple yet impressive ceremony that never grows old—the Pledge of Allegiance—while facing our beautiful national flag. Other organizations, like the Military Order of the World Wars, follow the same pattern.

They remember how it was in combat in their day and—perhaps unconsciously—realize the part ceremonies played in generating that "cold glitter" for them. Their programs with ROTC units are calculated to develop intangibles, not just mechanical skills.

It is no accident that militaristic nations place great emphasis on parades, reviews, and spectacular military displays with pomp and ceremony. They strive for the best weapons, and accent field training and the acquisition of the best technologies—but they also use great marching ceremonies and colorful displays to reach out for and inspire the "cold glitter" in the eyes of the nation, as well as their soldiers.

We have our own Armed Forces Day, which serves the same purpose in a decentralized fashion, with a defensive national security slant.

Many things we consider normal military routine are, in effect, ceremonial actions. These include exchanging hand salutes and, in some foreign armies, an exaggerated arm swing and goose-step marching. Indeed, what we call "military courtesy" is an important ceremonial procedure, too.

It seems clear that military ceremonies and procedures take many forms. American Indians had their martial ceremonies, called "war dances," to produce their "cold glitter" for battle.

Just as "man does not live by bread alone," battles are not won by hardware alone. While there are some who may deride their value, in my view ceremonies serve a real purpose—they are not just empty gestures.

23

Bulletin Board Principle: An Action Tool

AMONG THE MULTIFACETED aspects of experience is the curious fact that often the empirical lessons and principles you learn have future implications not recognized at the time. One such lesson resulted from my tenure as coach of our battalion basketball team on my first active-duty post. When twelve of my fifteen-man squad decided not to play basketball unless excused from Saturday inspections, I accepted their resignations.

Then I prepared a brief message, including a time and place for new basketball candidates to report the next day—with a copy to be placed on all company bulletin boards that afternoon. When the notice appeared, however, the reluctant dozen decided they did want to play basketball—and go to Saturday inspections. If there had been no company bulletin boards available, the solution to my problem would have been far more complicated.

At that point I did not realize I had discovered a flexible and effective tool for exercising command, leadership, planning, and organized control that would prove invaluable throughout my career. Consider the extracts from my active-duty service that follow.

For five wonderful years I was a company commander—Company G, 26th Infantry, Plattsburgh, N.Y., and Companies F and D, 19th Infantry, Schofield Barracks, Hawaii. In those years, our bulletin boards were an indispensable control and communications system. Inherent in that system was the requirement for every individual to read the bulletin board daily and comply with all instructions or report immediately to the orderly room if there was any problem.

In July 1942, the exigencies of World War II jumped me (only fifteen months removed from a captain and company commander) to eagle colonel and chief of staff, 24th Infantry Division, Hawaii. Though I had seventeen years of service, it was those five years as a company commander that prepared me for this challenge—especially in early 1944 in New Guinea, where it was my responsibility to stage manage preparation of an amphibious order for the Noiseless Landing Force of 33,000 to land in Tanahmerah Bay.

I had no experience or training that answered the specific question, "How does a chief of staff go about preparing the amphibious order for such a complex operation?" The bulletin board–oriented command and communications system came to my rescue. That procedure goes a step beyond the war room idea of just posting maps and other information on which oral briefings can be based.

As a point of departure, I read the field manual on amphibious operations, and noted the step by step requirement that certain units and staff sections must prepare their plans first, so that other commands and staffs will have the necessary information on which to base their plans. Next I took a piece of paper about three feet square and laid out a phased planning schedule.

That is when the company bulletin board principle came into play. First I arranged for a plans room and a fine young lieutenant to administer its operation. Then, based on my phased planning schedule, he laid out on vertical wall surfaces the spaces where each segment of the amphibious order would be posted—with dates indicated by which each would be posted.

Then instructions were issued:

- Each commander and staff section chief was responsible for seeing that his part of the order was in place by the date indicated.
- It was the obligation of all concerned to keep informed of progress in this planning control room—and to notify me if any problem developed.

With this bulletin board principle established, the chief of staff could sit back and monitor the progress of work by others (which included getting a little unhappy on appropriate occasions)—and the amphibious order wrote itself.

A challenging situation existed when I assumed command (briefly) of the 82d Airborne Division (1953), after serving as regimental commander of the 505th Airborne Infantry, and then as assistant division commander. The problem, as division commander, was a retest in the field of Exercise Falcon, under the aegis of an evaluation team from The Infantry School—because the first field test had been rated "Unsatisfactory."

Exercise Falcon was designed to test a new organizational concept for infantry regiments. Two basic elements were essential for the test: the number and assignments of personnel in the test regiment, and the number, type, and distribution of equipment, weapons, and transportation.

It was mandatory, for the test to be viable, to have the required personnel and equipment on hand in the test regiment and for those who were evaluating the test to know this and be able to verify the facts. So I directed that a control plans room (war room) be established by division, using the bulletin board principle.

Since the success of the plans room would depend in some measure on the ability of the young lieutenant assigned to administer it, I called on a regimental commander not involved in the test, told him of the requirement, and said:

"I want the best lieutenant in your regiment for the duration of the test. This is a priority division responsibility, and I hold you responsible for the officer you select to do the job." (Sometimes you have to put the bee on somebody to get what you need.)

That officer, and representatives of the test regiment and division staff, were charged with establishing the bulletin board plans room. This included an organizational chart of each unit in the test regiment on the walls of the plans room, showing visually:

- Personnel requirements—with transfers from other regiments to fill vacancies.
- Significant items of equipment, indicated by visual symbols, to include status for each item—using a color code.

If a unit had two kinds of radios, for example, one could be represented by a circle for each item and the other by squares. If the item was on hand and serviceable, the circle or square was to be filled with green; if it was on hand but in need of repair, the circle was half filled in green. If the item was authorized but not on hand or requisition, the symbol was to be filled in red; if it was not on hand but on requisition, the symbol was to be half filled in red.

This visual display of the status of personnel, weapons, and equipment was thus available to all concerned at any time. As division commander, all I had to do was admire what others were doing and, on appropriate occasions, apply a little heat to spark more action in trouble spots. The retest of Exercise Falcon was a success.

The war rooms described above were the two major ones in my war room career; however, you might say I was war room happy—not just initiating but improving those existing.

As deputy chief of staff for personnel, Headquarters, U.S. Army, Europe, my war room was a wall cabinet with vertical leaves, hinged to swing outward; thus both sides of each leaf were available for posting personnel information. As Deputy Commandant, Army of the Armed Forces Staff College in Norfolk, Va., my mania took the form of a demonstration theater–type war room for an amphibious operation.

At my last duty station, as chief of staff, U.S. Continental Army Command (USCONARC) at Fort Monroe, Va., we had multiple war rooms. The operations war room was amplified from both showcase and functional angles. The comptroller established a facility that featured information on the walls around a conference table, and the post commander developed a war room to meet his alert and emergency responsibilities.

The war room that saved me the most trouble was the one with the Very Important People (VIP) plans wall. Nothing caused me more trouble as chief of staff than snafus in handling VIPs—and there was a parade of them through USCONARC from around the world. My VIP problem disappeared when one of the finest officers and gentlemen known to me, Lt. Col. (now Colonel) Leon Cheek, U.S. Army retired, was named custodian of VIPs, with a war room wall where schedules for each visit were posted—*and kept up to date*—for all interested parties to see.

Obviously, the reason for my longtime addiction to bulletin board–type war rooms stemmed from the simple fact that they helped me get my job done in varied situations. Often overlooked among war room functions was that chiefs of staff sections and unit commanders were brought into the action, not just their action officers. That war rooms greatly facilitated passing on information incident to reassignment of personnel was also often overlooked.

With due respect for computers and other complicated technologies in our modern Army, certain basic tools of our trade—like rifles and war rooms—cannot be replaced in appropriate situations. Maybe you have a war room opportunity in your zone of action.

24

MP Experience Helps Solve Tough Cases

IF EVERY OFFICER could serve two years as a lieutenant in the military police—as it was my good fortune to do—many disciplinary, command, and administrative problems in the Army could be prevented. For instance, the widely publicized "NCO club scandals" could never have developed as they did. Since it is impossible for all officers to serve as MP lieutenants, a spot check of my experience may be helpful.

My detail in the Hawaiian Division's military police, at Schofield Barracks in 1933–35, came about in somewhat unorthodox fashion as a result of getting into an automobile accident. Apparently, not every day did a lieutenant report an accident, and know the regulations involved, so within days I was wearing crossed pistols on my collar as a military police lieutenant. My duty assignment: traffic officer—responsible for safe driving on the post.

There were three other lieutenants, each of us doubling as detective and general troubleshooter, rotating on twenty-four-hour tours as military police officer of the day. The MP officer of the day handled all cases during his tour, following through perhaps for days or even months. Sometimes you got a puzzler—like this one handled by my friend Edwin M. Van Bibber.

Ed had a local Ellery Queen reputation as a detective. One day the provost marshal (PM), a crusty lieutenant colonel in his fifties with a submerged sense of humor, sent for Ed and tossed an obscene postcard on his desk.

"Mistuh Van Bibber, find out who mailed that."

The card was unsigned, addressed to a man in Detroit, and—since there were twenty thousand possible senders on the post—the PM thought he was handing Ed an unsolvable riddle. But several weeks later Ed reported to the testy old PM with a soldier in tow, and tossed the obscene postcard back on the colonel's desk.

"Sir," he said, "this man mailed that card."

"Did you?" the colonel asked.

"Yes, sir," the soldier replied.

Whereupon Ed picked up the postcard, saluted, and left with his culprit. Some hours later the provost marshal sent for him again.

"All right, Mistuh Van Bibber," he said. "You win. How did you do it?"

To quote Ed, "It was a shame to tell him   took the mystery out of it. I just wrote the Detroit chief of police, gave the name and address on the card, and asked for a plainclothesman to see if the guy knew anybody in Hawaii. He did; just one man.

"So I descended on the fellow, flashed the card under his nose, and he confessed. Nothing to it."

What he did not say was that many an "unsolvable" case has a simple and logical solution, if you set your mind to think it out.

My first case came on my first officer of the day tour, when a soldier from the 35th Infantry reported a gold ring stolen. He was sailing the next day for the mainland, and valued that ring highly because it was a trophy awarded members of the team that won the Schofield Barracks football championship.

Since he had no reason to suspect anybody, it looked like a lost cause. Not knowing what else to do, I asked questions and learned:

(1) The ring had been stolen from his packed suitcase, which lay on the floor between his bed and the next one in the line of bunks near the squad room wall.

(2) That morning his suitcase was neatly arranged just as he had packed it, and he discovered the loss by chance when he decided to look at the ring.

Since the suitcase appeared undisturbed, it could indicate the thief knew where the ring was packed. Ruling out the adjacent neighbor in his own line of bunks, the man best positioned to see where he had packed the ring was the occupant of the bunk in the center line, across the aisle, who could see between the bunks on both sides of where the suitcase lay on the floor.

This was tenuous reasoning, so I said nothing about it. But the soldier was so upset about his loss that I got two MPs and returned to his company with him in the hope he would at least give me an E for effort. After checking in at the orderly room we went to his squad room, where I told my MPs to search the bunk and footlocker across the aisle from the suitcase. When the third pair of socks in the locker was unrolled, out popped the ring!

As we walked from the squad room, leaving a happy soldier reunited with his prized ring, we passed a group in the aisle who had watched the search.

"Sherlock Holmes!" one stage-whispered to another.

"Naw," came the sotto voce reply, "Hawkshaw!"

I was just as surprised as anybody, but there seemed no reason to say so.

Of course, there were some serious crimes, too. How could it be otherwise among 20,000 men for two years? But simple cases point up the same principles and take less space. An interesting angle is that if unit commanders had had military police training, many troubles would have been solved without calling in the MPs—like the last case that came my way on my final night as OD.

At about 8:00 P.M. an older company commander from an infantry regiment came in to report a .45-caliber pistol missing from his supply room. The loss had been discovered three days before during a weapons inventory after the company returned from an extended field maneuver. He was sure the pistol was taken while the arms racks were left unlocked, so that men returning from the field could put their weapons there.

Further, he knew it was stolen and not lost in the field, because that pistol had not been issued to anybody. Finally, he said he had made a shakedown search of the company, in every nook and cranny, so there was no need for me to come looking for it. He was merely reporting it missing as required by regulations.

After writing a report for our records, I gave the matter some thought. Apparently the captain had searched for the pistol like a kid looking for Easter eggs: using his eyes and legs but not his head. It seemed unlikely the soldier who took the pistol would keep it in the barracks. So I sent for the supply sergeant.

From him I learned that when men placed their weapons in the arms racks on returning from the field, they also picked up their brown paper–wrapped packages of clean laundry from a pile nearby. Thus the pistol may have left the supply room hidden in a package of laundry. When asked if any man who picked up laundry (except married NCOs) lived away from barracks, the answer was, "Yes, sir. A man on special duty sleeps in one of those long shed-like buildings near the gas storage area."

At around 11:00 P.M. I arrived at that building with two MPs, and the soldier there cooperated in the search. In fact, he even lifted out the empty tray of his footlocker so one of my MPs could check through clothing in the bottom. As he replaced the tray, I turned away to think about where I would hide a stolen pistol in that building.

Then the possible significance of the empty tray—something I had never seen in a soldier's footlocker before—hit me: so no one would question his picking it up during a search. When I turned back and overturned the tray there was the stolen pistol, fastened to the bottom by strips of cloth anchored with thumbtacks.

The point of interest here is the difference in mental approach between the company commander and a trained MP lieutenant.

We have space for another case, but instead of detailing one of the more serious problems that MPs deal with, we will look at how some people feel about MPs.

Six years later, during my second tour in Hawaii, I was squiring a tall, slender blonde around. One night we were having dinner at the Royal Hawaiian Hotel, to be followed by dancing and a floor show—at a price even an Army captain could afford now and then.

During our before-dinner cocktails I noticed a couple of ladies, several tables removed, trying to beckon me over their way. I did not recognize either of them, so I gave undivided attention to my dinner partner, who was not too pleased by the obvious effort the ladies were making to get me to come over there.

My blonde really began to steam when a waiter brought me a note from the ladies. But she cooled off when I handed it to her.

"Are you," the note read, "the same red-headed SOB who used to be an MP lieutenant at Schofield Barracks?"

These fragments of military police experience suggest three ideas:

(1) When facing an unusual problem—including the endless variety of troubles human beings cause each other—the fact that you

have never faced such a situation before should not be unduly disconcerting. Think out what to do and often there will be a simple solution—like that of my friend Ed Van Bibber, who wrote one brief letter and found the sender of that obscene postcard.

(2)   Where money is involved, or anything that can be converted to money, carelessness invites theft or loss—which will be illustrated by cases from my later service, involving Army post club operations.

(3)   When you deal with trouble it is never pleasant, and sometimes offenders will make things unnecessarily disagreeable. Such people often attempt to avoid the consequences of their own failures by trying to pressure you into the offense of neglect of duty. That is a sucker gambit; don't fall for it.

On other assignments military police training was valuable for the rest of my service, because that background was very helpful in handling trouble and troublemakers. Here is a little penny-ante case, but it illustrates the principles involved in smoking out dishonesty: You first have to realize it is there, then think out how to tie the can on the chiselers.

When you move around like we do in the Army, nothing replaces cocktail parties to get acquainted and to know each other. While stationed in Washington my wife and I decided to have a party where we lived in Arlington, Va., in 1946–47. To free my blonde to enjoy the occasion more, I arranged for a caterer to pitch the party at our house, with liquor supplied by me. After the guests were gone I went into the kitchen to tip the two men and a woman from the caterer.

The head man pointed to two cases of assorted liquors I had bought for the party, indicating he had put the empties back in the cases.

I took one look and said, "We did not drink that much!"

"Colonel," he said, "how can you say that when the empties are right there?"

At the moment I had no answer, so I tipped them (to my later regret). After they left I looked at those empty bottles, and all my logistical experience told me we had not drunk that much. And my bump of MP experience palpitated. I decided I had been had; the question was, how? That's where my MP days came in handy.

First I emptied the trash container on the kitchen floor and put corks back in empty liquor bottles. This showed four corks missing. Next I lined up empty quart soda-water bottles and put the metal caps back on them—ending with four caps left over.

Then I remembered they had brought a small suitcase with them, and the answer became clear: A gallon of my liquor—in the missing soda-water bottles, corked with the missing corks—had gone with them in that suitcase.

When I went to the caterer, he offered to pay for my loss. I declined, because that would not stop their little racket, and accepting money would place in question my primary motive. I wanted those chiselers fired, which was done after I provided a written statement to justify it to their union.

We will always have dishonesty in the Army—as we do in civilian life—in proportion to the lack of supervision and controls in money matters. How could it be otherwise? But since our standards are so much higher, and our controls of appropriated funds so strong, we depend too much on duty and honor to replace supervision and administrative controls for non-appropriated funds.

In 1948, after getting settled in my office as deputy post commander at Carlisle Barracks, I looked up the procedure for taking money out of the slot machines in the officers' club (they were legal then). The officer of the day was supposed to supervise the club steward, who would empty the machines after the club closed at night—which meant a different supervising officer each night.

Late that evening when I walked into the club, the officer of the day was not there, but the steward was taking the money out of the slot machines—alone. Obviously, this was an unsound system—and there were slots in the NCO club, too. So I reported the situation to the commanding general and added that, as a former MP, it was my opinion the present system invited the money loss I was sure had been taking place.

"What do you recommend?" he asked.

"Take the responsibility from the rotating officer of the day, and give it to a single officer on the staff," was my reply. "Also all keys to the slot machines should be collected by that designated supervising officer and kept in the safe here. Then, once a day, at times set by him, the officer will open the slots, monitor the club steward as he takes the money out, and keep a separate record of it."

"All right," the CG said. "We'll do it that way. He won't like it, but make Major Soandso the supervising officer."

This change in system almost doubled the take from the slots in the two clubs, an increase of about six thousand dollars a month as I recall—well worth the limited time required of the supervising officer.

There was a little sandwich shop back of the post exchange, so I dropped in there for a cup of coffee and cased the joint. Questioning developed this information:

- Average money taken in was about sixty-five to seventy dollars a day.
- There was no accountability system. Supplies were drawn from the storeroom as needed and money in the cash register was taken out by the post exchange at the end of the day.

I designated a lieutenant as mess officer for that little lunch bar, in addition to his other duties (which did not make him happy). He was required to use the old Form 85 for company messes, with added columns necessary to establish a relationship between supplies drawn and money taken in. The average money taken in jumped to about $120 a day.

My next duty station was Fort Campbell. The officers' club was not doing too well financially, and I soon found myself on the board of governors.

At the first meeting my old MP awareness, that things are not always kosher, was actuated by the fact that the main club mess was being subsidized about six hundred dollars a month—another way of saying it was losing that much. On inquiry, it developed that the system in effect was the same as at that Carlisle Barracks sandwich bar: Supplies were drawn as needed from the storeroom and no accountability check was in effect to relate the money taken in to the supplies drawn.

The club officer was directed to install an accountability system based on the Form 85 principle, modified as required. More paperwork, of course, but the money loss in the mess was eliminated.

However, our "country club," a weekend branch of the main club, continued to lose money. It turned out that the club officer had not extended his accountability system to that operation because, he said, "I did not think it necessary."

As a demonstration for him, and to confirm my own ex-MP opinion, he was directed to follow this procedure for the dinner there on Saturday night:

(1) Make a quiet but careful inventory of supplies issued to the country club for the Saturday night dinner.

(2) Place an officer, who would appear to be making a night of it, at the bar in a position where he could see each dinner brought from the kitchen. The officer was also to keep doodling on a piece of paper and, in a code of his choosing, keep track of each dinner that came out of the kitchen: steak, roast beef, chicken, or lobster tail (sold at different prices).

(3) Balance the money in the restaurant till against the number of dinners served and paid for.

(4) Subtract the dinners served from the supplies issued and inventory the supplies left to see if they balance.

The results made a believer out of the club officer, because the money taken in fell far short of that paid for in cash and coupons to the waiters for the dinners served. I do not remember the sum, but it was on the order of eighty dollars for that one meal.

The inventory of supplies in the kitchen fell short, too. Part of this shortage resulted from the fact that one of the cooks liked lobster tail, so he had eaten five of them—and lobster tail dinners were priced at $1.75 each, which was real money then.

The slot machines (still legal) were also checked and, again, there was skulduggery. The only thing I remember now is that some of them had a small hole, barely noticeable, bored through the metal in back. By inserting a wire through this hole it was possible to do what is called "milk the tubes," causing money to fall out the coin delivery chute.

There seems no limit to the ways money will disappear unless there is adequate supervision and an effective system of controls. There must also be a certain mental attitude. I call it "awareness," though some may call it a "suspicious mind"—unworthy of one soldier toward another. But where money is concerned, idealistic Pollyanna thinking cannot change a basic fact: In the Army, and in civilian communities, there is a difference between unfounded suspicion and normal alert awareness.

After looking back over thirty-five years of commissioned service, including many happenings in addition to those mentioned here, these comments are offered:

- Money and dynamite are alike in that they not only require careful handling; they must both be guarded. They are also alike in that not only their legal custodians are responsible; anyone who sees or has reason to believe they are not being properly safeguarded is responsible for questionable situations. If there had been a general such awareness among officers and NCOs, along with acceptance of reporting responsibility, dishonesty could never have evaded detection long enough to create the so-called "NCO club scandals."
- Serving as an MP lieutenant was wonderful training in how to handle trouble and troublemakers because in a brief period you faced more of both than you would normally meet in a lifetime of service. However, to paraphrase a line from a bawdy poem by Ogden Nash: If you have never served in the military police, you can make yourself a self-appointed MP in your attitude and thinking.
- Those who make military service their careers live in a type of "fool's paradise," so far as money and general honesty are concerned, because our standards are higher than those in civilian life. To protect these standards from the few spoilers in our ranks, who will always be present among a large group of men, requires the same kind of alertness and awareness necessary to avoid accidents, fires, property damage or loss, compromise of classified material, and other hazards. It is a state of mind, a personal attitude, and a calculated way of thinking.
- Habitual unfounded suspicion breeds an unhealthy atmosphere of distrust among friends and associates—in or out of uniform—and has been condemned by thinkers down through the centuries. But there is another side of the coin. More than a hundred years ago Charles Simmons said, "Discreet and well-founded suspicion avoids a multitude of evils, which credulity brings on itself." And more than four hundred years ago Sir Philip Sidney said, "The only disadvantage of an honest heart is credulity."

• Obviously, there had to be a lot of credulous people with honest hearts—including some of high rank—to permit the NCO club corruption in Vietnam to reach the degree eventually exposed. So there must be a balance between undue suspicion and naive credulity. To me it comes out this way: Be as alert and aware in administrative matters as in combat, especially where money or things of money value are concerned, giving calculated thought to what you should do about any untoward situation observed or brought to your notice—and do not shirk the responsibility to become involved.

25

Are Stars Born, Developed, or Picked?

ONE READER HAS posed a question I have heard before in various guises, but he presented it in a new fashion. Instead of writing or raising the issue at a cocktail party, he called me long distance and asked, "How do *bad generals* manage to reach that rank?"

Here we go again. I have delved into that quicksand before, but the question will not go away. Technically, it is just another version of the old booby trap query, "When did you stop beating your wife?"

More often than not, however, there seems to be a sincere interest in how generals are selected. Some of the material that follows is adapted from the first chapter and the epilogue of my book *What Are Generals Made Of?*

Since last ruminating on this subject ("Stars: 'Little Hard Pieces of Metal,'" "The Forward Edge," *ARMY*, November 1979), I have acquired some added information and had new thoughts on the problem. I remembered that after my retirement a civilian neighbor said to my wife, "I cannot imagine how Aubrey became a general, because he is so quiet and polite."

In my defense, Dorothy explained the mystery this way: "But you do not know him very well yet."

Apparently, most people have ambivalent convictions about the composition of generals. But enough of these esoteric views about the composition of generals, and on to the more balanced question, "Who gets the stars, why, and how?"

The best broad answer to that question was stated by Pulitzer Prize–winning journalist Hanson W. Baldwin: "The shaping of a general, like the making of a soldier, is a complex process that defies definition or consistent pattern. Like the miracle of man, it can be examined but never completely analyzed."

He then adds, "Great generals, like great writers, poets or artists, are born, not made, yet the influences that touch their lives unquestionably shape their careers."

Now we are getting somewhere: ". . . *the influences that touch their lives unquestionably shape their careers.*"

So we will leave genetics to others and take a retrospective look at environmental influences and selective promotion procedures. In due course it may become clearer how some men interact with these influences better than others, in ways that lead to their eventual selection for star rank.

History is replete with records of how background and experience lead to success in military command. Consider these outstanding examples:

- Alexander the Great's father was King Philip of Macedon, who built the army and trained his son for the command and leadership role he was later to play in conquering the known world of his day.
- Similarly, Hamilcar Barca of Carthage played an analogous role in setting the stage for the great campaigns of his son, the matchless Hannibal of Cannae fame in his Italian years.
- In our own time, we have General of the Army Douglas MacArthur, born on an Army post as the son of Arthur MacArthur, Medal of Honor recipient who reached the then top rank of lieutenant general. As in the cases of Alexander and Hannibal, the son eclipsed the father.

Of course, these are exceptional cases, and the truly great ones are born. Yet, situations and influences also had to be there that lifted them to stellar greatness. So what about "the general run of generals"? How did they get where they did and under what influences?

Since I am one of them, subject to the same influences that resulted in the selection to general officer rank of uncounted numbers of generals, it may be I can cast a little light on the influences and the process of selection.

One of the first considerations to understand is that officers have some control over the influences that will shape their careers. For instance, the choice of branch of service is a major consideration and, in my view, the combat arms offer the widest opportunities. If your natural bent is toward one of the technical services, however, your star chances may be better there—a potential chief of one of the technical services may not be as well suited to a combat branch and vice versa.

I had my choice of branches on graduation from West Point; however, any thought of possible star rank had nothing to do with my going infantry. It was simply the right place for me. I liked working with people, in peace or war, as opposed to manning long-range weapons or operating machines, or handling technical services or supply forces.

I do not advocate stargazing as a consideration in choosing your branch of service—or remaining in one if you want to transfer out. Every general officer I knew was interested in and happy with his branch and was a strong advocate of its virtues and capabilities—as I was with the infantry.

Another way in which individuals can in some measure choose the influences under which they serve is in deciding whether or not to specialize in duty with troops or in staff assignments.

As a footnote to history, three infantry officers on the general staff of my division during World War II asked for and received command in combat with infantry regiments—and those three, and only those three, became generals in later years.

Another interesting illustration of how choosing a particular environment may enhance the chance for star rank is the future of those who volunteered for airborne forces. Five members of my 1925 class at West Point volunteered in later years to become paratroopers, and four of those five became major generals. Genetics, environmental influences . . . or is some other factor involved?

According to an old Chinese saying, "It is easy to find a thousand men, but hard to find a general." Finding enough *average* generals is not the real problem in the U.S. Army; World War II proved our school system (the best in the world) and training programs provided more than enough qualified colonels when much larger numbers of generals were required. So our problem becomes how to select the *best qualified* from our reservoir of fine colonels.

The peacetime machinery for promotion to general officer rank is simple under laws passed by Congress. It is based on a system of selection boards for one- and two-star generals, like the one on which I served to pick colonels to be nominated for brigadier general.

The board consisted of ten major generals chaired by a lieutenant general, relieved from all other duties for thirty days and assembled in the Pentagon to review the records of all eligible colonels. These records are detailed and extensive, with regular efficiency reports and supplementary documents from citations and other favorable papers to disciplinary actions (if any).

For one- and two-star ranks in peacetime, promotion action must begin with a selection board. The "chosen few" names then go up the chain of command to the commander in chief, the president, for approval and nomination. They must then be confirmed for promotion by the Senate of the United States.

Notice that while this procedure permits names to be deleted during the confirmation process, none can be added from the ranks of those who were passed over by the board. I cannot think of a better or fairer system—though no system can be perfect that must, of necessity, be based on one man's opinion of another.

As to selection to three- and four-star ranks, I did not serve at that rarefied level and thus have no comments.

For wartime general officers, the situation is totally different and includes spot promotions to meet existing situations. Experience, personal and professional qualities, and other factors, however, were the same as ones on which stars depended in peacetime—although chance did play its part as far as one's being at the right place at the right time. The primary difference was that stress of war brought these qualities to the surface more quickly in some men.

To reply to the above question about "bad generals," perhaps the same answer applies that my wife gave our neighbor who had doubts about my star qualities: "Maybe you just did not get to know him very well."

Our system of selection boards for general officer promotions, based on their records of service, has its limitations. For example, the records of all candidates can never be based on the same service under the same rating officers, but nobody has been able to devise a better system.

26

Mutual Good Faith:
A Key to Change

ALICE SAW SOME wonderful things after she passed through the looking glass. I know how she felt, because last year I made a visit to the 1st Battalion, 29th Infantry, at Fort Benning, Ga.—nearly fifty-six years after reporting to Company B of that great "We Lead the Way" regiment as my first duty station. And, viewed through the backward looking glass of memory—compared to how things were fifty-six years ago—I saw some wonderful things, too: changes.

Before we look at the greatest and most fundamental change in the Army, let me parade in retrospect some changes that paved the way to our Army of 1982.

A clear memory of my day is the first Christie tank, a single prototype, which demonstrated on our drill field its speed, maneuverability, and operational capability over obstacles. But I did not have the vision to foresee the great armored divisions of World War II.

At 11:00 A.M. one sunny day we watched a scheduled death-defying event high above the dusty drill ground, between Gowdy Field (baseball stadium, still there) and the steel jump towers (present to-day, not imagined then). An airplane soared overhead and a single white parachute blossomed as the "daredevil" drifted down to the hot sand and dry grass where the Christie tank had cavorted.

I did not imagine then that this signaled future airborne divisions in our Army—much less the XVIII Airborne Corps, or the 11th and 82d Airborne Divisions—or that I would serve in both of them.

In May 1981, recalling that first Christie tank, the single parachutist, and the future they presaged, I witnessed a demonstration of the first infantry fighting vehicle issued to the 1st Battalion, 29th Infantry, with others to follow. It is first cousin to a tank, with revolving turret, small rapid-fire cannon, and machine gun; it is proof against small-arms fire to include .50 caliber, with a crew capacity of nine who man all-around defensive fires—including firing ports, TOW antitank missiles, and two means of providing smoke.

Once again, I was seeing a single unit of the wave of the future. So is this the great change in our Army that I've been leading up to? No. It is a major development, but not the great fundamental change to which I refer.

In my 1925–28 years at Fort Benning there were two infantry regiments on the post: the 29th Infantry (white), operating with The Infantry School; and the 24th Infantry (black), operating with the post. The only activity they shared, that I recall, was that each regiment (of two battalions) entered two baseball teams in the battalion-level post baseball league.

At that time, there was no talk of Armywide "integration." The guardhouse and hospital were integrated, yet I do not remember considering this as a step toward future full integration.

During my May visit last year I noted integration of the 1st Battalion, 29th Infantry—which appeared about 50-50–and recalled a recent newspaper item reporting our Army as being 32.7 percent black, or about one in three. But it is not the percentage figure per se that counts; it is the established fact of integration itself—surely, the most fundamental change during my lifetime.

Before commenting on the implications of this change, here are incidents from my experience after Fort Benning.

I was wounded during World War II in the Philippines and evacuated by hospital ship to New Guinea. The jungle hospital there consisted mostly of open-air wards under thatched roofs covering two rows of iron cots. Several days after my arrival, a black lieutenant, wounded in one knee, was brought in on a stretcher to a cot one removed from me.

Both of us were completely bed-bound, but with a difference. The nurse greeted me with a cheery word when taking my temperature, but extended the thermometer toward him in silence. It was the same with the orderly who brought our meals—and the lieutenant said, "Thank you."

After two days of this, an ambulatory patient (from Georgia) assumed the initiative. As the nurse arrived with the thermometer, he strolled by, placed a magazine on the bed by the young lieutenant, and said, "Something to read." Later he stopped to chat briefly as an orderly brought the lieutenant his breakfast.

Overnight, the "situation" disappeared. It was a dramatic demonstration—with goodwill on both sides—of instant integration. Nor did I miss its long-range significance for the Army.

Four years later (1948, at Carlisle Barracks, Pa.) my old wound caught up with me, requiring an emergency operation in our post hospital by a civilian surgeon. In due time I was ordered to Valley Forge General Hospital for determination of my future duty status.

Since Valley Forge was not much over a hundred miles away, a staff car would take me and two more patients. When it picked me up the other patients were in the back seat—a white soldier and a black woman (obviously, a military dependent). My attempt to establish an easy conversational relationship did not appear welcomed. So I gave it up until we arrived at a roadside diner, and the driver said, "Colonel, we generally stop here for coffee. Is it okay?"

Of course it was, and the two soldiers promptly dismounted and entered the diner. So I opened the rear door and invited the lady in for coffee, which she declined. On entering the diner I sat at the opposite end of the counter from the two "gentlemen," but somehow could not enjoy my coffee.

Another four years later (1952), after my return from the new unified command in Iceland, it was my good fortune to assume command of the 505th Airborne Infantry, 82d Airborne Division. An interesting feature of the "Five-Oh-Five" was that we had two white battalions and one black battalion, with two officers' clubs.

Soon after my arrival President Dwight D. Eisenhower ordered the military services integrated. So I decided to do two things: not wait for instructions to integrate my regiment; and begin with my officers—and do this by holding an integrated "Prop Blast" (an airborne term, from the fact that jumpers dropped through the propeller airstream backwash).

The Prop Blast is an initiation ceremony for newly parachute-qualified officers to get them socially qualified. It is a semi-hazing affair, including the consumption of alcoholic beverages (there is a substitute testing concoction for nondrinkers)—the drinking being a formalized procedure involving imbibing in a cadenced routine from a Prop Blast mug—and a demonstration of parachute landing falls.

Making this my first integrated formation was designed to meet the problem—if there was one—in the middle of the road. As a first step, I reported to my division commander, Maj. Gen. Charles D. W. Canham, and briefed him on my plan.

When he said, "Why are you in here, Colonel?" I replied, "My regiment is part of your division, and you can tell me not to do it."

"You are the regimental commander," he said.

So I left to issue the orders, and, incidentally, dropped a word here and there that anyone causing trouble at the Prop Blast would have a date in my office the next morning.

But there was not the slightest hint of trouble. Just as in the hospital in New Guinea on the other side of the world eight years before, the key element was mutual good faith.

The subsequent national integration of our armed forces since 1952 is a matter of history, not just "in the ranks," but at the military academies and up to and including multistar-level senior officers. These comments are relevant:

- It is a matter of great pride to me that the Army in which I served (and the other military services) led the way in setting an example for our country in this great national change. Perfection? No, but almost unbelievable progress.
- This skips over the subject like a flat rock across a broad pond, without following the widening and converging ripples from each contact, but the principle and result are clear. As a former regimental commander of the 505th Airborne Infantry, I can say that from the day we had three integrated battalions— replacing the two white and one black—we became a stronger and more effective fighting force.
- Similarly, the greatest single fundamental development in the overall fighting strength of our Army has been successful integration, but, most emphatically, it is *not* a substitute for the draft. No change of this complexity and magnitude can be implemented without turbulence, but, to paraphrase a popular saying, "Year by year, in every way, we are getting better and better."
- There is a greater problem in civilian life, not only because the overall situation is more complex, but also because the

authority to manage the change is more diffused. However, our great country is making reality out of the motto of the United States: *E Pluribus Unum,* that is, *One Out of Many.* Or expressed another way: "In unity there is strength," and we are a unified people today as never before; thus, a stronger nation, in uniform and mufti.

27

Learning to Talk in Public as Career Plus

AS A YOUNG officer something in my nature made me shrink from public speaking—just as I instinctively recoiled from touching live snakes. But, when I visited Ranger training in later years and witnessed students handling live snakes to overcome that instinctive fear, I tried it, too. It works. Further, it worked that way for me with public speaking, but the shrinking was harder to overcome.

My friend Col. Edwin M. Van Bibber attended a reunion of the 1st Infantry Division (between the two world wars) when the late Maj. Gen. Paul B. Malone was the speaker. Ed remembered these spellbinding words: "Marble is not hard enough nor alabaster pure enough to enshrine the glowing deeds of the noble 1st Division!"

And, Ed said, "There was not a dry eye in the house."

Such glowing flights of noble oratorical phrases are not for you and me, but the ability to stand on our two feet and make a speech that holds the interest of an audience is a valuable professional asset. Bernard Duffy, assistant professor of speech at Clemson University, put it this way: "As an art, public speaking is not readily reduced to a list of hints and suggestions. However, a brief discussion of the steps to making a good speech should provide some help."

So, in furtherance of the good professor's thought, a little pontification on my case history seems permissible.

The difference between a public talk and giving drill instruction was demonstrated to me in unforgettable fashion shortly before World War II. On moving from my happy home as commander of Company D, 19th Infantry, to G2 of the Hawaiian Division, one of my fringe duties was as Schofield Barracks' representative in the local Rotary Club.

The guest speaker program at lunch meetings was a practical demonstration (good and bad) of how to give a public talk. Of particular interest to me was a talk by the only military speaker: a flat and wooden collection of monotonously presented generalities.

As a result—realizing that advancing age and rank would eventually require me to give public "talks," in military and civilian life— I put this notice in the Schofield Barracks daily bulletin: *PUBLIC SPEAKERS' CLUB—All interested officers come to the Officers' Club at (time and date).* Unfortunately, World War II brought that enterprise to an end before it really got off the ground.

After the war, students in the National War College (1946–47) worked on problems in twelve- to fifteen-student seminars. When the solution of my seminar on the national budget was selected for presentation to the whole college, seminar members designated me for the job. Believe me, that all-too-brief exposure to public speaking in Hawaii came in handy. And again, as in the Rotary Club, it was an education in public speaking to hear the distinguished guest speakers there.

The same was true with a different speaker program at my next station, the Armed Forces Information School at Carlisle Barracks (where I was director of instruction). I volunteered to give the lecture series on psychology, thus deliberately touching the snake of public speaking that my nature recoiled from—and changed the approach from academic technicalities to case histories of how psychology was applied in the military service. Finally, as Deputy Commandant, Army, at the Armed Forces Staff College, I sat through another series of guest speakers—as well as platform presentations by faculty members. And it was there that I evolved a "formula" for the "average speech" or public talk that worked for me on active duty and in retirement. It is simple:

- Do not read your talk, but speak from notes. (Exceptions: classified briefings, talks "for the record," and certain talks by senior officers to insure accuracy, especially when possible publicity is involved.)

- Do not speak in generalities or parade facts and figures (although these are normal elements for the drill field and classroom).
- Do not open with a funny story that has no relevance to your subject or the occasion, but do search your mind for some *relevant* incident, story, or anecdote that is interesting and helps set the stage. If it can include humor, that is a big plus.
- Write out and polish in detail your opening, to be sure you have it just right; then add necessary reminder notes for the body of your talk that support the theme, such as:

(1) First day on duty—Sergeant Fugate
(2) Keep your cool—trash box case
(3) Butch qualifies with the rifle
(4) Etc. for other incidents, anecdotes, and case histories

- Write out in detail the ending to bring it all together, and close the talk with a logical and clear signing-off.
- Rehearse your talk aloud, to include checking the time length.
- Of course, you must sometimes make speeches on short notice or even extemporaneously. But the more you give carefully planned talks, the easier it is to meet the challenge of quickies.

As a sample opening, here is the one I used at the Command and General Staff College some years ago:

Gen.————, members of the staff and faculty and student officers, it is a proud privilege for an old soldier of yesterday to address you.

It has taken me thirty-two years to move from where you sit to where I stand. Being here reminds me of my first day in the airborne jump school at Fort Benning, when I was old enough to be the father of others there—which is also true with regard to the student officers here today.

In mid-morning of my first day at jump school, after intense physical conditioning and training exercises, I sat down gratefully on the sandy soil in the hot Georgia sun, sweltering in my own sweat. After a brief silence the eighteen- to nineteen-year-old soldier nearby turned and said:

"Sir, reckon why they sent you here?"

That was a good question then, and it is a good question here today. The answer must begin with the mission assigned me, stated this way: "Under the elective course titled Advance Staff Direction, examine staff operations from the perspective of the commander, the chief of staff and the section chief." It was further stated that in doing this I should "Relate your experience in the variety of staffs on which you have served."

It is on that basis that I am here. Thus, this talk covers selected segments of personal experience, including what I think are the implications of this experience. It presumes to be no more than that. Each of you can then determine how much of what I remember from the past is of benefit to you today.

This opening was designed to establish a meeting of the minds between speakers and audience as the first step. This is a prerequisite for the opening of any good talk. Of course, selection of incidents, case histories, and personal experiences *that support the theme* is a matter of judgment, and the success of your talk will depend upon your skill in this selection (including research when necessary). It also takes time and reflection.

Like the beginning, the ending should be carefully considered and written out to be sure you have it right. Many a fine talk has been sabotaged by a lame and faltering conclusion. The following is how I tried to solve this problem, ending my talk a year ago at the dining-in of the infantry officers' advanced course class (captains) at Fort Benning:

Your mission today is the same as it was in my long years as a company-grade officer, beginning here fifty-six years ago:

- *To train, command, and lead men* in peace and war.
- Weapons change, equipment changes, customs change, but let nobody tell you different: *people do not change.*
- Never forget the human element; use it, do not abuse it.

As I look round me here tonight, and as I moved about the post today, one thing was just as it was when I reported here in 1925. I saw the same look in the eyes of officers and men, the same readiness to meet the challenges ahead—that has not changed, as you lead the way into an uncharted future.

Since I've gone this far in my case history, let me pontificate a little more in these comments:

- One reason I've ventured into this somewhat controversial field is that at no time in my commissioned career did I receive training in this skill. The only time I saw it given was in the "charm" school scheduled for new faculty members at the Armed Forces Staff College.
- In that charm school, after a lecture on the subject, each new instructor was required to give several talks—and was *critiqued in detail*. Items stressed were elimination of distracting mannerisms, especially meaningless gestures that most neophytes tend to make; voice pitch and tone in using the mike; and the mechanics of how to prepare and use notes.
- The requirement is not to be an orator; only on special occasions is oratory appropriate, and even then a good talk is almost always better. In fact, a real threat to an effective talk is the temptation to be overly dramatic in voice and gestures. (Note the adverse effect when your local TV weather forecaster goes dramatic when there is no drama.) So easy does it—after careful thought and meticulous preparation.

28

Paperwork: New Slant from the Top

ONE OF THE standard complaints about Army administration is excessive and unnecessary paperwork. To examine the validity of such allegations, we can invoke the case of a certain circus elephant.

This elephant was one of the animals that escaped when a circus train was wrecked in the wide open spaces of the western plains. All other animals were soon recaptured, but the old elephant wandered miles away from the railroad and found himself hungry from his travels. When he chanced to see the vegetable garden of an old widow who lived way out there, he lost no time in helping himself to the fine cabbage patch. He would curl the tip of his trunk around a big cabbage, snake the succulent leafy head from the ground, stuff it in his capacious mouth, and consume it. Then he repeated the process.

The old widow, who had never seen an elephant before, looked out the window and saw what was happening to her cabbages. She stared in disbelief for a moment, then rushed to the phone and called the county sheriff.

"Oh, sheriff," she said, "come quick—there is a tremendous, big, strange animal in my cabbage patch!"

"What is he doing there?" the sheriff wanted to know.

"He is pulling up my cabbages with his tail," she said.

The sheriff needed more information about this so he asked, "What is he doing with your cabbages then?"

"Oh, sheriff," the old lady replied, after taking another look, "if I was to tell you, you wouldn't believe me!"

Her failure to understand what she was looking at stemmed from the same basic trouble that often causes younger officers to misjudge the nature and need for some of the paperwork that emanates from higher headquarters. They are evaluating it simply from where they stand, without considering it from all sides and both ends—including the higher headquarters end as well as their own end of the elephant of paperwork that does exist.

It is true that there is, and always will be, some needless and excessive paperwork from higher headquarters. But just as "all is not gold that glitters," similarly, all allegedly needless paperwork from the viewpoint of lower units—especially at company level—is not always as unnecessary as it seems. So a closer look at the problem seems in order.

Some twenty-odd years ago I read an article by a captain in a military journal about what he called "The Paper Blockade." His premise was that excessive and needless paperwork from higher headquarters interfered with his efforts as a company commander to do his job. A key element in his proposed solution to the problem intrigued me.

He suggested that division screen and shortstop all papers from higher levels, passing on to him only such extracts as pertained to him and his company. What this would do to paperwork in division headquarters did not seem to bother him; he was just looking at his end of the paperwork elephant.

Since divisions have many kinds of companies, this solution would entail a complicated extraction and republication process. There was the further angle that his idea presumed the staff officer(s) engaged in this work could anticipate every facet of higher headquarters regulations and directives that might apply to his company and eliminate all that did not apply—which would take a superman to do in most cases.

Finally, since he had never been at the division end of the problem, he did not yet realize that, *when feasible and practicable,* division headquarters simplifies and republishes regulations and directives from higher levels. I have often wondered what the captain thought of his own article when he himself arrived at higher headquarters in his later years.

Another aspect of paperwork, as viewed by a company-grade officer, was recently brought to my attention in a long-distance telephone call from a captain. He was previously unknown to me, but, as a reader of "The Forward Edge," he called because he thought I would be interested in his ideas about excessive and obstructive paperwork. In this he was correct, because his phone call sparked me to assemble these comments about the paperwork elephant that will always be a major part of any modern army.

From our phone chat I learned he is in charge of an Army Reserve unit motor pool and believes that personal visits by commanders are preferable to requiring him to make written reports.

Specifically, he cited one such report that required four hours to prepare—but, he said, a fifteen-minute personal visit by the commander could have provided the same information. On another occasion, he said a different commander made a personal visit without calling for a written report. He considered this evidence that his thesis was sound: Higher headquarters should not require him to spend hours on paperwork but come down to get the information in a personal visit.

So here we see another young officer, more than twenty years later, looking at the paperwork elephant in his cabbage patch without considering all sides of the paper problem in the exercise of command.

There are times when nothing can replace a personal visit to see and absorb facts on the ground. But there are also situations in which there is no substitute for a written report. Neither can replace the other. You cannot file a personal visit for future reference; nor can a piece of paper give you the kind of information obtainable by a timely visit to the motor pool.

So it is a matter of perception and good judgment as to how to reduce paperwork. Here are some thoughts on the subject:

- In "Don't Write, Don't Telephone, Go See" (*ARMY*, June 1970), I discussed the advantages of "foot coordination" that accrue from a personal visit. But as you rise higher in the rank structure there are wider and more varied responsibilities that make demands on your time, so that you must depend far more on the chain of command and the written word.
- It is not enough to reduce the number of written regulations, directives, and reports. Excess words in each paper should be eliminated in a clearly organized and concise style.

Some twenty-five years ago I wrote a 500-word article and tried to sell it to several national magazines, but there were no takers. Convinced the point was valid, I edited the article down to 250 words, but still no sale. Finally, revised to 92 words, it sold for twenty-five dollars—a clear lesson.*

Even though you have a captive readership for official papers of all kinds, the same principle applies: One of the best ways to reduce the paper load on readers (lower units) is by careful editing and revision to reduce reading time.

- When I was a student in the wartime (1943) "quickie" General Staff Class No. 13 at the Command and General Staff College, one of the first things they gave us was a concise summary of how to read and study in order to handle the mass of reference material for each day in class.

  In general, the technique was: (1) look over the lesson assignment to see what the problem was; (2) glance through all the reference material to see what was there; (3) scan the pertinent parts to locate what to study in detail—then read those parts carefully. An elementary technique? Sure, but it can save you time in the chore of coping with the paper wheels on which Army administration moves.

- I was a company-level officer for fifteen years (including company commander for nearly five years) and, during that period, I must admit to the old widow's view of paperwork initiated by higher headquarters—wanting to be "just let alone to do my job." But in the nearly twenty years that followed I looked at the elephant of paperwork from higher headquarters and discovered it to be an animal often maligned by those who had not yet had a comprehensive all-around look at it.

- Finally, if I may be permitted a pedantic comment: The best way to deal with the river of paperwork in our modern Army includes the following: (1) learn by assiduous practice how to scan, speed-read, and study papers from higher headquarters selectively; (2) develop your own skill at writing concise, well-organized papers, which requires revision, not just quickie first drafts; (3) wait until you reach higher headquarters and see the

*See Chapter 52.

paperwork end of the elephant from that angle—and then decide what, if any, changes are needed that fall within your authority.

It is possible you may find that the paper cabbages up there are more logically handled than you had thought when viewed from lower levels.

Members of the Clemson College (now university) 1921 basketball team. The author is second from right in the front row.

West Point's Class of 1925 "Hop" managers. The author, who was Senior Hop Manager, is seated at center.

The author as a first lieutenant in the Hawaiian Division Military Police Company in 1934–35

The author (right) poses beside 2d Lt. Richard Mayo during training for the modern pentathlon in the 1932 Olympics. Mayo went on to win the bronze medal (third place). Lieutenant Newman was an alternate on the team and did not compete.

Pfc. Jimmie Reeder, one of the soldiers of Company G, 26th Infantry at Plattsburgh Barracks, N.Y., in 1938 when the author was commander.

The sergeants of Company G, 26th Infantry during then Captain Newman's tour as commander from March 1936 to November 1938.

Members of Company G, 26th Infantry photographed at Plattsburgh Barracks, N.Y., in August 1936. The soldier at left in the middle row is Pfc. Samuel E. McGarvey (see Chapter 1). The author is seated at right in the front row.

The author as commander of Company D, 19th Infantry in Hawaii (July 1940 to February 1941). The command was his third and last at the company level.

First Lts. Howell Barrow (left) and Paul Austin served as company commanders in the 34th Infantry, commanded by the author during Gen. Douglas MacArthur's famous "return" to the Philippines on Red Beach at Leyte in October 1944.

The blown bridge over the Palo River after American engineers gave it a "quick-fix." Just upstream, soldiers of the 2d Battalion, 34th Infantry forded the Palo—packing only their weapons and whatever supplies they could carry—and began the drive to Jaro.

The author (left) meets with Maj. Gen. Franklin P. Sibert, commander of X Corps (center) in the Philippines during the waning days of World War II.

The author accepts congratulations from his Pentagon boss, Maj. Gen. Willard G. Wyman, chief of the Army Ground Forces (AGF) G2 section. The occasion was the author's departure from the Pentagon after completing a tour as chief of the AGF G2's Training Division.

The author, while serving as assistant commander of the 82d Airborne Division, is shown here presiding at a Prop Blast "social qualification" ceremony. Here he congratulates a participant who successfully completed all of the requirements.

General Newman poses at his desk during his final tour of duty—as chief of staff, U.S. Continental Army Command, at Fort Monroe, Va.

General Newman is greeted at the Manila airport by a Philippine general during his 1977 visit for the "Reunion for Peace."

Most writers gain insights from a good informal critic—a role Dorothy Newman filled for the author. Here the couple sit beneath their portraits in their apartment overlooking Sarasota Bay in 1977.

29

What's in a Name? Plenty!

WILLIAM SHAKESPEARE ONCE said, "What's in a name? That which we call a rose, by any other name would smell as sweet." One can also put this another way: Stinkweeds by any other name would be as obnoxious. This principle applies equally well with animates in uniform and inanimate flora—not just in regard to legal names, but to nicknames and group classifications, which often carry implications about the so-named people.

Consider this extract from my files, written as a captain in the 19th Infantry at Schofield Barracks, Hawaii, prior to World War II:

We Need a Few

There are those who say I am soured on life, and the efficiency of my digestive processes has been a matter of conjecture. But the most popular explanation of my manner in official matters is that I'm just a plain sonofabitch. It is confusing, because I'm good and kind to all things that live and breathe, except maybe second lieutenants. And so I've tried to be modern and analyze the situation.

My conclusions are as simple as they are definite. Both soldiers and officers have developed feelings and finer sensibilities. You must handle them "tenderly," as distinguished from "fairly." Once upon a time fairness was the thing that mattered. When somebody needed to get his ears bent he got 'em damn well bent. When a soldier or officer is out of step there ought to be hell to pay. Then a lot fewer people would get out of step.

Those who don't tell you your faults don't cure you of them either. The more polite and tactful an officer is with his junior, the poorer that young man's efficiency report is apt to be.

Maybe I am turning into an old so-and-so before my time. But of this much I am certain: year by year the number of so-and-sos in the Army is diminishing. And any army is a hell of an army without a few so-and-sos in it.

That was penned more than forty-two years ago, but the passage of time, and wider, more varied experience—along with the pickling effects of age—have mellowed, although not changed, my opinion of that military fundamental. Actually, I belong to another classification, too, as evidenced by my name in a recently published paperback titled *The Red Head Book.* Also there are more group classifications such as "softies," "disciplinarians," "old fogies," and others. But it's time to look at some different types of names.

There were the names painted on a Jeep parked near the airfield in Hollandia, New Guinea, in World War II, after our division had liberated that area.

In the narrow area under the windshield, just above the center of the hood, the single word "Mary" was carefully printed in neat, prim white letters.

On the front fenders were names like "Marian" and "Margarette"— one painted in flowing red and the other in seductive pink letters.

On one rear fender, "Mabel" was carelessly lettered in dull blue paint.

So what's in a name? Well, there seemed to be something in the placement, color, and lettering of those names that said something about the individual ladies. Also, I took another look at the driver, who at first glance had seemed a young and quiet soldier—but the implications of those names belied his deceptively quiet look.

Then there are names of individuals that fall into two classes: legal names and nicknames. Legal names can have varied connotations, including national, geographic, religious, and ethnic nuances, thus providing speculative information about their owners. Examples include Karl (German), Juan (Spanish), James (English), Henri (French), -ski (Slavic), and Einstein (Jewish), to name but a few.

As to nicknames, a place to start is with some tacked on me. At my first post I took issue with a soldier over his foul language in my presence and won the name "Preacher." Some ten years later, as commander of Company G, 26th Infantry, at Plattsburgh Barracks, N.Y., my tag was "Big Red." As a division chief of staff in New Guinea, it was "That Redheaded SOB" and "The Great Red Father." Then, as a regimental commander in the battle of Leyte, it was back to "Big Red" again—nothing new, original, or revealing.

General George S. Patton, Jr., was known as "Old Blood and Guts" to his soldiers, stemming initially from his earthy prebattle pep talks. To his intimates, however, he was "Georgie," which carries a different connotation. But when soldiers after the war were asked what unit they had served in, they did not say, "Third Army," they said, "Patton's Army." And that has its implications, too.

The words "I like Ike" seemed to fit Gen. Dwight D. Eisenhower, but "I back Mac" did not seem quite right for Gen. Douglas MacArthur, which brings up the point that nicknames have to "fit." The absence of a nickname can be indicative, too, as was the lack of such tags for Gens. Omar Bradley and Mark Clark.

Another interesting facet to who calls anybody by what name is the fact (noted somewhere in my historical reading) that President Franklin D. Roosevelt, who had extensive dealings with both General MacArthur and Gen. George C. Marshall when they were chief of staff, addressed General MacArthur as Douglas, but did not address General Marshall as George. Both of those five-star officers had an imposing presence, but that little facet provides an intangible, inductive indication of their respective personalities.

As to other battle leaders whose names are writ large in the pages of history, consider these: "Stonewall" Jackson, "Unconditional Surrender" Grant, "Black Jack" Pershing, "Tooey" Spaatz, "Bull" Halsey, "Chesty" Puller, and others—including "The Little Corporal," Napoleon. From the nature of those names it appears their owners *earned* them in one fashion or another—although where "Tooey" could come from escapes me.

Since the above nicknames apply to generals and admirals, it appears in order to recount two echoes from the past that could indicate all of them may, to some degree, share membership in the general classification discussed earlier under the heading "We Need a Few." For instance, scuttlebutt has it that when Adm. (later Fleet Admiral) Ernest

J. (Ernie) King was called to Washington early in World War II to be chief of naval operations, he is reputed to have said, "When they get in trouble, they send for the sons of bitches."

Another Ernie, the late, great battle commander Maj. Gen. Ernest N. (Old Gravel Voice) Harmon, recounts this incident in his fine book, *Combat Commander* (Prentice-Hall Inc.). It happened when he commanded the 2d Armored Division in the Fort Bragg, N.C., area before going overseas in World War II. One rainy night when General Harmon was returning by car to his camp headquarters along a narrow, muddy road, his headlights picked up a soldier slogging along on foot, bottle in hand and weaving.

Ernie ordered the soldier picked up and seated in front with the driver "because he is one of our own, and we should help him home." Once seated, the soldier paid no attention to who might be in the rear seat and became alcoholically loquacious, offering to share his bottle of champagne. When this was declined he launched into a critique of his superiors, beginning with his platoon leader and working upward. Some of them he liked and some of them he did not like, and he said why. Finally, the soldier's ramblings reached the level of division commander and he paused.

"Well," he said, "he is a general and, I guess, more or less a son of a bitch."

So what *is* in a name? To paraphrase Shakespeare, a general by any other appellation would be unchanged—even if he is some kind of one. But, regardless of the nature and implications of various sobriquets, there is one name vitally important to every person's professional success and personal happiness: his or her good name in the eyes of all with whom he or she serves. Thus, there is plenty in your good name, hence these comments:

- Your good name in uniform is what you make it, beginning with your first day on duty. If you sow wild oats, including the bottled kind, they are in your name to stay. Similarly, if the first half of your service is spent drifting on the tide with little effort or initiative, that will permeate your good name, too.
- Even your nickname is a part of your good name (for example, if you are a kid called "Stinky"). Further, the nature and scope of your SOB content is an important element. If it is totally absent, you may be a fine gentleman and good guy, but the odds

are against your reaching top rank. The same is true if you are too much of an SOB.

- There are all kinds and types of SOBs: the born kind; the self-made type; the stupid, unnecessary model; the brilliant, selfish, and lazy vindictive; the hard-nosed professional; the jealous incompetent. Then there is the reluctant and considerate SOB; the kind and thoughtful SOB; the interested and square SOB; also the efficient, fair, and empathetic SOB.

So maybe your SOB content should be carefully reviewed, because it will be an element in your good name. Or you may call it the iron in your soul. But by whatever name, you need enough—but not too much.

30

Talk Is Good, but Writing Is Better

AT COFFEE CALLS and cocktail hours on military posts, a standard topic was—and I am sure still is—new ways to make the Army better. It is easy to talk about new ideas, but hard to get one adopted Armywide. Few know the circumstances under which I sired the Aggressor Army concept now used to represent the "enemy" and provide intelligence training in field maneuvers, so it seems time to regularize the paternity of my brainchild. There are also angles involved that may help you with your ideas.

In the late 1930s I endured the confusing exercise in futility of being handed a bunch of colored flags—usually white, yellow, and red—with instructions to take my company out and "represent the enemy" in a maneuver. In those exercises the only persons who seemed to know what they were doing were the G3 who wrote the problem and a few commanders and umpires briefed by him.

As S2, 19th Infantry (1939), and G2, Hawaiian Division (1941), I asked for intelligence play to be written into field exercises. My requests were brushed aside, partly because there was no established technique to do this, but also because I did not say exactly what I wanted—not knowing myself how to go about it.

The first step toward a solution came in a large Hawaiian Department maneuver in 1941. As division G2 I issued intelligence bulletins based on imaginary combat intelligence and coordinated with the scheme of the maneuver.

These started by announcing movement of enemy ships, as reported by my imaginary aerial reconnaissance and submarine sightings. Ships sighted by shore observation posts (OPs) followed—based on what I imagined these posts would report. Finally, as the exercise progressed, so did my imaginary intelligence—including how enemy action set fire to oil storage tanks near Pearl Harbor, with windblown smoke limiting visibility on part of the shoreline we defended.

I was surprised at the interest created, but had a moment of misgiving when the older and senior G3 came into my office with the bulletin about oil smoke.

"Where did you get that information?" he asked.

"Well, sir," I said defensively, "the enemy would probably hit those tanks. The wind would drift smoke that way."

He stood staring at me a moment, then held up the bulletin. "These are good," he said. "Keep it up."

This helped me recognize the principle that would lead to the Aggressor Army concept: that even one intelligence-trained man can produce acceptable maneuver intelligence out of all proportion to the man-hours involved.

When Pearl Harbor was attacked, I was G2 of the 24th Division at Schofield Barracks, and thus learned the kind of information needed in an attack on Hawaii. So, in a large maneuver early in 1942, I used more trained personnel to introduce intelligence into the exercise:

- The division G2 (myself) was designated intelligence umpire at that level.
- S2s were intelligence umpires for their units, to introduce combat intelligence at their levels—anything consistent with the maneuver plan.
- A master movement plan was prepared for enemy ships approaching Hawaii—in diagram form, with dates and hours indicated. It was thus possible to fix the locations of ships at any time.
- A system of "reverse transmission" was used at battalion level. If an acting S2 called his shore observation posts for what they could see—and completed the communications link—the intelligence umpire consulted his ship-movements plan for what OPs could see. This information was relayed to OPs for entry in their

logs and processed by the S2, as though obtained by observation at OPs.
- At division, air-reconnaissance and submarine reports were handled in a similar fashion, but only when the acting G2 asked for them.

This system produced G2 and S2 situation maps at division and lower levels *before* the maneuver battle began, as would be the case in actual operations. When the maneuver progressed into simulated landings, intelligence umpires (G2s and S2s) continued to supply information in various ways, using their imaginations—always coordinated with and designed to advance the maneuver plan.

The result was more realistic combat intelligence. It was still far short of what could be done, but the principle proved sound: A small number of *intelligence-trained personnel*, starting in advance with a definite plan, can produce effective maneuver intelligence.

Two simple ideas dawned on me. If the G2 wants combat intelligence in maneuvers it is up to him to figure out how—not expect G3 to do it. If it helps to develop the maneuver as G3 planned it and leads to a more realistic exercise, G3 and all others involved will cooperate.

In early 1946, with World War II combat experience behind me, I reported for duty in the Pentagon. Duty assignment: Chief of Training Branch, G2 Section, Army Ground Forces. Thus, it became my duty to develop means to correct the lack of adequate intelligence training.

Within two months, based on my Hawaiian G2 maneuver experiment and founded on battle experience, the Aggressor Army concept took shape in my mind. Over one weekend in my Pentagon office, with the phones silent and no interruptions, I reduced to writing the Aggressor Army idea in staff project form. My boss, Maj. Gen. Willard G. Wyman, approved it. Next step: to staff Aggressor for "concurrencies" in our headquarters.

The first stop was at the office of the G3 training branch chief—who refused to concur. So I went to the G3 himself, Maj. Gen. Clarence R. Huebner, one of the great battle leaders of World Wars I and II. He gave me the okay. After that it was smooth sailing, with nobody having anything to add, subtract, or change—except one officer who did not like the word "Aggressor," but had no better name to offer.

My next task: draft a formal letter-directive to the commanding general of Sixth Army requiring him to test the idea in a large West Coast amphibious maneuver scheduled for early fall 1946. That directive delineated at length the plan for Aggressor. In addition to general instructions, my staff study was attached as an enclosure, including specific details like these:

- Design a flag as a national symbol for Aggressor.
- Use recognition symbols on vehicles, aircraft, naval vessels, and the like.
- Prepare technical data and a training manual for Aggressor—with uniforms, insignia of rank and branch, and other items.
- Compile an Aggressor order of battle.
- Base Aggressor uniforms on our old ones by using a distinctive-color dye. A selected shade of green, both in paint and dye, was suggested.

There was much more—eleven single-spaced typewritten pages' worth. This included specific details of required combat intelligence, and techniques for working them into a maneuver.

That field test was a success, resulting in adoption of Aggressor for Armywide use. In the meantime, however, I was ordered to the first class (1946–47) at the National War College, and so I was not present at the test. When Aggressor Army later appeared in large maneuvers in Tennessee, there was much publicity in newspapers and magazines. But until now the circumstances of the birth of the Aggressor concept have not been recorded, although some writers wrongly attributed the idea to the Aggressor commander in those maneuvers.

Four comments are pertinent:

- Discussion of new ideas over coffee is a fine Army custom, and an oral briefing for your boss is excellent procedure. But your bright idea may die stillborn unless you get it down on paper, and its survival may depend on how clearly you express the idea in writing.
- In this case, the power of the written word is demonstrated by the fact that my staff study and directive operated to bring Aggressor to enduring life even after I left the scene.
- If you think highly of an idea, keep a copy even though your boss turns it down. When you get another commander, try it

out on him—after some careful restudy and further evaluation to be sure your proposal is valid.

- Sometimes the question of "claiming credit" will be a factor. It does not appear on my record that I originated the Aggressor Army idea, possibly because the successful test had not yet taken place. My thought then was, and still is, that when your boss knows what you have done, you have received credit.

31

All Inevitable: Death, Taxes, Retirement

SOON AFTER WORLD WAR II an eagle colonel chaplain at a post where I served retired at age sixty-four, then the retirement age. But instead of accepting this with happy anticipation as a well-earned reward, he left the post a disgruntled man with no retirement plans— complaining that his long experience only enabled him to preach a better sermon.

But that was not the point, or in legalese it was "irrelevant and immaterial." He had known since the day he was commissioned that he must retire at age sixty-four. For every career military person, retirement joins death and taxes as an inevitable eventuality. Also, just as there is more than one way to divest a cat of its hide, there is more than one way to prepare for retirement. What follows is a backward look at one man's erratic path, with the hope it will focus attention on the problem for career soldiers early in their service.

Some people are smart, some are lucky, and circumstances make some look smarter than they are. For me, an amalgam of bad luck and fortuitousness pushed me in the right retirement direction, but not until late in my career. The bad luck—a combat wound that placed my future active duty in question—was the catalyst.

Money in the bank (or its equivalent) is a salient factor as you enter retirement, a little matter often overlooked on active duty, especially by young military men. That is not surprising, since active-duty paychecks (including allowances) arrive every month, every man and woman is a member of the club, and medical care is available.

Anyway, after five and a half years' service this second lieutenant had a savings account of one month's pay when three things happened: (1) promotion to first lieutenant—before the Great Depression freeze on promotions, (2) a 15 percent pay cut, and (3) my anemic savings account disappeared in the wave of bank failures at a time when there was no federal insurance to protect me.

It would seem this would make clear the desirability of finding a safe way to establish a financial anchor to windward for the long run. But since this critique is limited to facts, it must be stated that after World War II, with more than twenty years' service, I arrived in Washington for duty with total liquid assets of barely three thousand dollars—and most of that from my wife's efforts.

This situation had a critical influence on my "sunset years" because my wartime wound might force retirement at any time, and a quick decision was necessary: to rent an apartment or buy a house? In that situation it seemed logical to buy a small home (with attached mortgage); thus, if sudden retirement was in the cards we could drop anchor and stay there.

So how to go about it?

As a wartime division chief of staff, loose-leaf notebooks were my favorite planning tools, so we rented a room, and I bought a loose-leaf notebook. We then studied newspapers, clipped homes-for-sale advertisements, and pasted each likely looking ad at the top of a page in the loose-leaf book.

Our next move was normal staff procedure. We visited potential homes, made notes about each under the ad on its page in the notebook, then held an executive meeting to decide, after considering our notes, on which house to lay our nest egg as a down payment.

Why all this tedious detail?

Well, when we left Washington a year and a half later we had doubled that original nest egg by selling the house at a profit—in addition to living in it for the cost of maintenance and taxes. The point is that when you buy a house in lieu of living in on-post quarters you can make a profit—or face a loss. This is still true even in these times of high inflation when managing to acquire a home is much more difficult.

The way to lose money is to buy under pressure and in haste, and sell the same way. To achieve the victory of a profit in buying a house there is no substitute for careful planning, looking until you know the local values, and the good judgment to buy a house with resale in mind.

It was at our next post that we saw the colonel retire at age sixty-four, unhappy, with no plans for his retired life. When he got in his car and drove away to an uncertain future, that crystallized the problem for me because I had no plans for retirement either and a still-anemic bank account—after twenty-three years' service.

When my wound required a sudden emergency operation, I asked myself, "Where are *you* going to retire—and how big a mortgage payment can we afford on 60 percent of my pay and no allowances?" The arithmetic was enlightening. Although the operation was a success, I kept asking that question and reviewing the arithmetic. I also started asking people, "Where are you going to retire, and why?"

A year later, an Air Force officer when asked that question replied, "Sarasota, on the west coast of Florida." He had five acres on Siesta Key Island, fronting on Sarasota Bay, and he explained why he was going to retire there.

So I flew down, conducted an on-the-ground reconnaissance, including the road net and proximity to a beautiful Gulf of Mexico beach, and bought the available five acres next to the Air Force colonel. At thirty-five dollars per front foot that gave my wife pause. But she accepted my reconnaissance report, we put most of our nest egg in a down payment, began paying on a mortgage, and nine years later sold it for six and a half times what we paid for it.

The proceeds bought another and better waterfront location with a small house on it on Longboat Key, to which we retired a year later. Then (with a mortgage) we added a major addition and, after living there seventeen and a half years in retirement, we sold the house for three times our investment.

We now live in a luxury beachfront apartment, free and clear—because, after living like the proverbial summer grasshopper for more than twenty years, the misfortune of a combat wound pushed me into planning for retirement. Not a brilliant saga, more of a seventh-inning rally, but it's dangerous to wait for the seventh inning—and more of a struggle. Fortunately, the "extra innings" of thirty-five years' service also came to my rescue.

Space limitations prevent inclusion of more details and reflections. Since fate seldom gives you more than one time at bat, these comments seem in order:

- When each of us enters military service we know the day will come for retirement, and should begin planning for it. On active duty we have all kinds of plans: attack plans, defense plans, supply plans, intelligence plans, alert plans, disaster plans, among others, and we place much stress on *advance planning.* Yet my observation has been that all too many military people do not apply that basic principle to one of our most important campaigns: Operation Retirement.
- Be certain of one thing: *Money,* repeat *money,* holds a new and unique place in your life in retirement. If you can buy a home with cash your whole life will be much simpler, because a mortgage obligation under sky-high interest rates, subtracted from an already radically reduced paycheck, really puts a financial monkey on your back.
- How you get that money is up to you. Maybe you bought gold when it was thirty-five dollars an ounce, or perhaps your thing is stocks and bonds (we fiddled a bit in that and got fiddled a little, too), or maybe you have this great job in mind that's waiting for you—although those great jobs on the distant horizon sometimes evolve into mirages.
- Several of my friends accumulated a nest egg in their early years on active duty, then bought or built a home—via the down payment and mortgage route—which they rented, and owned free and clear when retirement arrived. One Navy officer did this twice in his thirty-year career, selling the first one at a profit to send his daughter through a top-level college, and the second one was there free and clear when he found the "sun over the yardarm" of his career.
- If you do follow the own-a-house route, be sure your head rules the buy. On one occasion, knowing I was due for an overseas "no dependents" tour, we put our kitty into a nice home for my wife to occupy in my absence, in a nice area with nice landscaping and nice neighbors. And we ended with a nice little loss, too, because we did not buy with *appreciation* (thus resale) in mind.
- So what is the answer to the need for money in the bank (or its equivalent) when you retire? I can only emphasize the need—but, like buying a hat, the solution must fit your head. Only you can pick the method best for you, yet a program to pro-

vide working capital, especially today, is basic. Whatever your method, if you do not already have a kitty, start a Tuckabuckaway Program.

Don't just stand there for twenty to thirty years—start saving and planning. But only as an extracurricular activity, never at the expense of your military mission: soldiering.

32

Clemency in Military Justice

THOSE RESPONSIBLE FOR good order and military discipline often decry legal technicalities written into our Uniform Code of Military Justice (UCMJ). Technicalities *do* exist, but is *that* where we should focus our attention?

Fifteen years ago I was president of a general court that tried a soldier for murder under the then relatively new UCMJ—with its ritualistic gesture of isolating the law member from other members of the court. Evidence, including that of eyewitnesses to the crime, proved beyond conceivable doubt that the defendant was guilty of premeditated murder, cold-blooded and unusually reprehensible. He was convicted and sentenced to death.

Later, I said to the law member, "Military reviewing authorities will approve the finding and the sentence. But when it gets to the civilian review board in the Pentagon they'll throw it out."

"Why?" the law member asked in some astonishment. "He is guilty; it's a proper finding and sentence. I've bent over backward—we all have—to protect the legal rights of the accused."

"Yes," I answered, "but as lawyers they are steeped in technicalities. That the evidence proves ten times over he is guilty, and that the sentence fits the crime, to them will not be the critical things. Nor will they be reviewing the rights of the dead man, nor the best interests of the military service. They will examine the record of trial in a legal vacuum, looking for technicalities. With that approach they will find one—and throw the case out."

And they did.

It is such distortion of legal technicalities until they override established facts of the crime that has sparked much of the criticism of the Uniform Code of Military Justice. Although there are flaws in the UCMJ, our court-martial system is still so far ahead of civil court procedures there's no comparison. For proof of this we need look no farther than stories constantly trumpeted in the press of legal shenanigans and miscarriages of justice in civil court actions.

Hence we should recognize but not unduly magnify flaws and failures in our Uniform Code. Further, in spite of its shortcomings, the UCMJ retains the great cornerstone of military justice: It does not convict the innocent. Because of this—and its unique features like pretrial investigations and the way members of the court (our jury) can ask questions—we have the finest legal system in the nation. Thus, our primary attention should be focused on making it work better.

There are many ways to do this, but the most important is in the exercise of clemency. Here it is not technicalities that count, but judgment founded on the best interests of the military service—and a capacity for empathy and human understanding of special circumstances faced by the accused.

Years ago when I took command of a regiment it occurred to me that men in the guardhouse were then being held in confinement on my authority—because I had special court-martial jurisdiction, and so could exercise clemency and release them. Yet I knew nothing of their cases, had never seen any of them.

So I arranged for a visiting schedule at the guardhouse after supper at nights, the men coming in to talk with me one at a time in a room there. It took three or four nights, but was more than worthwhile.

I discovered, among other things, that most were AWOL cases, an appreciable number of whom were there because they had become homesick kids. One result of my guardhouse visits was to reduce some AWOL sentences. Several were released, it being my opinion that the ends of justice and discipline had been served.

But the most important result was that I made it my policy thereafter to talk personally to soldiers tried and convicted by court-martial before I approved their sentences, if the sentences included confinement. After I had reviewed the legal papers, the regimental adjutant scheduled interviews in my office. This took little time but vastly improved my understanding of the cases. Nothing can replace information gained through a face-to-face meeting unhampered by rules of evidence and legal technicalities.

In one interview (later, in another regiment) it developed that after the soldier had returned from leave his sweetheart had written asking him to come back and "do the right thing." When his company commander refused another leave so soon after the first one, the soldier went AWOL—which might have been predicted. Then, as the soldier said: "After we were married, and since I was already AWOL anyway . . . well, you know, Colonel. I just stayed on a while."

I consulted my empathy, decided I did know, and that the soldier's young company commander should have. Under the UCMJ, clemency was not merely something I could exercise; it was a stern duty where warranted. The young soldier had done what he thought was right by his sweetheart, under the circumstances; so I did what I thought was right by him, under the circumstances.

Of course, no commander can set himself up as a patsy. He must be sure his decisions are based on facts, not imagination. Further, there are occasions when the courts-martial manual should be examined for the best way to lower the biggest possible boom on a surly or wise-guy offender.

Like the time, when I was a company commander, that a soldier went AWOL for one day—thus missing a twenty-mile hike under full pack, an overnight bivouac, and the march back. His idea was to forfeit three days' pay for that one day AWOL, then give the company the horselaugh when they returned, streaming sweat from marching dusty miles.

But it didn't work that way, because you can't temporize with that kind of business. This soldier was charged with deliberately skipping out on a scheduled march, or arduous duty, and got two months in the can. So not all legal technicalities operate in the wrong direction, and in some cases "reverse clemency" is in order—at the time charges are prepared.

In deciding whether or not to exercise clemency, it's not enough to consider the past record of offenses. It's the man, and special circumstances not in legal papers. That's why, if a soldier's liberty is taken away by a stroke of the pen of the reviewing authority—who has never seen the soldier—it may be legal justice, but it's not military justice in its truest sense.

I think that when a court-martial sentence includes confinement it should be the Army's policy (but *not* a legal requirement) for the reviewing authority to see the accused in person before finalizing the sentence—if the situation makes this practicable (sometimes it may not be if travel is necessary, or during wartime). In most cases interviews will be brief but the results far-reaching. Men of all ranks will react favorably to their commander's personal interest, and have greater confidence in the fairness of his decisions—including those where severe sentences are approved. This does not blur disciplinary standards, but sharpens them.

Finally, there is an important collateral benefit from personal interviews: The alert commander will gain a better insight into areas that cause trouble within his unit. This will often suggest corrective measures to reduce or eliminate similar offenses in the future.

When military justice stumbles, as it sometimes does, the legal rigidity of the UCMJ is frequently the cause; but there are also human errors by those who use "the book." Hence the broadest area for immediate improvement lies in better implementation of our existing UCMJ—especially as regards greater emphasis on personal contact in the exercise of clemency.

Now, fifteen years after that murder conviction was thrown out because of a legal technicality, my viewpoint has been rounded by broader experience and clarified by hindsight to realize that we must live with unwise legal technicalities in the UCMJ—at least until time or the next war forces needed revisions. In the meantime, however, "Ask not only how we can improve the UCMJ, but also ask yourself how you can better carry out its provisions *now* within your area of responsibility."

The place to start is in the exercise of clemency—where the commander remains uninhibited by technicalities, free to exercise authority and judgment in the best interests of his unit, the soldier, and the military service.

33

Stop Selling G2 Short

DURING MY ACTIVE-DUTY years (1925–60) our Army sold G2 (combat intelligence) short, and it still does—but not as far short. My experience in some measure clarifies why it was that way.

Prior to World War II I served in five infantry regiments where command and staff intelligence training was conspicuous by its absence. Nothing unpleasant happened when intelligence officers either didn't exist or failed to function, which is why intelligence was a staff stepchild.

The attitude toward intelligence is reflected in my assignment as G2 of the Hawaiian Division in early 1941—a Table of Organization and Equipment (TOE) slot for a lieutenant colonel. It had previously been occupied by the Army's senior colonel, who was replaced by the CG's aide (first lieutenant) *in addition to his other duties.*

I was a company commander who had been regimental S2 for six months, with primary duties as athletics officer, and I was a friend of the CG's aide. Since the G2's responsibilities included doubling as public information officer, and I had been writing for a local newspaper, you can see who became the logical man to take over when the CG's aide got tired of playing G2.

By the time a division field exercise came along I had studied intelligence manuals, found the classified intelligence SOP, and conceived the odd idea that they should be followed during the maneuver. When they were not, I went down to a brigade headquarters (we were a "square" division, of four regiments) to inquire into the matter.

No brigade S2 was assigned. The S3 had S2 functions as an additional duty. When I took this business up with the combination S2/S3 —a somewhat older officer whose major's leaves ranked my captain's bars—his reaction was crisp and to the point: "Why don't you go gumshoe somewhere else, so you won't be in the way?"

This was my first controversy as G2, but not my last. I recount it here because it pinpoints the prevailing attitude toward G2 training at the time.

On 1 October 1941 the Hawaiian Division was redesignated to form the 24th and 25th Infantry Divisions. I was G2 of the 24th Division when the Pearl Harbor attack came on 7 December—and that brought a dramatic change in my status. From the staff nuisance G2 I became Somebody: What was the enemy situation? And—most flattering— what did I *think*?

When, eight months later, I became division chief of staff, it wasn't the new eagles that were the valuable result of those sixteen months as G2. It was my personal knowledge of intelligence gained during the frustrating struggle to get my G2 job done—an understanding of the part combat intelligence should play in battle operations. Nothing, absolutely nothing, was of more value to me when commanding an infantry regiment in combat.

During World War II the standard of combat intelligence was below our other battle techniques—a natural result of peacetime neglect of intelligence training. This was by no means confined to G2, for in combat all officers are in some measure responsible for and need intelligence. Yet, when fighting begins, "intelligence awareness" among officers can't be developed overnight and automatically integrated into staff and command operations. Thus, the G2 was often shunted aside by those who most needed his help. Further, G2 was not a highway to top rank; hence many avoided it.

If a G2 on an army staff was promoted to general officer during World War II, I'm not aware of it. In particular, the G2s of Patton's famed Third Army in Europe and of Krueger's Sixth in the Pacific wore eagles, not stars. Both were outstanding officers, well known to me.

In my opinion this unwritten policy had a major effect upon the caliber of intelligence, resulting in too many passive types as S2 and G2. Their primary preoccupation seemed to be in keeping journals and files of information, so they could find facts already in the record—if asked for them.

On a number of occasions my own intelligence background enabled me, as chief of staff, to come up with an angle about the enemy situation that the G2 should have discovered. One incident, simple and basic, illustrates the importance of transmuting information into intelligence.

On this occasion the G2 overlay of estimated enemy locations and numbers showed a force of 10,000 on our left flank. If correct, this was a serious threat. When called upon to justify his estimate, the G2 produced identifications of units in that area, mostly from enemy dead. Then he looked up those units in our enemy order of battle and multiplied each by its TOE strength. Sure enough, the figures added up to approximately 10,000. He didn't have the kind of mind or training to realize that here was merely a motley collection of several hundred disorganized stragglers from those units in that area.

The continued tense international situation since 1945—including Korea and Vietnam—has prevented intelligence training from decaying to its pre–World War II state. But when I retired, we were still below par, for the same fundamental reasons:

(1) Nothing much goes wrong in peacetime when the S2 and G2 fail to function in combat intelligence. Even in battle, G2 failures often pass unnoticed.
(2) Because of this we continue to sell G2 short in the rank and caliber of officers we assign, which is further aggravated by able officers trying to avoid intelligence assignments.

Now new factors are working to remedy the situation.

The growing complexity of military technology, with greatly increased speed and flexibility of movement and striking power, has placed a higher premium on adequate and timely information: the enemy's capabilities and intentions, the nature of terrain, and other factors in far-flung areas.

Operations in Vietnam are focusing attention on these new factors in battle.

This is not merely my opinion. Battle experience is demonstrating this, as graphically described in a letter that recently came to my attention. I may be overage and Over Here, but he was in command in combat Over There when he wrote:

". . . battles are short and violent and decisions must be made quickly and orders issued accordingly. Helicopters have made this both possible and necessary.

". . . in a war without a front it's the G2 who really determines where we go, then G3 must figure out and recommend how to do it. . . .

". . . in earlier wars terrain was often the object, whereas in this war it's the enemy. This is why G2 has become so important, if not more important than G3.

"On occasions I moved the division, based on intelligence reports which proved incorrect. On the other hand most of our major victories followed rapid movement on the basis of my G2's analysis of enemy locations and intentions.

". . . we are always concerned about enemy capabilities; but a good G2 also deals with enemy intentions."

The time has come to recognize a basic truth: There is an interdependence between G2 and G3 that exists among no other principal staff officers.

This suggests an obvious solution: Make it policy (but not immutable law) that when an officer serves a tour in G3 he should next serve in G2 before going back to G3—and vice versa. If an officer is not good enough to be a G3, he is not good enough to be a G2.

When an assignment in either G2 or G3 leads to an assignment in the other, this establishes them on a career parity—an intangible but important consideration, if intelligence is to be fully integrated into fast-moving modern operations.

An equal-rank basis would then follow naturally. The imbalance in rank—particularly at general officer level—sells G2 short and lowers the importance of intelligence. Of course, a good man is a good man, but let's not kid around: Rank *does* make a difference.

The policies I have suggested are designed not only to correct past weaknesses, but to anticipate complex new requirements for better intelligence in the vastly more difficult, fast-moving, and varied situations of modern warfare.

I'm aware these observations and ideas lay me open to attack: from G2s who think I've maligned them; from G3s who don't want to share their prestige; from commanders who say, "It wasn't that way in my outfit," and who object to suggestions about how to assign officers; from certain active-duty officers who believe that on retirement an officer's lifetime of experience should disappear with him into limbo, without trace.

But it would be craven to hold my strong convictions, yet be afraid to hold them up for public review and evaluation.

34

Measure of a Soldier: How He Carries Out Orders

A CORNERSTONE ELEMENT of your professional military life is how you carry out orders issued by your superiors. This is underscored by the definition of discipline: the instant and willing obedience to all orders and, in the absence of orders, to what you think those orders would have been.

Consider the case history of one of the finest soldiers of any rank I have ever known, William H. (Big Bill) Biggerstaff. He was a sergeant in the 29th Infantry when I joined in 1925, and we next served together when he was a warrant officer in the 19th Infantry in Hawaii before World War II began with the attack on Pearl Harbor in 1941. In mid-1942, I became chief of staff of the 24th Infantry Division and he was a first lieutenant (later captain) in the adjutant general section.

When I wanted anything done on his side of the staff house, all I had to do was send for Biggerstaff and tell him. But I also had to be sure that what I told him was what I wanted, because he would have it done before I could change my mind.

Unfortunately, the road to promotion was blocked to him in our division, so I reluctantly approved his transfer. However, it gives me much pleasure to report that Big Bill ended World War II as an eagle colonel, adjutant general of a corps.

Not many men after nearly twenty years of enlisted service began World War II as a warrant officer and came out of it an eagle colonel.

There is no question in my mind that the way Big Bill Biggerstaff carried out orders with energy, initiative, loyalty, and careful attention to detail was a major factor in his outstanding success.

In one of the seven divisions in which I served, there was a unique demonstration that how a commander's order is carried out often determines whether or not the purpose of that order is achieved. This came about when the division commander decided that intensive-training disciplinary camps were more appropriate for young minor offenders—like homesick recruits who went AWOL—than confinement in the post stockade with hard-shell offenders. So he issued orders for establishing intensive-training camps at regimental level.

One regimental commander selected the best company commander in his regiment to establish their camp, and gave him some of the regiment's best NCO drill instructors. He also selected a site for the tent camp in a good training area.

As a result, the intensive training intended by the division commander was achieved, as well as the needed disciplinary effect. Further, as an extra bonus, this camp had good morale, and those who went through the fine training there returned to their companies proud of their new military competence.

Another regimental commander established his camp on a routine basis, pretty much as though it were just another unit. Thus it lacked the intensive-training value, as well as the intended disciplinary effect. Consequently, the men in it returned to their companies pretty much as they were to begin with—besides feeling like they had "beat the guardhouse rap."

The third regimental commander openly disparaged the order and set up his camp with an I'll-comply-with-orders-but-I-don't-like-it attitude. His camp was a failure: officers and NCOs running the camp on a loose training schedule, including some "realistic"-type "training" that was more punitive than beneficial, militarily.

The establishment and operation of those three camps revealed a fundamental principle: The value and excellence of an order is often in direct ratio to the loyalty, ability, and intelligence of the subordinates who carry it out. Further, to sabotage an order by poor implementation is an insidious type of disloyalty that, if discovered, should be dealt with firmly.

Of course, there are times when an order is received that it becomes the loyal duty of a subordinate to request it be changed, or even to appeal a refusal to change the order. I was an interested witness to such a case in wartime when my division commander, Maj. Gen. F. A. Irving, did just that when his battle plan for the amphibious landing in Tanahmerah Bay during the New Guinea campaign was changed by higher headquarters (see "Military Tact Tactics," *ARMY,* February 1966). As a result of his strong and repeated requests for a change in orders to permit him to follow his plan, the order was changed—and he was proved right by subsequent events.

That is the key to obtaining a change in orders you believe are wrong or unsound: You have got to be right!

The same applies when you take a radical step without orders. An outstanding example of this was the prompt establishment of martial law by Maj. Gen. Frederick Funston in San Francisco at the time of the great earthquake and fire of April 1906.

Of course, there are isolated extreme cases where the correct action is to flatly disobey an order when time is a factor and you have information unknown to the commander who issued the order. But you are shaking hands with the court-martial manual when you do this, unless you are right beyond question—and I have no personal knowledge of such a case during my active-duty years.

Another interesting angle to carrying out orders is the matter of how far you can go in adding supplementary details in the implementation. For this we will look at a case history where I was not an eyewitness.

Usually in reporting some story relayed to me, I do not identify the place or names of those involved. The case that follows, however, includes names and identifies the place because it seems necessary for an understanding of the incident.

As told to me, this happened when Maj. Gen. Maxwell D. Taylor (later Army chief of staff, still later chairman of the Joint Chiefs of Staff) was superintendent at West Point. One of his subordinates was Col. (later Lieutenant General) Robert F. Sink, who had been an outstanding regimental commander under General Taylor in the 101st Airborne Division during World War II.

The occasion was the visit of a special VIP to West Point. As reported to me, Bob Sink was in charge of arrangements, and General Taylor told him to give the VIP red-carpet treatment.

My grapevine source said all arrangements were carefully planned and implemented, with this special feature when the VIP guest arrived at the officers' club for lunch: There was a red carpet where the VIP dismounted from his car, extending along the walk to the entrance of the officers' club.

Everything went off fine, and it is reported General Taylor remarked with a quiet smile, "It looks like Sink took me literally."

I do not know who the VIP was, but I'm sure my friend Bob Sink took the visitor's personality into account when he injected this bit of submerged humor into the details of his reception. Yet, somehow, a red carpet fits into the atmosphere of classic stone buildings and the beautifully manicured grass of West Point's famous parade ground on which those buildings face. But a red carpet would be ridiculous on posts where World War I–type buildings peel their paint in the sun. At the West Point of that time, however, with the personalities involved, there was no discordant note, though it took a Bob Sink to see this and act accordingly.

This underscores again the principle that in carrying out orders it is not enough just to do what the man says, no more and no less. Nearly always, supplementing instructions are required. And a good subordinate will supply them—often from specialized knowledge of the situation that his chief does not have or might not think of.

I do not recommend that you add eye-catching red-carpet angles to your plans to implement orders you receive—unless you have the sure flair of a Bob Sink. Let's face it, few of us do.

Some comments:

- There is no finer measure of a soldier than how he carries out orders, especially when the success or failure of an order to accomplish the intended result depends upon the initiative and ability of subordinates.
- The parrot-like, wooden "compliance with orders," without supplying the push and guidance of supplementing instructions required, is at best the mark of a mediocre subordinate—or, at worst, a disloyal subordinate who does not want the order to succeed.
- It is normal to give careful thought to orders you initiate, knowing the imagination and judgment they reflect on you will polish your apple for efficiency report time. On the other hand, if the same careful thought, imagination, and judgment are missing from your implementing instructions to carry out orders you receive from above, then you are cultivating the worm of apathy or mediocrity or disloyalty for your apple at efficiency report time.

35

Things Are Not Always What They Seem

IN 1929, AS a second lieutenant with the 31st Infantry in Manila, I put on my white tropical civvies and took a *calesa* (two-wheeled pony cart) out to see a Philippine country fair. Among other things, there was a wrinkled old woman smoking a homemade cigar, her ankle-length skirt tucked under her knees as she sat on her heels. Beside her was a basket of what appeared to be goose eggs.

Between puffs on her cigar she announced, *"Volutes! Volutes!"* At least that is what it sounded like.

Never having eaten a goose egg, I was about to ask if they were hard-boiled, thus edible on the spot, when a Filipino man bought one. He broke off half the shell and I started to laugh—because there was a little hard-boiled gosling in it, near hatching size. However, like fabled "Little Audrey," he knew all the time what was there and proceeded to eat it.

But this is not a gourmet discussion of esoteric foods. The principle involved was stated like this in the parody of a long ago popular song: "The girl of my dreams is not what she seems." Many who sang the words did not realize the depth of heartbreak in them or give a thought to the principle.

The principle that sometimes things are not what they seem is true not only in love and war and country fairs, but also in peacetime military service. The results vary from small embarrassments to major career damage, or even great disasters in war.

In 1934, as a military police lieutenant at Schofield Barracks, Hawaii, I checked the polo field on the upper post one day where MPs were handling parking for a polo game. Thus, I saw a tough sixty-year-old regimental commander try to park in a reserved area and one of my MPs require him to move.

By chance, I saw another MP walk over soon thereafter and shake hands with the MP who had moved the regimental commander. This looked to me like a little harmless horseplay between two fine soldiers. But next day the provost marshal ordered me to investigate a written complaint from the old regimental commander.

His beef was that an MP had made him move at the polo field for no other reason than to prove he could. Then another MP had come over to shake hands and congratulate the first MP on getting away with it.

My inquiry discovered that the accused MP had just been promoted to private first class. The second MP had noticed the new stripe and had come over to congratulate him on his promotion. So things were not what they seemed to the touchy old colonel.

But misjudging what you see does not always mean trouble or complaints, as demonstrated during a large maneuver in 1938 in northern New York near Watertown. I was commanding Company G, 26th Infantry, and all officers were supposed to stay in camp at night with the troops.

One day I visited another company commander in our battalion to help him inspect the coffee in his field mess. Captain Overweight was somewhat older and perhaps a bit more nonregulation, too. Anyway he said, "Nuts to staying in camp every night, Red. I've got a ride lined up and am going to have myself a night on the town."

Before reveille the next morning I visited Sgt. Long John Smith's field kitchen to watch his cooks fix breakfast for our company and, to avoid hurting Long John's feelings, sipped a cup of his fine black coffee. That is how I happened to see Captain Overweight enter his own kitchen tent from the wooded area in the rear, having taken the precaution of returning to camp that way from his night on the town.

I was also an interested spectator as he walked purposefully toward his tent, giving our battalion commander (who was taking an early morning walk) a snappy salute and brisk, "Good morning, sir," as he continued on his way.

Apparently our battalion commander failed to realize that things were not as they seemed. All doubt was removed at a regimental officers' call the next day. I was standing nearby as he said to another battalion commander, "Do you know Captain Overweight well?"

On receiving a noncommittal reply, our battalion commander continued, "Well, I've misjudged him. He has more on the ball than I thought. Yesterday, I saw him return from inspecting his company kitchen before reveille."

At higher levels in peacetime things are not always what they seem either. They are more complex, however, so would require too much space here. But the same principle and caution apply: When something surprises you or seems unusual or illogical, give it some free-wheeling thought—because things may not be what they seem.

While it is unethical to set up situations to mislead your superiors or fool your subordinates, the reverse is true with tactics and strategy in war. A basic principle of war is surprise, more often than not achieved by portraying a situation to the enemy that is not what it seems.

A classic example at the international level was the Kurusu "peace mission" to Washington that laid a negotiation smoke screen as the Japanese made their devastating surprise attack on Pearl Harbor to launch World War II in the Pacific.

At a different level, Gen. Douglas MacArthur set up a situation during the war that was not what it seemed in the Hollandia operation in New Guinea. He created the idea in the minds of Japanese commanders that our fighter-bombers could not reach the three airfields at Hollandia, by refusing to let our planes strike that far, when, in fact, the planes had new attachable, extra gas tanks that brought Hollandia within range.

He also had us planning for an amphibious assault in the Hansa Bay area. Thus, our division staff, which included me, sweated that one out every time we looked at aerial photos of the Hansa Bay fortifications.

Then, at the eleventh hour, General MacArthur ordered a quick conversion of our Hansa Bay amphibious attack plans to Hollandia, while our planes reached out suddenly and whapped enemy planes there on the ground. After our arrival, I saw from the air the cemetery of some three hundred burned-out planes on the airfields, especially around the fringes. We had achieved complete tactical surprise, and our two-division task force captured the Hollandia airfield complex with a minimum of casualties—because the preattack situation had not been what it seemed to the Japanese command.

Other comments are:

- History records many imaginative ways combat commanders have created situations that were not what they seemed. One of the most unusual was the Trojan Horse ploy that ended the long siege of Troy. As described in Homer's *Odyssey* and Virgil's *Aeneid,* the Greeks built a large wooden structure on wheels, in the shape of a horse, with a hollow belly that concealed several Greek warriors. Then the Greek Army seemed to lift the siege and marched away, leaving the big wooden horse in their deserted camp. Seeing this, the Trojans seized the abandoned horse in triumph and dragged it inside the walls as a trophy in their victory celebrations.

After things quieted down that night inside the walls, the Trojan Horse gave Caesarean birth to the hidden Greeks, who opened the interior gates of the city for their army on the outside, which had countermarched after dark to return. And that was the end for Troy, all because the Trojans had not applied the principle: Beware of Greeks bearing gifts; things may not be what they seem.

- Hannibal in 216 B.C. used this principle in planning the battle of Cannae. As Harold Lamb tells us in his great biography, Hannibal selected the plains of Cannae, with two areas of slightly higher ground on which to anchor his flanks, as the place for a climactic battle. His plan involved letting the Romans push him back in the center, thus setting up his double envelopment from what they thought was their penetration. He also had some brush and straw ready to light at the proper moment as a smoke signal to launch his cavalry from a concealed position to take the Romans in the rear.

To bring on this battle he set about terrorizing the Italian countryside, thus drawing a large Roman Army out to destroy him. Hannibal then appeared to retreat in fearful haste to his planned battle site; the Romans followed fiercely to attack and destroy his forces—but ran blindly into his brilliantly conceived booby trap, to their own complete destruction. They had failed to recognize that Hannibal's precipitous retreat was not what it seemed.

- Misleading situations are not limited to happenings like one MP's congratulating another, the before-reveille "inspection" by Captain Overweight, the Kurusu "peace mission," General MacArthur's concealing the range of his fighter-bombers, the Trojan Horse in the siege of Troy, or Hannibal's masterful planned battle of annihilation on the plains of Cannae.

So preventive thinking, based on alert awareness that sometimes things are not what they seem, is a military characteristic of incalculable value in war—and not to be sneezed at in peacetime.

36

On Military, Empathy, Civilians

THEY SAY (THOUGH I've never found out who "they" are) that nothing is sure except death and taxes. For career military men we must add *retirement*. Since "they" have said nothing about the need to adjust to differences of viewpoints between civilians and soldiers, especially in retirement, I'll give it a try.

Consider this active-duty case history, circa 1950, when I was chief of staff of the 11th Airborne Division at Fort Campbell, Ky. The nearby town was Clarksville, Tenn.; the boundary between those two states ran through the post.

One day a civilian friend from Clarksville arrived at my office with U.S. Congressman Pat Sutton, whose district included Clarksville. The last and only time I had seen Pat Sutton was on 20 October 1944, on Leyte in the Philippines when my regiment (34th Infantry) liberated the section of Red Beach where Gen. Douglas MacArthur was soon to land. The young Navy officer attached to my regiment as an underwater demolitions expert was named Pat Sutton.

I had personally contacted him at a critical moment in the landing, and later recommended him for a Silver Star for gallantry in action. So we had a pleasant reunion of "remember when."

About a week later the phone rang in my office. It was the editor of the Clarksville newspaper calling.

"Colonel," he said, "I understand you were Congressman Sutton's regimental commander in the war and that you said he was a good soldier. Would you talk to my reporter about that?"

My reply was to the effect that I had no political connections or interests (though both of us knew the congressman had been publicized as blocking certain legislation favorable to the Army), but I would tell anybody anytime—reporters included—that Pat Sutton had been a fine combat soldier.

The reporter arrived and I repeated what I had said to his editor—because it was true.

The next day the Clarksville newspaper had a two-column-wide story on the front page about Mr. Sutton's former regimental commander at Fort Campbell saying the congressman had been a fine combat soldier. The following day the congressman was reelected.

About ten days after that I attended a little cocktail party in Clarksville. As I sipped my first libation a civilian with white hair and an emotionally red face pushed up to me and said:

"You are not fit to be a corporal, much less a colonel!"

Taken aback, and not knowing who he was, I said something like, "You are entitled to your opinion—but why am I not fit to be a corporal?"

He replied with accusatory emphasis, "You got that man reelected to Congress."

It turned out that he was affiliated with the local radio station, whose politics were in conflict with those of the newspaper and Pat Sutton. At last, getting the point, I said neither the newspaper editor nor his reporter had mentioned to me the small fact about the imminence of an election, but that it made no difference anyway. As Pat Sutton's former regimental commander I would tell anybody he had been a fine combat soldier and that neither politics nor subsequent events could change that.

Without further beating the devil around a voting booth, let it suffice that there is some inherent incompatibility between politics and career military men. Both sides should, however, exercise a little empathy and recognize the point of view of the other, while adhering to what each believes is right without impugning the integrity of the other.

After eight years of wearing civilian clothes in retirement, my basic viewpoint and mental processes were unchanged. Although mellowed and more tolerant, I was still rankled when some of my civilian friends, especially on early acquaintance, persisted in telling me some story whose main point seemed to be that men in uniform were not overly smart—and also that they abused their military authority over subordinates.

So I assembled some thoughts on the subject in rebuttal. They were published (18 February 1968) in the "Sounding Off" (personal opinion) department of *Tropic,* the Sunday magazine of *The Miami Herald,* as follows:

Why Do Civilians Portray
Soldiers as Bunglers?

Many civilians have a peculiar complex towards military men which displays itself in a compulsive urge to lacerate with biting words the hand that defends them. Since there are thousands of active and retired armed services people living in Florida, this is a matter of special interest here.

For many years I have read ludicrously distorted diatribes against the military but followed the usual service tradition and ignored them.

Now retired, I have a closer look at civilians, and am free to express my opinions. Since civilians run the U.S. mails that is a good place to start.

On a Florida island near the one where I live (we are connected to the mainland by bridges) three little towns rub elbows, each with its own post office instead of one town and one post office. This principle, applied nationally, is undoubtedly a factor in the current postal rate increase.

So I enquired why three small towns so close together (with three mayors and three police forces) would not be better off unified. It seems civilians, like the military, have a peculiarity called human nature, because the answer was, "Well, there was a lot of friction about it."

Civilian courts and laws are snarled in a tangled proliferation of legal technicalities which appear to benefit lawyers, jeopardize the innocent and protect criminals. If I am ever falsely accused I want to be tried by court-martial. But if I am guilty—move over, make way for another civilian.

The all-pervading theme in civil life can be summed up in two words: self interest. Consider a federal court, in ordering reapportionment of the state legislature, cited this fact: "The five most populous counties average one representative for each 106,000 people. The five least populous counties average one for each 3,266.

Civilians explain this to me by saying, "That's politics."

While I'm trying to understand civilian ideas and become one of them, this is an area in which I am backward—and expect to remain so.

When military authorities decide to close a no-longer-necessary Army post as an economic measure, local civilian interest soon rears its head. There is much pulling of influential wires, which sometimes results in a politically appointed civilian executive in Washington overruling the military. Naturally this is seized upon as "confusion in the Pentagon." To old John Q. Public, that means the military and nothing else.

This curious quirk of blaming military authorities for civilian decisions remains a puzzle to me, especially when applied to the Pentagon where the top two echelons of command are civilian not military.

The disdainful reference by civilians to confusion in the Pentagon is made on the bland assumption that only civilians can keep things straight. Yet in such a vital matter as divorce, to pick one of countless civilian towers of Babel, there is an unbelievable hypocrisy of commercial divorce mills in "liberal" states, with several weeks' "residence" all that is required. This makes everything legal?

A civilian reply might refer to the inflexibility of my military mind, because some civilians are always kicking that one around in print. Yet, if a lawyer has a legal mind, that's good. If a businessman has a sound business head, that's good. But when a military man has a military mind, that's bad.

For years civilians have told me, with a condescending manner, they would never be happy in the Army: no independence, too many orders. As I look around me now, however, I see civilian noses to grindstones and subject to a kind of dollar tyranny that does not impress me with its superior independence.

Since the day I entered the Army I have heard the words "drunken soldier" used by civilians in a tone that implied this is a condition peculiar to military men, but I have seen far more disgusting drunks in civilian clothes than in uniform. There is no Skid Row on military posts.

Don't misunderstand me. I like my civilian friends, my civilian community, and our American way of life. So let me finish by suggesting a common ground where all of us, military and civilian, can live happily ever after: "Forgive us our frailties, and we will forgive yours."

That was eleven years ago. And now these comments:

- What connection is there between that little active-duty, civilian-military contretemps at Fort Campbell and my defensive disputation in the *Tropic* Sunday magazine after my retirement? It seems to me they reveal an intangible, submerged, and largely unrecognized military-civilian adversary relationship.
- On my retirement I received a letter from a military friend who had preceded me in that estate, which began, "Welcome to the realm of the living dead!" But it is not that way unless you make it so. Retirement is just another duty station in life, with new requirements, responsibilities, and rewards that call for considered adjustments—mostly by you—to an environment that existed long before your arrival.
- The military is more cohesive, organized, and controlled than the civilian community nationwide. Thus, we are more capable of establishing a workable policy of mutual civilian-military empathy as a long-term objective. The cornerstone of the policy should be that above-stated common meeting ground: "Forgive us our frailties and we will forgive yours."

PART III

REFLECTIONS ON COMBAT SITUATIONS

37

Don't Dim the Glitter

TWO OF THE most basic items of the infantryman are the bayonet and the metal helmet. Descendants of the spear and casque, they have come down to the atomic age little changed in function since before recorded history. The helmet has grown in popularity. Even aviators who wore a leather hood back in the First World War and a "fifty-mission crush" in the Second World War now wear a hard helmet. But the bayonet has a different story.

In 1958, as chief of staff of U.S. Continental Army Command (USCONARC) at Fort Monroe, I discovered—to my amazement—that a decision had been made by USCONARC to recommend elimination of the bayonet.

As a former infantry regimental commander in combat and a life-time infantryman, I could not understand this. I learned that noninfantry-men did not understand that it is *mental* force that makes the bayonet so important, not the number of men impaled on bayonets.

Combat-experienced infantrymen know this, and there are count-less case histories to prove it. A battle action by Company F of my regiment (34th Infantry) illustrates clearly that, more often than not, the bayonet does its work before actual contact.

The occasion was an action at the Mainit River bridge on 28 October 1944. During the Leyte campaign, Company F, led by their gallant commander, Capt. Paul Austin, launched a bayonet assault—complete

185

with Rebel yell. That knife out front sparked the charge, and the view of oncoming steel collapsed the defense. A body count of stab wounds would have never evaluated the part played by the bayonet in that action.

In modern wars there is much close combat, and it's hard to visualize hand-to-hand fighting without the bayonet. Even within bayonet range, the rifle can and is fired—and should be. But this is not a valid argument for the elimination of the bayonet.

This "trial of strength" in hand-to-hand fighting is not a simple or easy thing to understand. "Shock action" is involved. True, the bayonet never runs out of ammunition, or gets unloaded or jammed in a melee; mostly, it's the "steel" in the mind and heart of the man behind the bayonet. That's why the will to close in on the enemy or the determination to stand and meet steel with steel is so often decisive.

When defenders are outnumbered two, three, or four to one they can stay in there, take punishment, and swap bullets with the enemy. But it is seldom indeed that the defense can throw back such odds in hand-to-hand fighting.

Infantrymen are proud that they are the men who close with the enemy in hand-to-hand assault. The bayonet constantly reminds them of this. It builds a mental attitude in training that results in the will to close in battle.

Another infantry general officer in Headquarters, USCONARC, shared my view that the decision to recommend elimination of the bayonet was a mistake. We requested that our commanding general—a much-decorated combat commander, but not an infantryman—reverse the decision, which had been made before he assumed command. As a result he appointed a board of general officers—headed by a lieutenant general who had been an infantry regimental commander in combat—to consider whether or not the decision to recommend elimination of the bayonet should be reversed.

To my surprise (as a member of the board) a representative of The Infantry Board from The Infantry Center concurred in the decision to eliminate the bayonet. However, he offered no compelling reasons to support his view. That still puzzles me (I do not know how The Infantry Center stands on this now).

The board called for a number of veteran noncommissioned infantrymen from widely separated units, whose campaign ribbons were encrusted with battle stars and flanked by decoration ribbons. They did not know why they were there, and were obviously puzzled by the question:

"Sergeant, what do you think of the idea that we should do away with the bayonet?"

All of them (questioned separately) first looked at us with an unbelieving stare, then stated in no uncertain terms they didn't think much of the idea. One put it this concisely: "Sir, when they take the bayonet away from the infantry, that's when I'm getting out of the infantry, too!"

Our board was unanimous that the decision should be reversed, the bayonet retained. And our recommendation was approved by the commanding general.

In the search for new and better hand-held infantry weapons, their form and effectiveness are bound to change. But the will to close with the enemy must still burn in the hearts of infantrymen. That's where the bayonet comes in. Redesign the bayonet to fit new weapons if necessary, but be sure infantrymen still have that sticker out front when close combat is imminent.

As I write this (9 June 1966) there is a front-page four-column headline in my morning newspaper—"BAYONETS THROW BACK REDS"— over a dispatch from Vietnam that begins this way: "SAIGON (UPI)— American paratroopers, charging with fixed bayonets, Wednesday threw back the greatest Communist offensive of the year in Vietnam." This is no isolated reference, for reports from Vietnam often mention the decisiveness of hand-to-hand fighting.

In these days many things are referred to computers for a decision. But the intangibles in the tremendous value of the bayonet cannot be programmed into a computer. In fact, those intangibles cannot be fully understood by anyone who has not experienced close combat, as distinguished from just standing away and exchanging shots with an enemy.

Sooner or later pencil-pushing analysts will count bayonet-wound figures on casualty reports and again come up with the idea that bayonets are obsolete. Do not let their figures fool you. General George S. Patton knew the fallacy in bayonet-wound statistics. That he recognized the all-importance of mental determination—the will to close—was made clear when he said: "It is the cold glitter of the attacker's eyes, not the point of the questing bayonet that breaks the line."

But General Patton never imagined an infantryman without a bayonet. If he were alive today I'm certain he would join in saying: "Don't take away the bayonet—or you'll dim that vital glitter!"

38

Combat Courage:
Where Does It Come From?

OLD SOLDIERS ARE like old athletes in saying that just as they understand what it is all about, they are relegated to the sidelines. Recently, looking backward from the sidelines of military retirement, I have given thought to the question: "Where do soldiers find the courage to face combat?"

This is not a new question of the atomic-electronic era, but one that has come down from antiquity. My favorite literary pundit, François Duc de La Rochefoucauld (1613–1680), put it this way: "No man can answer for his courage who has never been in danger."

On the other hand, President John F. Kennedy took a more positive but still nebulous view when he said, "The stories of past courage can define that ingredient—they can teach, they can offer hope, they can provide inspiration. But they cannot supply courage itself. For this each man must look into his own soul."

In my view, both La Rochefoucauld and President Kennedy are correct, but each states a premise that is so broad it becomes a truism. We need a more definite answer to the specific question: Where do men on the battlefield find the courage that sustains them—from patriotism, training, religion, egotism, hatred of the enemy, pride, ideals— or are some men just born with what it takes?

I believe that every military man wonders how he will measure up when the guns begin to shoot; certainly *I* wondered. Many factors are involved, but in my opinion the primary source of strength for me was the same for most soldiers. This may interest those who have yet to find out how it will be for them.

Obviously, when I went to the U.S. Military Academy, the challenge of battle, if that day should come, entered my mind. Even after four years of wonderful training and inspiration from the "Duty-Honor-Country" code, there was still that unanswered question that La Rochefoucauld so aptly posed.

On graduation, I was commissioned a second lieutenant of infantry, with my first assignment as a platoon leader in the 29th Infantry at Fort Benning, Ga.—under Platoon Sergeant Fugate. He had been decorated in battle and wounded three times during World War I.

Sergeant Fugate had truly met the battle test, but I could only wonder how I would face combat if that day ever came. During more than sixteen years of peacetime service, there was always that unanswered question.

The day of reckoning finally came during World War II, after I received the greatest honor and privilege of my life: command of the 34th Infantry, 24th Infantry Division for the amphibious landing on Leyte in Gen. Douglas MacArthur's "return" to the Philippines, 20 October 1944.

Several years after the war, I described this experience in "Command Performance," articles in the *Infantry Journal* (July and August 1948), under the pen name Colonel Riposte. Here are two extracts from the August 1948 issue:

I made my final preparations for exercising leadership as I leaned against the rail on deck at night. I looked down at the dark shapes of my men on the well deck below, and a heavy weight rested on my shoulders, the weight of responsibility for their lives and for our success in battle. Then I looked at the vague shapes of other ships where hundreds of other men sprawled in the darkness, all with their thoughts, just as I was with mine.

I remembered, too, how in the brief time we had together before we embarked I had tried to arouse in them a belief in me, and I hoped that in those ships on the dark sea there were men who felt a little better about the coming battle because they believed their commander was a competent soldier. But in their hearts there would be one unanswered question:

"What will he be like when the chips are down . . . ?"

... The last night before landing I wrote a letter to my wife ... saying a few things briefly that I wanted her to have as the last words she would ever have from me—if fate decreed it that way.

After finishing, I took another piece of paper and wrote down ... these words which had come to me:
I have the strength.
From where it comes I do not know,
But of this much I am very sure:
I have the strength.

Fear haunts any sane man as his first day in close combat approaches. When I won the struggle with the dragon that night, I did not realize then where the strength came from. The second extract from that after-action report, written nearly forty years ago, reads:

It is a great disappointment that the purpose of this story, and the space available, do not permit me to recount many examples of the skill, determination, and flaming battle courage of my men and officers of all ranks—such as the magnificent valor of a soldier who received a posthumous Medal of Honor; the company commander who led a spontaneous bayonet charge ... but, most of all, the never-to-be-forgotten courage of individual soldiers.

It did not occur to me then that they were gaining their strength from the same source that sustained me. Various facets of courage have engaged thinkers over the centuries. Here are some of their thoughts:

Jean Paul Richter (1763–1825): "Courage consists, not in blindly overlooking danger, but in seeing and conquering it."

William Jones (1726–1800): "True courage is always mixed with circumspection; this being the quality which distinguishes the courage of wise men from the hardiness of the rash and foolish."

James A. Broude (1818–1894): "Courage is, on all hands, considered as an essential of character."

Plautus (254–184 B.C.): "Courage in danger is half the battle."

Caleb B. Colton (1780–1832): "Physical courage which despises all danger, will make a man brave in one way; and moral courage, which despises all opinions, will make a man brave in another. The former will seem most necessary for the camp; the latter for the council; but to constitute a great man, both are necessary."

Each of these quotations has its own angle, yet none of them attempts to analyze the main source of battlefield courage. Respected military writer and historian Brig. Gen. S. L. A. Marshall is more specific and to the point in his *Men Against Fire* when he says, "I hold it to be one of the simplest truths of war that the thing which enables an infantry soldier to keep going with his weapons is the near presence or the presumed presence of a comrade."

For me, with reference to bravery in battle, the basic idea was best expressed by Maj. Robert J. Peterson when he quoted an infantry scout wounded at Salerno, Italy:

"You know the men in your outfit. The men are close-knit. They like each other and quit petty bickering and having enemies. They depend on each other—wouldn't do anything to let the rest of them down. They'd rather be killed than that. They begin to think the world of each other. It's the main thing that keeps a guy from going haywire."

In other words, you are not alone in battle; it is a group experience. You draw strength from others around you. Several comments seem pertinent:

- Training, physical condition, national motivation, leadership, good weapons, and many other factors go into how well a soldier meets the challenge of battle, but I believe the primary source of courage in combat is the intangible collective support of those there with you. One reason a well-trained unit fights better is that this invisible bond is more strongly developed through working together in mutual respect over a period of time.
- There are many special situations of sudden pitched battle violence where men react with gallantry and valor, often from reflex, sometimes from the will to survive. Also, a few men fit no pattern and respond to danger like a moth to flame—all too often with the same result. But what we are considering here is the primary source of courage in combat for most men, where any man in any squad moves out as directed—knowing he faces death at every step or crawl motion.
- In my view, the primary well of military courage is what might be called soldierly peer pride and confidence in each other, with

mutual respect and support between and among those with you on the battlefield. It is also a fact of combat history that all men do not draw the same amount of strength from that fundamental well.

- John Donne said: "No man is an island, entire of itself." That is how it was for me in combat—shared danger, shared fear surmounted, shared courage. I believe that is the way it was for most veterans and will remain that way on foreseeable future battlefields—because you will not be alone.

39

Essential Sleep: Personal Need, Military Duty

IN THE PROCESS of screening my files recently, I began reading my broadly based article "Sleep and the Soldier" (*ARMY,* October 1963), which defines sleep, describes the impact of its loss and the causes of sleeplessness, discusses how to determine the amount of sleep needed, and emphasizes the necessity of proper sleeping habits. My attention was caught by these extracts:

- In peace and in war the lack of sleep works like termites in a house: below the surface, gnawing quietly and unseen to produce gradual weakening that can lead to sudden and unexpected collapse. The Walter Reed Army Institute of Research puts it this way: "The daily experience of sleep constitutes one of the major cyclic events in man, and ranks with food and water as a major need demanding satisfaction."
- Science has produced fantastic new weapons, but it has found no substitute for judgment and other human abilities in the men who use those weapons—and those abilities can be damaged by loss of sleep.
- One of the serious damaging effects of sleep loss is the high and sometimes almost irrational degree of irritation it causes in dealing with others. One researcher concludes that "disturbances in behavior from lack of sleep closely resemble disorders from certain

narcotics, alcohol, and oxygen starvation . . . Values slip out of focus. We are literally 'not ourselves.'"

The words "literally not ourselves" brought my reading to an abrupt end because I suddenly realized that sleep starvation was my current problem—and had been for some time. The obvious need was for a good sleep schedule, which is now in operation.

I cannot explain how I was obtuse enough to fall into this sleep deprivation trap again—after the sleep lessons I learned during World War II.

A brief summary of my wartime sleep loss experience, however, reveals why this fundamental need has been and will remain an important factor in military operations.

The most spectacular demonstration I saw of the damaging effect of the lack of sleep took place in Hawaii shortly before World War II. Officers of the Hawaiian Department were assembled in a theater at Schofield Barracks for a briefing by a general officer on one aspect of the defense of Oahu.

He got along well until halfway through, when he began to stumble and flounder. He shuffled his papers, looked at us with a puzzled expression, said, "You will have to excuse me," and left the stage.

After a brief, stunned silence, the department commander rose and announced, "We will take a ten-minute break while the general gets his notes in order."

The speaker's aide rushed up to check the notes (they were in order), and the talk resumed. The general soon began a sentence he could not finish, however, so he left it hanging and started to discuss a visual aid—and got stalled on that. It was not stage fright; he just looked puzzled.

Finally he said, "I designed this aid myself, but I cannot seem to remember how it goes. You will have to excuse me." He left the stage again, abandoning the briefing. When the general was hospitalized for observation, it was determined that he was suffering from acute fatigue—*long continued lack of sleep.*

My own first encounter with sleep loss came the first day of World War II. I was intelligence officer of the 24th Infantry Division at Schofield Barracks. When the Japanese attacked Pearl Harbor on 7 December 1941, shock and uncertainty merged into automatic occupation of our planned defense positions. We will skip the details of false alarms (some on the ridiculous side, including parachute and glider landings) and the futility of fighting an enemy that had hit and run and thus was not there.

After two sleepless days and nights (chasing mysterious lights, among other nebulous things), an officer came in with a report after lunch. When I said, "Why didn't you tell me that this morning?" he gave me an astonished look and said, "But, Major, I did!"

Fortunately I remembered what happened to that general when he did not get enough sleep, so I took the necessary corrective action.

You would think this would, finally, get that sleep lesson straight in my head, but sleep starvation can happen in more than one way. It can inch up on you over weeks and months, while you remain unaware of the insidious damage to your mind and body.

The result of cumulative sleep loss was brought home to me in unforgettable fashion in the spring of 1943. After nearly a year as the division chief of staff, I traveled by air to Fort Leavenworth, Kan., for a nine-week quickie general staff course.

In the wartime urgency to get things done, I had been building up (without knowing it) what researchers call a "sleep debt." At Leavenworth, I began studying everything in sight, still unaware I was burning my sleep candle at both ends.

The payoff came ten days after my arrival. As I was reading the next day's assignment and turned a page, my mind went blank. I could not remember the preceding page. So I turned back, read it again, turned the page—another blank. After the fourth unsuccessful try, I recalled the general who had looked puzzled when he said, "I cannot seem to remember."

So I lay the manual aside, went for a hard walk, and then to bed. The start of a pressure-cooker course at Leavenworth is an awkward time for the sleep bill collector to say, "Pay up, now!"

Fortunately, by rigidly limiting my study and making a serious business of going to bed, I managed to get through the course—thankful to have learned my lesson in school rather than in combat.

During the amphibious invasion of Leyte in the Philippines, I commanded the 34th Infantry. After the landing on 20 October 1944, we were still trying to break out of the narrow beachhead when I was called to the phone late on the night of 24 October to receive this message from division headquarters: "Major elements of the Japanese fleet are entering Leyte Gulf, and bombardment of the shore may be expected momentarily. This is a warning from Sixth Army—no other information available."

It is a matter of history that in one of the most controversial sea battles of all time, the Japanese central striking force (including the great battleship *Yamato*) penetrated San Bernadino Strait and, at daylight, was heading directly toward our crowded Leyte beachhead and thin-skinned invasion fleet.

On the bridge of his command ship, a Japanese admiral stood on the threshold of immortality as he engaged lighter U.S. forces until he made one of the most amazing decisions of the war. Abandoning the chance to strike a devastating blow, he ordered a retreat.

Many (including myself) who have studied that great battle and the events leading up to it are convinced the apparently inexplicable error of judgment by the Japanese admiral was the result of failing to get enough sleep during the preceding tense days and nights.

In the meantime I, too, had a decision to make. My regiment had been fighting—in landing and ashore—for five days, and most men (except security forces) would be in the deep sleep of battle fatigue as best they could wherever they lay.

I passed on the warning message to my regimental executive, the regimental operations officer, and my battalion commanders with instructions not to awaken their soldiers unless the situation changed.

As it turned out, our regiment had an uninterrupted night of sleep.

An eyewitness described to me a wartime parallel in principle ("sleep when you can") on the other side of the world, during the Normandy invasion of France. At a critical stage in the operation, the commander of the 101st Airborne Division (then-Maj. Gen. Maxwell D. Taylor, later chairman of the Joint Chiefs of Staff) called in his second in command and said, "Tomorrow is going to be a big day, and I want to be ready. You take over while I get some sleep."

He did just that and, my eyewitness says, "General Taylor had a good night's sleep, and the next day when things really popped, he was on top of the action, and every decision was right on the nose."

Three comments are:

- In the Army, the importance of food and water is emphasized during training, yet the need for sleep by all ranks is not adequately recognized. This is so because that vital need is often unrecognized as the basic cause of many "human error" failures.

You can do without food much easier than without sleep. Animals have lived twenty days without food, yet died after five sleepless days.

- An experimental laboratory found that "with increased sleep loss, individuals consider fewer events in arriving at decisions . . . They are befuddled in situations requiring them to hold several factors in mind at once and act on them." This is the type of situation that commanders face in battle, where faulty decisions are paid for in blood and defeat. Thus, the "sleep where and when you can" principle becomes mandatory.
- Having looked at past lessons about loss of sleep in war with conventional weapons, one should realize that danger from sleep deprivation will be far greater in a nuclear war. Few will think of sleep then.

Time will be foreshortened and pressures increased beyond all past experience—yet the mental and physical need for sleep will remain the same. Not only soldiers but all Americans will face this problem, especially civilian leaders.

Therefore we must recognize that knowledge about proper sleeping habits and requirements is needed in military and civilian training, as a duty, as a command responsibility, and as a matter of stern self-discipline.

40

Why Orderlies?

AFTER I ASSUMED command of my first company, the first sergeant, a decorated veteran of World War I, came into my office and asked, "Captain, will you select your orderly, or do you want me to pick one for you?"

Of course I knew it was customary for the company commander to have an orderly—even in garrison in that day. But I replied: "Well, Sergeant, I live in the BOQ and take care of myself. There isn't much to do, so I don't think an orderly necessary."

The old sergeant stood silent a minute. Then, choosing his words carefully, he said: "Captain, the company will not like it that way. It's best you take care of the company and we take care of you."

So I got an orderly, who was also the company bugler and company runner.

Battle-wise soldiers know that if their captain is chasing his own chow in the field, caring for his equipment, running his own errands—plus using the first sergeant as a legman—the company will suffer as a result. In fact a company commander who operates in this way during combat will not only fail to take good care of his company, he might jeopardize their lives by poor decisions. His rank and responsibilities do not make him a superman immune to laws of time, space, and fatigue.

Professional soldiers, especially combat veterans, know this goes beyond physical factors—for a state of mind and a mental attitude are concerned. This does not happen suddenly after bullets begin to snarl, but is established during training, based on mutual respect and understanding.

Any outfit that has failed to gain this officer-enlisted relationship of mutual responsibility toward each other will be tremendously handicapped in battle. While the captain and his orderly are a symbol of this, it should pervade the whole outfit.

Unfortunately, distorted diatribes alleging universal abuse of orderlies appear in the public press from time to time. This deceives civilians about the place and function of military orderlies. It also misleads many inexperienced soldiers, officer and enlisted, who think in terms of privileges rather than multiplicity of duties and responsibilities.

The reality of need for orderlies does *not* condone their misuse or abuse, nor should we dignify absurd allegations by trying to justify them. In every endeavor involving large numbers of people there will be some poor judgment, some injustice. And orderlies are vulnerable to abuses. Proper corrective action in such instances is the elimination of errors, not emasculation of an operational procedure for which no adequate alternate has yet been found.

As to orderlies and aides in garrison for senior officers in peacetime, that is a different situation—beyond our discussion here.

Perhaps the function of military orderlies may be clarified by my experience when in command of a regimental combat team (more than 5,000 men) in the assault landing on Leyte. There was a regimental staff to help me, but I also had a personal enlisted staff of five:

One orderly in the command post responsible for my personal gear, laundry, meals, sleeping arrangements—anything that would rob me of time and energy, or distract my concentration from our battle mission—and to have coffee always available.

One orderly (bodyguard) with me everywhere I went. He was an armed fighter, but his primary mission was to conserve my strength in every possible way. It is amazing how much energy and time an alert bodyguard can save his commander—in addition to protecting him from enemy action.

One radio operator who followed me everywhere, instantly available when needed.

One jeep driver, ready day and night to take me anywhere.

One standby jeep and driver.

These five men were soldiers whose only job was to do my bidding, instantly, thus helping me carry out my heavy responsibilities. All of us had the same mission: success of our regiment in battle. They understood this and were picked men, proud of their jobs and eager to do their part.

Without any one of them I would have been seriously handicapped. Make no mistake: When you stumble back into the command post at sundown, physically and mentally exhausted, your heart bleeding from what you have seen, yet faced with the necessity of issuing orders on which many lives will depend—it is important that a cup of coffee come a-running, and that you need give no thought to food, where you will bed down, or other personal needs.

If these procedures are not established during peace, they will not suddenly be there during war. A state of mind, on both sides, is concerned that cannot be achieved by pressing a button; it is a feeling. Inexperienced officers and men who have never been in battle are likely to be deluded into getting the wrong feeling after reading some of the things about orderlies that appear in the public press.

Be alert to stop abuses, yes. But my veteran first sergeant stated a universal principle that is beneath the dignity of no soldier, and must pervade every good outfit if it is to achieve its greatest combat effectiveness: "Captain, it's best you take care of the company, and we take care of you."

41

The Unreasonable Is Sometimes Reasonable

AFTER WORLD WAR II, on one of my active-duty stations, I had a commander we will call General Shortfuse. He was a brilliant officer but, on occasion, a bit on the unpredictable side. One morning, I found this note on my desk, in his meticulous handwriting:

> Col. Newman:
> Your cat caught a bird yesterday (Sunday). As between cats and birds, the birds get the vote. Please warn your cat it is in danger of being ordered off the post.
>
> Shortfuse

This seemed unreasonable, because it is in the nature of all cats to catch birds when the opportunity arises. But there is a caution to be considered when faced with an apparently unreasonable order or decision; sometimes, it may not be as unreasonable as it appears. In such cases, it is advisable to search your mind and the situation for some fact or consideration that mitigates or even negates the apparent unreasonableness.

A good illustration of the need to evaluate apparent unreasonableness is the "unsatisfactory" grade I received on a "marked" problem, as a student in the World War II "quickie" general staff course No. 13 at Fort Leavenworth, Kan. It was a simple motorized troop movement problem in a reinforced division, but the commanding general's directive included the limitation, "Do not use trucks of the 424th Transportation Company."

The problem revolved around the fact that there were not quite enough trucks to meet the time and space requirements, even when kitchen trucks of the division trains were used (permissible in the static situation given); however, I included the kitchen truck of the 424th Transportation Company—and that got me the unsatisfactory grade ("violation of the commanding general's directive"). To me, at the time, the misuse of one truck did not appear to justify an overall "unsatisfactory."

That was my only "U," and I left Fort Leavenworth feeling it was unreasonable to have one trick question mar my record. Years later, reflecting on this "injustice," it occurred to me there was a fundamental angle involved I had not considered—over and beyond the cited violation of the commanding general's directive.

I had not asked myself the question, "What could be the result from the commanding general's view, and from that of the truck company, if that kitchen truck was not available?"

The answer removed the unreasonableness from the problem and made it a fine teaching exercise—because using that truck limited the possible use of the other forty-eight trucks in the company. If the 424th Transportation Company was suddenly ordered elsewhere or on another transportation mission, then the absence of their kitchen truck would be no small matter.

From that angle, we see this guideline: When receiving what seems to be an unreasonable order or decision, look for facts or considerations that could make it reasonable. More often than not, you will find that what may appear unreasonable at first is really your own failure to see all the implications involved.

That was only a school problem, so the next step is to consider real-life case histories to support our theoretical guideline. As mentioned here before, the simplest research by an octogenarian like me is to invoke memories from the long-gone years. The one that follows happened during World War II on Leyte in the Philippines, soon after Gen. Douglas MacArthur made his famous return there.

As regimental commander of the 34th Infantry, I faced a problem. We had captured our initial objectives. Several days after landing, the primary obstacle to our drive down the road across Leyte to Jaro was the towering mass of Hill Charlie on our right flank; so I gave the situation considerable thought.

Hill Charlie had a broad, steep side facing generally toward the road, which was largely screened by trees. The steep face of Hill Charlie itself was covered with tall *kunai* grass and low bush growth, which almost certainly masked the usual foot trails leading upward on that steep face—though I could not see them. The flank routes to the top of Charlie were wooded, thus providing natural approaches for an attack toward the top.

Another consideration was the fact that our division and corps artillery had periodically shelled that open face of Charlie and its top. Another factor was the momentum of our advance.

In view of these facts, and from what I could see, it seemed probable the Japanese were prepared for a flank attack but were not expecting a brazen frontal assault. Further, it appeared unlikely they had any observation over the sight-defiladed face of Charlie from its top and sides.

So my plan was based on one battalion making a frontal attack straight up the face of Charlie, with another battalion held in readiness to drive down the road toward Jaro when Charlie was captured.

The battalion commander ordered to attack up the open face of Charlie considered this an unreasonable decision and strongly expressed his preference for an attack up the usual wooded flank approach; however, I summarized my reasoning that the Japanese had almost surely vacated the top and face of Charlie because of our artillery fire and some air bombing—but were probably ready to give the commander and his battalion a hot reception on the flank approach. Thus, the "unreasonable" approach held, in my view, the best odds as the preferred route of attack. I was resolute in directing that the attack move straight up the front of Hill Charlie.

For the first time, I did not follow the attacking element of my command closely, because it was not the best place from which to control the overall action of our regiment. Therefore, I selected a place from which I could see our whole front, and thus noted that the attacking battalion seemed to be veering toward the flank. So I got on the radio to ensure that my order was carried out as issued.

Did it succeed? It sure did—or I could not use it here. During the action, I watched from my selected point of control. As individual soldiers threaded their way upward, my heart was in my throat, and I was lost in admiration for the way those unnamed combat infantrymen of my regiment met the challenge without hesitation.

In retrospect, I still swell with pride as an infantryman when I recall that slow but unflinching movement upward. Not a shot was fired until they reached the very top, which was captured without a single casualty. The fighting, too late, followed when the Japanese counterattacked.

Thus, the unreasonable had proved to be reasonable. If the "normal" attack route had been followed, there would have been casualties . . .and delay; to what extent remains conjecture. My wife, not for the first time, says that I tell this to make myself look good. Of course it is nice to look good, but, without false modesty, this is just the best illustration from my personal experience to validate the point under discussion.

Literature has covered the idea in various ways, including "Faint heart never won fair lady." But you cannot always win calculated risks by taking the bit in your teeth, full speed ahead—as I discovered a week later when a piece of Japanese steel relieved me of command of the 34th Infantry.

Some comments are:

- It has remained an unanswered question in my mind whether historical reading may have subconsciously influenced my decision on how to attack Hill Charlie, because I had read about a somewhat similar situation. This was the attack by British Maj. Gen. James Wolfe when he defeated the French under Maj. Gen. Louis Joseph Montcalm at Quebec in 1759, by a surprise attack that involved scaling the precipitous cliffs known as the Heights of Abraham—at a point inadequately guarded because it was such an unreasonable approach. The result changed history and cost the young British general his life, but his name lives on.
- The basic principle involved covers diverse actions, from a single soldier in combat to a theater commander. It covers everything from the great Medal of Honor exploits of Sgt. Alvin C. York in World War I to General MacArthur's spectacularly successful Inchon amphibious landing in Korea. The principle is the same: to see beyond the obvious physical danger to the calculated risk; that is, the capacity to see the possible, the judgment to assess

the odds, and the resolution to act. Without the resolution to act, however, the capacity and the judgment would remain mental exercises in futility.

- The principle was demonstrated in a different fashion by Gen. George S. Patton, Jr., in his famous change-of-direction attack in the Battle of the Bulge during World War II. To turn his great Third Army through ninety degrees and attack the flank of the Bulge, within a specified brief time interval, seemed an unreasonable decision. But he put everything in perspective when he said to his staff, "I know it is impossible—but you bastards are going to make it work anyway!" The result is history.

- If you only try the reasonable and safe course, if you cannot go for broke when the odds are in your favor—yet without being foolhardy—command in combat is not your métier. It is, per se, dangerous to be in battle. When that fact is accepted, it becomes much easier to accept the otherwise unreasonable risks to life as the reasonable requirements for combat success. Nowhere is the old adage "Nothing ventured, nothing gained" more true.

42
Lonely Lead Scouts

YOU DON'T SEE them in war pictures from Vietnam, because there are no photographers that far forward of the battle edge. But in front of those firing artillery guns and infantry mortars, in front of those advancing groups in approach march formations, there are and must always be a few lonely men—sometimes only one or two. These brave soldiers, so vital to battle and who suffer heavy casualties, have remained largely unheralded and unsung: They are the lonely lead scouts.

Yet every battle patrol has that man out front on the trail; every advance in the face of the enemy has those infantry lead scouts out there, alone. All too often a lead scout's job is done when he never hears the first shot—because you don't hear the one that hits you. Now, studying Vietnam photographs—and reviewing memory pictures from my time as a combat regimental commander—an idea comes of how we can give these men a measure of credit.

To see why this should be done, and how it can be done, consider these combat scenes from World War II in the Pacific.

Two soldiers were far out front, walking down a narrow dirt road, walled in by green jungle. The one on the left was armed with a tommy gun; the other, a few yards back on the right, was armed with a Garand. Each moved slowly with bent knees, weapon ready, finger on trigger, eyes restlessly scanning the thick growth on his side of the road.

When they came to some deserted native shacks along both sides of the road, their steps slowed but did not falter; nor did they look behind them. Their knees bent a little more, heads swiveled a little faster as eyes searched for hidden death at windows and walls as well as in the jungle.

For these were lead scouts, and I watched in silent admiration from the group behind them. Nothing impressed me more than this quiet courage of lead scouts—ready to step out from any infantry squad, day after day—walking steadily forward when each step might be their last, and often was.

Suddenly, the tommy gunner caught a movement in the corner of his eye from under one of the shacks. His crouched body whipped around, feet shifting in a boxer's quick shuffle, and the Thompson with its drum of .45-caliber shells shuddered in his hands as staccato sound thundered.

Three Japanese soldiers, surprised under the shack because they had not heard our guarded advance, were smashed before they could throw a grenade or fire a shot. After that long burst the gunner stepped back in short steps, eyes on the sprawled forms, while the man with the Garand faced down the road and to the other side—ready, cocked for action.

One enemy soldier moved, an arm reaching . . . grenade? Another burst of sound, and the mustard-colored uniforms twitched as .45 slugs struck again. Then motionless silence under the shacks. After a careful look the tommy gunner turned and the two lead scouts, without orders, resumed their characteristic tense movement down the road, in the face of death, as it was their jobs to do . . . out front, alone and vulnerable, offered as living targets in that tension-racked reaching for contact for which there is no substitute.

Another day I watched the 3d Battalion, 34th Infantry, attacking "Hill Charlie," a towering mass overlooking our main route of advance. As we neared Hill Charlie, corps artillery and air bombing blasted its unforested face. Then our own Div Arty dusted off its precipitous top.

The attack plan called for a bold advance straight up that cliff-like mountainside, believing that Japanese defenders would be in the de-filaded areas on the reverse slopes guarding logical wooded routes of approach on the flanks. It was an audacious plan, based on reasoned thinking.

But in spite of logic, firepower, bombing, and a thousand-man battalion in the assault, *somebody had to go first*. So in front of the lead company, that thin line of lonely men moved far ahead. This time there were three pairs, widely separated, pushing slowly through tall kunai grass in an area masked from sight above by the bulging face of the mountain. Then each pair of scouts found its own mountain-goat way upward, climbing toward certain death if discovered by the enemy above.

Fascinated, I watched in admiration. The very audacity of the plan brought success with relatively few casualties—and as a direct result of cold, quiet courage of lead scouts. These were not specially trained men, glamorized with colorful uniforms and insignia; they were just designated men in their infantry squads who moved forward to face eternity at the command, "Scouts out!"

The next day our drive continued across central Leyte. As always, two lead scouts, lonely and alone, were well ahead—one with a tommy gun, the other with a Garand. Cocked and alert, eyes ceaselessly scanning front and flanks, knees bent, steps slow but sure.

They, and all of us, knew contact would come momentarily, and violently. The road was slightly raised, with limited visibility over low kunai grass between scattered bushes.

Without warning the tommy gunner wheeled to his right, gun blasting .45 slugs into the Japanese soldier crouched behind a bush only yards off the road, grenade in hand. Then, backing in little crouched steps, the gunner loosed another short burst. Sure now the threat was eliminated, the scouts resumed their steady steps forward, ready for instant action. The grenade lay near the dead enemy's hand, which could not now toss it into the following group as he had planned.

Several hundred yards down the road (I now quote from *Children of Yesterday*, unofficial history of the 24th Infantry Division in World War II): ". . . the battalion point approached the village of Galotan on the outskirts of Jaro. The lead scout saw a bare-legged man scurry into a hut. He thought him a Filipino, and shouted for the man to come out. The answer was a bullet between the eyes . . ."

Early in the sharp fighting that followed against an entrenched Japanese blocking position, dug in under the shacks, the other scout was wounded. The enemy position was soon knocked out and our advance resumed—with two more lead scouts out front. Alert, intent, eyes sweeping right and left . . . alone and lonely, knowing the bullet they would never hear might strike at any moment.

That's what doesn't show in war pictures and TV reports from Vietnam.

But we can be sure these lonely men are out front again in Vietnam—in fact, more than ever before, because of incessant patrolling and "search and destroy" missions, with constant threat of ambush.

There should be a way to recognize the special battle contribution of these men who, without fanfare, perform this uniquely testing and dangerous mission.

Existing procedures point the way. The Air Force has its Air Medal, based on combat missions; those who repeatedly face danger are repeatedly recognized. We also have battle stars and arrowheads for campaign ribbons, and battle stars on paratrooper badges attest combat jumps. So why not a device on our Combat Infantryman Badge to identify lead scouts who have walked that spine-chilling lonely road out front?

My suggestion: Tiny silver stars stamped out of thin sheet silver (a size smaller than our present bronze battle stars) placed in the blue field under the rifle on our Combat Infantryman Badge. (They could be attached with one of these new glues.)

Requirement to qualify: To be a lead scout when contact with the enemy is made that results in dead or wounded men—friendly or enemy. One star for each such action, with a gold star to represent five of silver. The casualty requirement is necessary not only to give the little stars value, but to establish a clear line of demarcation between a true combat situation and routine movements in which there is little danger.

Administration: The platoon sergeant or platoon leader would simply write a field message, making the matter of record. (See my article on "Award of Combat Decorations" in *ARMY,* January 1967.)

In extended combat it is normal to rotate lead scout duty within squads to share the risk; thus, the result would be that these tiny stars on the blue field of our Combat Infantryman Badge would identify *very frontline infantrymen*—those who have experienced perilous duty in actual contact with the enemy. By the nature of lead scouts, officers would not qualify. Lead scout stars would be small enough recognition for these quiet, unheralded men who answer the call, "Scouts out!" by stepping forward to offer their bodies as targets for the first enemy bullets—so that their buddies can receive timely warning of danger.

In Vietnam today there are countless "lead scout situations." We can't make such awards retroactive to cover past events, but we can put the system into effect by issuing an order.

43

Loneliness Is a Factor in Command

IN THE SUMMER of 1950, I moved from chief of staff, 11th Airborne Division, to command the 511th Airborne Infantry—which, in one sense, was like going on vacation. Stated another way, I moved from staff work to command duty. One of my regimental staff officers, years later, recalled that time this way:

"Our 511th Airborne staff expected you [the author] to get into details and check everything, like you had as division chief of staff. However, except for orders when you wanted something done—and calling for a briefing now and then—you just circulated, sat back, and let us do our jobs and keep you informed."

But it had not been that simple. As the commander, I was under a specialized pressure they did not share: *the inherent loneliness of command.* This is a unique military application of the old saying, "Only those are lonely who build walls around themselves." On the other hand, there must always be certain invisible walls around commanders.

At company level, the sources of two basic walls for the commander are the silver bars of his military rank, which advertise and certify his authority—with consequent isolation and rank loneliness, and the sign on his desk, *Company Commander,* which announces a special loneliness wall—authority for decisions that he and he alone can make.

In my five years as commander of three companies, I was very familiar with these two walls. This was especially true when handling disciplinary cases. Always, when signing court-martial charges, there was that special feeling of responsibility because, in signing, I alone was taking this action against a soldier.

Consider this specific case from the 511th Airborne Infantry. Soon after I assumed command, court-martial charges arrived on my desk, signed by a young company commander against a platoon sergeant, for being drunk on duty and for going AWOL.

The man was a master sergeant with fifteen years' service, a Silver Star for gallantry in action, a Purple Heart, and multiple battle stars. But he had been transferred several times in recent years, so it looked like he was an alcoholic.

After some thought I called for the company commander to bring his sergeant in to see me, with the regimental sergeant major.

"Sergeant," I said, "your company commander wants these charges to go to trial. He says he has given you enough breaks, but I am going to give you a break, too.

"I know your length of service and fine war record, but you have been transferred several times recently. It looks like you have a bottle problem, and transferred to keep from being tried. But it will not work that way here.

"I will hold these charges, pending your good behavior. However, if there is a next time, both sets of charges will go to trial—and you will probably end up as a private."

Within weeks, more charges were filed. He was tried and transferred out of the regiment—as a private. Since he was married, this was a real hardship. You cannot, however, establish a policy that married sergeants with good war records have a license to get drunk and go AWOL.

For the commander who signed the final papers, it was a lonely burden that would not fade away and in fact still lingers after thirty-six years.

Situations that affect command loneliness are unlimited in number and variations. Also, they are traumatic in war, where men's lives and success in battle are involved.

When I commanded the 34th Infantry in the 20 October 1944 invasion of Leyte in the Philippines, our regiment captured its last beachhead objective on 25 October. The walls of command had been strongly drawn around me by hard decisions since our landing. This intensified when I relieved the commander of the 1st Battalion, increasing my aloneness. But fate was kind, since a truly great soldier, Lt. Col.

Thomas E. (Jock) Clifford, Jr., was the replacement commander of the 1st Battalion.

In the late afternoon of 25 October, I anticipated a change in regimental boundaries that would make the road across Leyte to Jaro *inclusive* to the 34th Infantry. So I positioned the 2d Battalion in readiness. Also, since we had to ford the Palo River to reach the road, my orders called for hand-carried weapons and supplies—a real hardship for soldiers carrying the heaviest loads, including the fifty-three-pound tripods of our water-cooled machine guns.

The morning of 26 October we were cleared by our division commander, Maj. Gen. Frederick A. Irving, to ford the Palo River (actually a large, knee-deep stream at that point) to lead the drive to Jaro. Our mission was to prevent Japanese reinforcements from landing on the west coast of Leyte, so time was a vital consideration.

I accompanied the 2d Battalion on its five-mile drive to Santa Fe, and spent the night in a foxhole there. Thus, the morning of 27 October I was aware of the situation and leapfrogged the 1st Battalion ahead of the 2d Battalion. Since we were through the Japanese lines, meeting only straggler resistance at the moment, Colonel Clifford and his battalion were fighting against physical exhaustion as they pushed on toward the Mainit River bridge.

By this time, my command posture—the status of my invisible walls— was established; but, by the same token, my command loneliness was increased. When you issue orders that put men's lives at risk, especially if the line between professional judgment and taking gambling chances can be questioned, your loneliness becomes acute.

Fortunately, there were supplementary invisible walls. I was a grade higher than my commanders (full colonel "eagle" versus lieutenant colonels). Also, my nineteen years of service and training, over their seven to eight years, was a consideration. These intangible command walls were helpful in the late afternoon of 27 October.

As sundown neared, we had not hit the strong organized delaying position I was expecting and our first vehicle arrived, a jeep for me. At this point the 1st Battalion halted for the night, on Colonel Clifford's order—to which I took immediate exception.

His reason was simple and clear: His soldiers were completely exhausted, especially those with the heaviest loads, like the punishing machine-gun tripods. My point was that sweat and struggle were preferable to loss of time, with subsequent enemy fire—and I wanted to get a patrol ahead in the newly arrived jeep.

When Colonel Clifford demurred about that, I decided to go—at which point he took over the patrol and started to get in the jeep himself. But I did not want him in the patrol, whereupon he said:

"Colonel, you tell me to send out this patrol, but I decide who goes in the patrol!" He had me there. The jeep rolled away and soon received fire, made a U-turn, and came back—with a wounded man in the jeep.

With contact established, and night coming on, the battalion settled into a perimeter for the night, and our artillery began ranging in. The first two rounds were long "overs," but the next was a "short" about ten yards from me, and several men went down.

At this point, I was standing on the shoulder of the road from where Colonel Clifford had led his patrol and returned with a wounded man, and now this. All eyes turned my way with those invisible walls around me and my command loneliness. My orders had produced these results—it was my responsibility, because I was in command, and it was truly lonely where I stood.

After a deep-breathing moment, I noticed the artillery forward observer not far from where that artillery "short" landed, and the commander of our attached 63d Field Artillery Battalion (now retired Brig. Gen. Cornelius Lang) moved toward him. So I stepped forward and said to "Tommy" Lang, in substance:

"You have given us fine support. I know these things happen and that you will take the corrective action required, and then bring fire down on the area to our front."

No further orders or explanations were expected from me, as our troops settled into a defensive perimeter for supper and sleep, preparing for the next day while our division artillery searched the area in our front with fire.

I carried my command aloneness with me, for supper and sleep, too. When daylight came, Jock's battalion was on the road again without opposition, as the artillery had done its work. Thus, my loneliness eased a little, until the next time—at the Mainit River bridge later that day.

Some comments:

- In general, command loneliness stems from the requirement in some situations to take what you consider proper action, knowing that some others will not agree.
- I do not recommend that regimental commanders lead a motor patrol or permit a battalion commander to do so. The result in this case, however, was the quick capture of the Mainit River

bridge the next day before it was adequately defended. This illustrates the fact that aggressive but risky combat decisions often work out well . . . but somebody must issue the orders.

- Experienced officers, active and retired, will have their own memory files of loneliness as a factor in command. Young officers, with their command experience ahead of them, will surely face their own testing situations that require decisions that accent the inherent loneliness of command.
- When faulty decisions are paid for in blood, reactions are magnified. Those walls mentioned above can be helpful in coping with the resulting lonely adversity. Nothing is worse, however, than to dither over a decision in fear of the loneliness of possible blame, then suffer the most bitter loneliness of all—the failure of failing to act.

44

Time and Timing:
Both Critical in Combat

SOMETIMES IT TAKES a jolt to make you recognize previously unnoticed side effects from your past actions. That happened to me at
the annual reunion of the 24th Infantry Division in Cincinnati, Ohio,
in 1985. There I was privileged to meet again (after forty-one years)
several veterans from World War II. So, in time-honored fashion, we
shared memories of different situations in our battle experiences—from
our varied viewpoints.

My most memorable contact, briefly at the Saturday night banquet,
was with a retired colonel. He had been a fine young battalion commander in the 34th Infantry when I was regimental commander in our
drive across Leyte in the Philippines in October 1944. It was he who
gave me the jolt.

After a quick handshake to span the years, our shared memories were
inhibited by the occupied seat between us. But he did manage to comment,
"You refused to allow me time for a reconnaissance before moving
out in the flanking attack at the Mainit River bridge."

This confirmed my growing feeling that I was happier to see him
than he was to see me—not an entirely new experience.

Anyway, time was indeed the crux of the battle situation at the Mainit
River bridge. Remember the story of the sick bear? When the zookeeper
placed a paper tube containing powdered aspirin between the bear's
lips, the keeper slowly drew in a deep breath preparatory to blowing

the aspirin down the bear's throat—but the bear blew first. That illustrates how a good plan of action depends on timing for its success.

There is a difference between the principles of *time* and *timing,* however, especially in combat. Consider these quotations by two of history's greatest battle captains:

Napoleon Bonaparte said, "Time is the irretrievable factor in war." He also cautioned, "Ask me for anything but time."

General George S. Patton, Jr., put it this way: "Death in war is incidental; loss of time is criminal."

These statements indicate the immediacy of the principle of *time,* as differentiated from the selectivity inherent in choosing the best *timing* for planned actions. This brings us to the reason for my adamant order for the battalion to move without prior reconnaissance.

With the 34th Infantry leapfrogging battalions on the main road across Leyte, the leading battalion was stopped cold at the Mainit River bridge. I was following closely with the battalion commander of the next battalion in line, which was ready to move quickly to the right or left.

We could see the steel girders of the bridge, and it was clear the bridge and heavily overgrown banks of the river could not be forced directly and quickly. Further, the bridge was surely prepared for demolition when its capture was threatened.

I recall that moment clearly, because the ball was now in my court. It was not up to the leading battalion alone, since two more battalions were uncommitted. Our division commander had come forward, too, but made no move to preempt control. The situation was clear, and I was in command; but before I could issue orders, happy chance gave me exactly the information I needed.

The Philippine scout, Vicente Sydiongco, was there at this moment of decision. He quickly pointed to the light but clearly defined footpath leading off to the right and said, "This trail leads to a ford over the river."

On hearing this, my years of active-duty training plus the vital time element coalesced in my mind with these considerations:

- In river crossings, you try to flank the defenders in the face of strong resistance.
- That path led directly to an ideal flanking crossing—a ford.
- The scout's manner was such that I believed the ford was there.

- Because of the speed of our advance, the Japanese may not yet have discovered that ford—so minutes, even seconds, might be decisive in getting us across the river unopposed at the ford.

Therefore, the situation involved the *time* principle personified. Not only did I refuse time for the battalion commander (later my reunion banquet friend) to make a reconnaissance, but when the leading company commander wanted to brief his platoon leaders before moving out, I called on the battalion commander (rather forcibly perhaps) to get him going at once.

I then followed the leading company down that trail to make sure it got across the Mainit River without delay—if the ford was not defended. It did cross, without a shot fired, and captured the bridge intact.

This was a specialized battle situation, but the time principle applies in peace as well as in war. Most such situations develop from putting off a recognized required action.

Anticipation to avoid a time crisis is routine procedure for effective leaders in garrison and in combat. For example, if I had studied the map closely on Leyte, the Mainit River bridge would have been an obvious danger point. Thus, a flanking movement could have been planned, with my battalion commanders briefed in advance on this possibility.

Good leaders are not just decisive crisis managers; they do their homework before the situation can reach the crisis stage. Of course, every leader also needs a crisis busting capability—because there will always be times when nothing else works.

Three comments follow:

- After our Cincinnati reunion, I received a letter from Paul Austin, who commanded the company that led the way across that undefended ford. In substance, he wrote:

    When you ordered the battalion down that trail to cross the Mainit River at the ford, I wanted to assemble my platoon leaders to brief them. But you demanded we move immediately. As we moved down the trail I felt out of control of my company, and was upset—not understanding and, frankly, resenting having no chance to brief my leaders.

Now, however, I understand. Although we crossed the river without being fired on, very soon a Jap came running toward us, unaware of our presence—and we shot him. We also killed another one near the ford who had an automatic weapon. This makes clear to me why you were in such a hurry—to get to the ford before the Japanese. And we did . . . but just barely.

If only one sniper had fired on us as we entered the waist-deep water, that would have changed everything—because we could not have crossed and taken them by surprise with our bayonets before they set off the explosive charges on the bridge.

Maybe I was not too tactful, but in time-sensitive tactical situations celerity of action takes precedence over amenities. It was a mistake, however, to give no explanation. Although I thought the situation was obvious, it would have wasted no time to have said, "We have got to get to the ford first!"

• The importance of time at the Mainit River bridge did not stem from the local situation alone, but was part of the big picture. The primary concentration of Japanese forces was on the northern island of Luzon, but selection of Leyte for our landing in force made that the decisive battleground. To lose Leyte was to lose the Philippines.

As a result, the Japanese needed to reinforce Leyte, and with our Navy controlling the waters off the east coast the only way to do this was through land reinforcements on the west coast. So our mission was to cross Leyte before those reinforcements could land there, and the Japanese mission was to prevent this.

Two days later, north of Jaro, the 34th Infantry ran head-on into the Japanese 41st Armored Infantry Regiment (as I recall the number; I was wounded in the initial collision). It was a classic meeting engagement: two units on the same road with directly opposing missions. The Japanese had recognized the time factor, too, sending this force ahead to help existing forces gain time and cover their west coast landing.

Although the 34th Infantry, backed by our division artillery and attached tanks, largely destroyed the Japanese 41st Armored

Infantry Regiment, the regiment had accomplished its mission. We were delayed long enough to give Japanese reinforcements time to land, and the battle for Leyte was materially lengthened, with increased casualties for our side.

- It is fascinating to note how this principle of time pervades all military history. In the complex battle of Waterloo, there were multiple situations on both sides where loss of time resulted in lost opportunities. In World War II, the most publicized lost opportunity resulting from loss of time was the failure to close the Falaise pocket during the race across France after the Normandy invasion.

Conversely, one of the most publicized successes resulted from seizing time by the forelock, thus capturing the great Remagen bridge over the Rhine River—on the other side of the world from our modest bridge over the small, fordable Mainit.

Nothing in all the diversified and radical innovations in weapons and technologies of modern armies has changed the time principle. Actually, the *time* factor has been foreshortened and sharpened, but the basic requirements remain the same: the perception to see the time opportunity, the judgment to evaluate the situation, and the resolution to act.

45

The Commander's Proper Place in Battle

THE OCCASION WAS a Ranger dining-in at Fort Benning, Ga., in June 1974, where I was the guest speaker for the thirtieth anniversary of the World War II landing on Omaha Beach in Normandy. The steep cliffs close behind the beach there were a major obstacle until Brig. Gen. (later Major General) Norman D. Cota issued his famous order, "Rangers, lead the way!"

After I talked for my dinner, we viewed a movie showing those precipitous cliffs behind Omaha Beach and then settled into the informal part of the evening. In due course, a young captain came up to me, glass in hand and wearing ribbons attesting his combat service in Vietnam.

"General," he said without preamble, "you have received a lot of publicity for leading the way off that beach in the Philippines—but, as a regimental commander, I don't think that was your job."

I counted slowly to seven and lowered the level of the liquid in my glass, then decided that one drink debating with another on that topic—considering the difference in age, rank, experience, and combat situations—was not a good idea. So I changed the subject by asking, "What was your combat assignment in Vietnam, Captain?"

That little gambit worked—he was happy to talk about it. So I did not explain to him that the company commander had been killed where I landed on Red Beach at Leyte, the battalion commander landed elsewhere, and that the potential for publicity—plus the fact I was an eagle colonel and regimental commander—in no way changed the fact I was a combat infantryman facing a situation that called for immediate action.

This illustrates a specialized angle to the overall question: What is the proper place for a regimental commander in battle? Before commenting on that, I will summarize what I know about regimental commanders of the 24th Infantry Division in the Philippines during World War II, what I have learned about the commanders of those same regiments in the dramatic fighting during the early days of the Korean War, plus a little historical research about where combat commanders elsewhere have placed themselves in combat.

As to the regimental commanders of the 24th Infantry Division in the Philippines during World War II, the record for these primary names reveals:

19th Infantry: Col. Thomas E. Clifford, Jr., two Distinguished Service Crosses, Silver Star, Purple Heart (killed in action).

21st Infantry: Col. William J. Verbeck, three Silver Stars, two Bronze Stars with V (for Valor), three Purple Hearts.

34th Infantry: Col. Aubrey S. Newman, Distinguished Service Cross, Silver Star, Purple Heart; Col. Chester H. Dahlen, two Silver Stars, Bronze Star with V, Purple Heart.

Similarly, when the 24th Infantry Division was ordered into Korea in late June 1950 to slow the powerful North Korean surprise attack, these same three regiments were literally ground into the battlefield by overwhelming forces, but saved the vital Pusan beachhead to support our counterattack. The battle records of key regimental commanders are surprisingly similar to those who commanded the same regiments in the Philippines:

19th Infantry: Col. Guy S. Meloy, Distinguished Service Cross, Purple Heart; Col. Ned D. Moore, Distinguished Service Cross, Silver Star.

21st Infantry: Col. Richard W. Stephens, Distinguished Service Cross, Silver Star.

34th Infantry: Col. Robert Martin, Distinguished Service Cross, Purple Heart (killed in action).

It is an intriguing fact that the six surviving regimental commanders listed above all became general officers—Meloy, a four-star general; the others, major generals. There were other commanders of the three regiments, too, but those Distinguished Service Crosses, Silver Stars, and Purple Hearts tell their own mute story, revealing the place in combat these commanders selected for themselves, in the situations they faced.

Before considering why these regimental commanders appeared in the forefront of battle, consider the following footnotes to history.

Historian Martin Blumenson summarized Gen. George S. Patton, Jr.'s, view this way: "Success in battle was due to 'indomitable will and tremendous energy in execution,' together with commanders who held the hearts of their troops by displaying personal valor."

The great German commander in World War II, Field Marshal Erwin Rommel, summarized his ideas:

> There are always moments when the commander's place is not back with his staff but up with the troops. It is sheer nonsense to say that maintenance of the men's morale is the job of the battalion commander alone. The higher the rank, the greater the effect of the example. The men tend to feel no kind of contact with a commander who, they know, is sitting somewhere in headquarters. What they want is what might be termed a physical contact with him. In moments of panic, fatigue or disorganization, or when something out of the ordinary has to be demanded from them, the personal example of the commander works wonders, especially if he has had the wit to create some sort of legend around himself.

In the early stages of the German drive toward Dunkirk in World War II, Gen. (later Field Marshal) Erich von Manstein was a corps commander. A condensed extract from his book *Lost Victories* is relevant

> Next I paid a visit to the right-hand regiment of the corps. Though ready to advance, it was waiting to see what effect the artillery had on the village of Coisy to its front and the adjacent high ground and wooded perimeter. Reconnaissance reports were not available. As I had the impression that neither the village nor the high ground and woods were occupied, I ordered the regimental commander to advance on a broad front, but in well dispersed groups. If there were enemy out there they would show themselves, and be beaten down by artillery. . . . Since the commander evidently harbored doubts about my appreciation of the situation I went on ahead in my *Kübelwagen*.

At the entrance to Coisy the way was barred by a barricade, but it was unmanned. . . . After a brief observation, we drove into the village and found it had been evacuated, as had the high ground and forward edge of the woods. So I returned to the regiment, which was now ready to advance, and suggested they make arrangements to do their own reconnoitering in the future.

Although corps commanders are not meant to do the work of scouting patrols, I felt it necessary to set a drastic example, particularly as the fighting troops did not know me yet.

On 9 May 1943, the Allies closed in on Bizerte in North Africa, and the commander of the 2d Armored Division, Maj. Gen. Ernest N. Harmon (Distinguished Service Cross, two Silver Stars, Purple Heart) thought the end of the battle was near, so he set out in a jeep to see how his forces were doing. On the left flank, he saw our tanks driving into Bizerte. He then moved to check the right flank and found a cluster of tanks firing bravely but not moving forward. There was incoming machine-gun fire, but he got out of his jeep to talk with the tank commander, who said they were being held up by machine-gun and tank fire.

"All right," General Harmon said, "you follow my jeep forward," and climbed back in his jeep. This embarrassed the young commander into action, and the tanks began to move. General Harmon then continued along the road, ran into a company of Germans taking cover from our artillery fire in a deep cut—and realized he was about to be captured!

But he recovered mentally and began to yell for the German captain to go back with him to call off the artillery fire and arrange for their surrender . . . and that is the way it was done.

Note: The division chief of staff at the time was Col. Maurice Rose. Later in Europe, as a major general commanding an armored division, Rose was killed in a similar foray out in front. Luck in battle cuts both ways.

Comments on the place of regimental commanders in battle follow:

• I cannot improve on Field Marshal Rommel's summary of the place of the commander in battle: up front; that means at the critical moments, at the hot spots. To me, the decorations (especially those Purple Hearts) of the listed successful regimental commanders of the 24th Infantry Division in the Philippines and Korea are prima facie evidence.

- The battle decorations of commanders do *not* mean day-to-day frontline exposure on the same basis as lower ranks but, rather, selective appearances at critical times and places where their personal influence is not only needed but may be decisive. Regimental commanders and above have a broad knowledge of the front, which often enables them to judge the situation at hot spots with better overall understanding than the local commanders.

- These key commanders cannot be readily replaced and are doubly valuable after they know their commands, have been tested by fire, and are known and trusted by their soldiers. The captain at the Ranger dining-in at Fort Benning was a veteran, too, and he was right in principle—that regimental commanders cannot be a "one-man army," and thus should not take unnecessary risks.

Later in the Leyte campaign, I made the exact mistake he was talking about—the greatest mistake of my career. I took a needless and unjustified risk out of impatience . . . and was suddenly changed from an effective commander to just another burden to be taken care of.

46

Who Gets the Combat Decorations?

THE REASON IT is difficult to award combat decorations uniformly and fairly is that no exact criteria can be established and each award becomes a matter of judgment. But judgment directly depends upon the information available to the judge and this brings us to the critical point: How can we improve procedures so as to make better information available?

During the Second World War, when I was chief of staff of the 24th Infantry Division during the Southern Philippines campaign on Mindanao, the division commander, Maj. Gen. Roscoe B. Woodruff, required this staffing of recommendations for combat decorations:

(1) Our G1 packaged recommendations in batches, binding them together with an Acco fastener.
(2) On top of each "book" the G1 placed a cover sheet, lined into columns with headings (left to right): *Names, Unit Commander's Recommendations, G1 Recommendations, C/S Recommendations, CG's Decisions, Remarks.*
(3) The G1 then listed in the left column names of men recommended for decorations. He also filled in the columns to show unit commanders' recommendations for awards in each case, and his opinion of what the awards should be.

(4) The file next came to me as chief of staff to indicate my ideas of the proper decorations.

(5) Finally, the CG entered his decision for each award.

When I saw the first such book my reaction was to think it needless duplication of effort. I quickly changed my mind. In an appreciable number of cases there was a divergence of opinion as to whether to downgrade or upgrade the unit commander's recommendation. One night I picked up a file of recommendations and soon reached the name of Sgt. Charles E. Mower, 34th Infantry.* His unit commander had recommended a posthumous award of the Silver Star, and the G1 had agreed.

As I read the sketchy supporting evidence, my mind tried to bridge gaps and visualize the action in which this brave soldier had given his life. I noticed that the actual battle incident (an enemy ambush at a stream crossing) had taken place months before, so most of the eyewitnesses may have been killed or wounded, then or later.

After reading the paper I decided: If this happened the way I think it did, Sergeant Mower deserves not the Silver Star, but the Medal of Honor!

The CG agreed this possibility should be investigated. When queried by phone the regimental commander pointed out that there had been much fighting since Sergeant Mower died, and that available evidence would support only award of the Silver Star. Further, it would require two eyewitness accounts for award of the Medal of Honor, and there were no such witnesses still with the regiment.

It was not surprising to discover that witnesses to the action had been killed or wounded at the time, or in subsequent months of fighting. But necessary witnesses might be in hospitals somewhere. The regimental commander was therefore directed to search out names of possible wounded witnesses evacuated to hospitals, and to fly someone back to take their statements.

Before learning what came of this effort I returned to the United States and thus did not know the results until six months after the war. One day I picked up a DA general order from my IN basket at the

---

*See Appendix A.

Pentagon, and there it was in print: Posthumous award of the Medal of Honor to Sgt. Charles E. Mower!

So the only difference between award of the Silver Star and one of the Medal of Honor for Sergeant Mower was adequate administrative action.

Granted, this is an unusual case where, so long after the event, follow-up paperwork did, eventually, bring America's highest honor to the soldier who had earned it at the cost of life. But Sergeant Mower's case is by no means unique. From Maj. Gen. George E. Martin (now retired) I learned that he had had a similar experience as a division chief of staff in Italy. A recommendation for award of the Silver Star had reached his headquarters, and there, after further investigation by division, the recommendation was changed to award of the Medal of Honor. This time, however, the soldier lived to receive it, though he had lost an arm.

In past wars uncounted thousands of soldiers have failed to receive deserved decorations due primarily to lack of detailed information on which to base necessary paperwork. With Americans fighting in Vietnam today the problem remains: how to obtain better information so that heroic men will receive well-earned recognition, often posthumously. Now, more than twenty years after World War II, examination of Sergeant Mower's case suggests a way.

Combat is not violence prolonged for weeks or months, or even for many days in a row. There is always time, though at irregular intervals, to sleep and to eat, to answer calls of nature, to write messages. *That's* the word: messages! The system for placing information in the record exists; it's only necessary to use it.

It can be done like this:

(1) Announce a policy that, from platoon sergeants and platoon leaders up, it be accepted procedure to write on a field message form any battle action deserving special recognition.

(2) The message would then be filed in the unit journal like any other battle action report or message.

(3) In addition to a telegraphic summary of facts, the message would list other witnesses, who might sign their names, or even attach supporting statements, especially if it were a possible award of the Medal of Honor.

In this way unit journals would not only be more complete battle records, but would also serve as basic references in preparing recommendations for combat decorations.

Further, this system would act as a spur to expedite paperwork. Such a field message might read:

To: CO, Co A, ——th Inf   15 Oct 1966
When lead scouts A R Jackson and W M Smith advanced down the road near Bong Son enemy MG opened fire. Est range 250 yds. Jackson badly wounded, fell in road. From cover in roadside ditch Smith saw bullets from second burst kick up dirt near Jackson. Smith jumped out of ditch, pulled Jackson to safety in ditch and, while doing this, was himself wounded in left arm by bullet from third MG burst. Recommend Smith for combat decoration.
Other witnesses: Sgt Frank Ames, Pvts Rex Black, Tom Lawson, John Leathem.

(signed) MORGAN ANDERSON
PSG, 2d Plat

If this field-message-to-unit-journal procedure is followed it will eliminate current loss of information when witnesses are killed or wounded in subsequent fighting—or when commanders are killed, wounded, or transferred before the paperwork phase is reached, which should not be a factor, but often is. It would also provide means of checking official recommendations, which must remain the foundation for finalizing all awards.

Finally, I believe the system required by General Woodruff—obtain two different viewpoints in his own headquarters to support the unit commanders' ideas of the proper awards, or suggest variations from them—is sound procedure in a decision headquarters. For a division, however, I suggest that the assistant division commander (when available) replace the chief of staff. The ADC not only has less paperwork to do but is free to roam the combat areas, so normally he should have better knowledge of battle actions described in statements. Also, his star would lift decorations paperwork out of routine handling, and he has two aides who can be got off their duffs to verify or seek facts.

Looking backward, I wish I had thought of integrating battle decorations information into the field-message-to-unit-journal system when I was a combat regimental commander. Such a procedure could have resulted in well-earned battle decorations for many men of my regiment whose heroism went unrewarded.

Of course, any new idea—no matter how well reasoned—must be battle-tested to prove its worth, and to discover what, if any, undesirable side effects may develop. Such a test in Vietnam now would provide a positive evaluation of this proposed system.

If it proved successful in combat the system could be adopted for future Armywide use by including it in unit training, especially in the company. No new equipment or techniques are required; messages for unit journals would be similar in form and general nature so as to present intelligence messages, patrol reports, and the like. I think the result would be that frontline heroism would be better and more equitably recognized in the future than it has been in the past, because more complete, authentic, and timely information would be readily available.

47

The Draft and the Will to Win

THERE MUST BE a sadistic element for some writers in the art of stringing words together to portray an idea. How else explain our tendency to stretch a simile on the rack to serve our purpose, or distort the import of an anecdote to make our point?

Anyway, I'll invoke my writer's license to link a pre–Pearl Harbor incident in Hawaii with a footnote to history that preceded the Leyte landing of Gen. Douglas MacArthur's famous "return" to the Philippines. Then we can examine how these vastly disparate happenings can be related to our present pressing need for the draft in our military services.

The incident took place more than a year before the surprise attack on our Navy at Pearl Harbor. I was a captain on the staff of the 19th Infantry at Schofield Barracks, and our regiment was having a sort of tea dance at the officers' club. You know, with receiving line and music and refreshments. Very nice.

The party was one of those 5:00 to 8:00 P.M. affairs, but, being a bachelor, I decided to stay on to make the most of an evening begun so pleasantly. Thus, in my dress-blue uniform, I was still in the club when two things happened: The club suddenly announced it was closing for the night, and I heard the retreat gun fired five times, which was the signal for a "general alarm."

So I passed the word along, received the reply it was "just another alert"—and was asked, "How many shots have you had?" But since alerts were supposed to come by phone, I elected to report at once to my regiment, which was only a couple of hundred yards away.

Of course, being in blue uniform posed a problem, but I decided if "this was it" there was no time to get properly dressed for the occasion. When I arrived at regimental headquarters, it was dark and empty. So I called the guardhouse and ordered the sergeant of the guard to send runners around the quadrangle to turn out all companies, and told the sergeant to call all officers of the regiment. Then I called the regimental commander, told him the "general alarm" had been fired, that I had the regiment turning out—and assured him the situation was well in hand.

That accomplished, I went to my office where I kept a campaign hat and one of those old double-strap, field-type Sam Browne belts hanging on hooks behind the door.

So I donned the campaign hat, and put the double Sam Browne on over my blue uniform. Then I got my pistol ammunition. The supply sergeant took a look at my blue uniform, campaign hat, double Sam Browne—and said he didn't have any ammunition. We had a few words. I got kind of emphatic and ended up with the ammunition. One clip went into my pistol and the other two into the pockets on my belt.

Back in my office—loaded and ready for bear—I sat down, stuck my feet on the desk, tilted my hat at a belligerent angle, and nonchalantly lit a cigar. A few minutes later the adjutant came striding into headquarters, looked in my office, and said, "Well, General Grant, where did you come from?"

It soon developed that the "general alarm" had been fired by mistake, and so everybody kept on "alerting." Pretty soon the regimental commander arrived and was briefed on the situation. One of his first actions was to tell me he thought I could spare the time to go home and change uniform.

Well, they called me General Grant for quite a while—but since 7 December 1941 I haven't been quite so apologetic about jumping the gun on World War II.

Later in the war (via Australia and New Guinea) I found myself commanding the 34th Infantry Combat Team, loaded on ships in an immense amphibious force, steaming inexorably on toward Leyte Gulf and the sandy Leyte beaches where General MacArthur would return to the Philippines on 20 October 1944.

I was with the battalion that would lead our landing, aboard the APA *Fayette*—Captain Lester, USN, commanding, Commodore (captain, USN) Taylor aboard. Since I had my meals in the captain's mess with them, I was privileged to see classified messages delivered there. That is how, two or three days before the landing, I saw this message (repeated here from memory):

My intelligence informs me of major concentrations of Japanese naval strength to the westward of the Philippines. If the central passages of the Philippines [that is, San Bernadino and Surigao Straits, to the north and south of Leyte] *are left unguarded, the result could be disastrous.*

I do not know to whom that message was addressed, but clearly General MacArthur was warning the Navy not to let the great Battle of Leyte Gulf develop the way it did. But the main great Japanese striking force did transit San Bernadino Strait to the north of Leyte, and caught our Navy by complete surprise.

What would have happened if Vice Adm. Kakeo Kurita had not lost his nerve and turned back will always remain a matter of debate and conjecture. But the situation remains a vivid memory for me, because the night of 24 October I received a phone call from division headquarters:

This is a warning. Major elements of the Japanese fleet are entering Leyte Gulf, and bombardment of the shore may be expected momentarily.

You can be sure that recent message aboard ship jumped into my mind—but shore bombardment never came, because our Navy intervened with a great naval victory, including complete destruction of a Japanese force in Surigao Strait.

Well, so warnings did not serve to prevent surprise attacks in these two World War II footnotes to history, but what has that got to do with the price of baloney and the pressing need to reinstate the draft—*now*? Just this: The dangers of surprise attacks at Pearl Harbor and through "the central passages of the Philippines" were obvious to anyone who examined the facts surrounding these situations; but there were strong odds against the dangers developing into actual explosive reality—if you can call that an excuse.

But when the dangerous world situation today and relevant facts vis-à-vis the draft are examined, there can be no doubt about some of the intangible but very real dangers that are already developing into realities—right now, before our eyes. Yet, it is not too late to regain control, if we take the obvious corrective measure: reinstate the draft. Consider these comments:

- The facts of the money cost of the all-volunteer Army, including projected future obligations, are simply a matter of putting the figures down on paper and doing the arithmetic. To paraphrase Li'l Abner in the former Al Capp comic strip: "Any fool who will make the effort kin do thet—even I kin."
- After a generation under the all-volunteer system the experience of service in uniform will be largely lacking for those in top legislative and executive positions in our nation—and that generation is now well on the way.

  Maybe you will not like the idea, but it is my considered opinion, and there is no way to sugar-coat it: Among those who come into the Army *for a career,* some will reach high military rank as dedicated soldiers, but those who come into the Army for the money are unlikely to get out and reach top legislative and executive positions in our national government. And it is our civilian leaders, not our military men, who make basic decisions in our national defense.
- In any analysis of a nation's military strength, the will of individuals to serve and fight when called is of incalculable importance. Although the principle of an all-volunteer Army is a wonderful theory, it works only when the situation makes it a feasible operating solution. But "Let GI Joe do it, we will pay him for it" is not a viable solution when a nation faces a serious military threat. It raises a generation of young adults without the priceless will to serve and fight when called—and we are now doing just that.

  The potential damage from surprises at Pearl Harbor and Leyte Gulf were short term, which could be remedied by further military action. But the loss over an extended period of years of the will to fight, in a nation governed and led by legislators and elected executives who will increasingly lack military experience—for that there is no short-term correction.
- It is our heritage that "everybody is free to do his own thing"— but that privilege is not unlimited and presumes willingness to fight to preserve that freedom. That our elected representatives now see this is evidenced by the current requirement to register, which presages a return to the draft, sooner or later.

48

The Battle Catalyst: *Endure**

THE CAPACITY TO endure is the matrix that binds other battle qualities into the flexible strength of a fighting man. It is the catalyst that merges military skills with mental and physical attributes to meet the test of close combat. To dare briefly is not enough.

In referring to this basic principle in an article for another journal (*ARMY,* September 1970), this author wrote: "The sudden flame of raw courage must be there when needed, but combat calls for the capacity to endure cumulative, pyramiding stresses: loss of sleep, hunger and thirst, long-continued physical effort to utter exhaustion, living with gnawing fear for yourself, and the terrific strain of responsibility for the lives of others—for hours, days, weeks, and months."

Several months ago I visited the U.S. Army Ranger Camp at Eglin Air Force Base. In order to document this *endure* principle, and to supplement my own combat experience, I talked with Vietnam veterans—including their outstanding, battle-wise commander, Lt. Col. James Tucker. These men discussed case histories and ideas that illustrate how the capacity to endure permeates the battlefield.

Captain John LeMoyne told how Americans endured the unique dangers and pressures of war in Vietnam. In his unit, each company, except

*Published in *Infantry,* March-April 1972.

the one in reserve, sent out ten squad-size ambushes each night. Reserve duty was rotated to give all companies a break in the cumulative tensions of night ambushes. Additionally, inexperienced lieutenants and new NCOs—with as little as eight months' service—were often leaders of the independent ambushes. These operations sometimes lasted three to seven days. The procedure involved sleeping in the morning, reconnoitering for night sites on accessible routes to their zone in the afternoons, and lying in ambush through the black jungle night.

One surprising result of this successful program revealed that the battalion suffered casualties from day contacts, but no fatalities in night ambushes. Another feature involved intensified pressure when a large enemy force came along. The leaders had to decide whether to shoot or just sit and hope they would not be discovered.

These on-your-own missions subjected inexperienced leaders to tensions that gave them, and their men, self-confidence and the will to persist. "The first dragon is always the hardest to kill." Once a soldier has killed that first dragon—enduring personal fear, dread of failing his men with faulty decisions, suspense, and self-doubt—subsequent operations will be easier. However, the will to endure must remain.

Captain LeMoyne said that two enlisted men and one officer failed to endure through those months of night ambushes. "One man took the indirect way out, by reenlisting for six years—anything to get away. The other could not bear the long, continued strain and had to be evacuated. The officer 'wilted' in a similar fashion, even though he had been a successful company commander in the States."

After six grueling months, combat pressure was not lessened, but suddenly increased when the battalion was committed to the Cambodian operation. As Rabelais said, "Necessity has no law." In a war zone the necessity to endure knows no rules or schedule. One must meet every situation.

Of course, patrol-size units also ambushed trails in daylight. Captain Dennis Rosenberry told about one team (six men) operating in the area of Task Force South, twenty kilometers northwest of Phan Thi.

The team took a break in the mountainous area by moving about thirty meters off the trail. The group was well hidden in dense jungle when a company-size Viet Cong force came down the trail—armed with AK-47s, machine guns, and grenade launchers. As if this was not enough pressure, the enemy company pulled off the trail into an open place, downhill and opposite from where the patrol lay hidden, and sent out reconnaissance parties to check the area. One party came within ten meters of the dense growth concealing the patrol.

While the enemy company rested for two hours, the six-man team endured the hostile presence without trying to sneak away. By "low voice" radio transmission, the patrol leader warned helicopter gunships to stay away. Finally, when the Viet Cong force moved farther downhill into a ravine, he called in the gunships. The patrol opened fire on the enemy moving back toward the trail, causing added casualties and dispersing the larger force. The friendly patrol suffered no casualties.

This victory was not achieved by sudden violent bursts of heroism, or by retreating from danger. It resulted from the patrol leader and his men enduring the imminent threat without panicking. They were able to think under pressure and decide on a plan to destroy the enemy force. They did not surrender to their fears, but repressed them—thus carrying out their mission against heavy odds.

The patrol, however, did not do all the sweating. Captain Rosenberry was on the other end of the radio link, in a staff capacity, and could have ordered the patrol out. Instead, he warned other patrols of the enemy location and left the decision to the patrol leader. In so doing, though not in physical danger himself, he had to endure tormenting worry about the patrol's fate. He was not only concerned for their safety, but also for possible blame if the patrol was destroyed.

Also, when the task force commander learned of the decision and situation, he demanded more information than was available, thus adding command pressure to the operation. This is a type of stress that staff officers will recognize as commanding with a chance factor—being second guessed. They endure continued and repeated risk of censure if things go wrong, knowing that credit will go to the commander if the ball bounces right. Little drops of sweat and little grains of blame produce an insidious strain and a familiar name: "jittery staff officer."

Captain Richard White, a veteran from the 4th Infantry Division, said cumulative mental pressures, endured for months, were a greater test than physical fatigue or short periods of imminent danger. He recalled days, weeks, and months of patrolling that Vietnam required of combat units—always with a "point man" out front. That lonely lead man had to endure the strain of knowing each step might be his last. Doing this, day after day, adds layer on layer of silent, soul-searching tension, pyramiding the requirement to endure. Duty as "point man" was rotated to reduce the intensity of strain on any one soldier.

Captain White identified "command tension" as an intangible long-term need to endure. This is a many-faceted pressure for commanders, from squad and patrol leaders on up. Command tension builds from responsibility for the lives of men, balanced against actions necessary to accomplish assigned missions. It includes agonizing decisions; the duty to provide supplies, ammunition, medical care, and other needs in changing situations; and increased human friction that comes with authority. These tensions and others (including the commander's worry about his own life, his own success or failure) call for a broadened ability to endure. Some fine peacetime commanders fail under converging and conflicting combat pressures.

Sergeant Tommy Duncan agreed with Captain White about the demanding need to endure by the "point man" in patrol and advance guard formations. "In the point, men had to sweat it out, which is what you call *endure*. That puts you through the wringer, with your nerves ready to jump out of your skin. But after that first shot is fired, reflexes and instinct take over," he explained.

There is a frustrating tension that follows a warning of pending enemy attack, an uneasiness that results from enduring long-continued alert status—and nothing happens. Captain Stephen Bowman's experience is a good illustration.

In July 1969 his company was operating in the Ashau Valley, usually in mountainous jungle surrounding the valley. In August the company moved to fire support base Berchtesgaden, on the western edge of the valley, to secure the brigade Tactical Operations Center (TOC) and two artillery batteries. This was to have been a rest break for the company. However, soon after their arrival, an intelligence report warned that one of the first support bases in the Ashau would soon be hit.

The company went on 100 percent alert at night. The schedule began at dusk, with the men awake all night. An hour after sunrise, they would sleep (except for enough men to provide security) for approximately five hours. The afternoon was spent hauling ammunition, working on defensive positions, and maintaining equipment. They also sent out local reconnaissance patrols.

This grinding schedule continued for three weeks. Then the company caught a reinforced enemy sapper company in the defensive wire with a small-arms "mad minute." Results of the action were thirty-seven enemy killed, twelve RPGs, and six AK-47s captured, and scores of satchel charges captured and destroyed. The cost was three friendly killed from a direct hit by a mortar round on a fighting position, and six wounded. By enduring sustained alert status without relief, B Company successfully carried out its mission.

To get things in perspective, we'll look at the other side. Captain Frederick Jelnek spotlighted the obvious fact that one of the great strengths of the Viet Cong is their ability to endure. This goes to extremes often hard for Americans to visualize.

In one area where his unit operated in open country, they discovered a VC bunker—dug into the ground and protected by a flimsy camouflage cover. It was just a slit trench about two feet wide and four feet deep, which contained five men packed in like sardines. They had been there, surrounded by Americans and subject to being crushed by cruising armored vehicles, for *six months*!

Their mission was to spread propaganda and serve as guides for infiltrators. They holed up during the day like a family of moles, coming out only at night. Their normally brown skins had faded from lack of sunlight. They had faced the constant danger of discovery and death, surviving on food that barely sustained life, in the sanitation of a pigpen. Amid all this, they had accomplished their mission, for all those months.

This brings out the fact of life in Vietnam that we are highly aware of: The Viet Cong have conditioned themselves to an almost inhuman capacity to endure years of mental and physical stress. Their tactics take advantage of this. By their willingness to endure, they have infiltrated supplies and replacements throughout Vietnam, while keeping Americans and the South Vietnamese under pressure from mortar attacks, booby traps, and hidden mines. Consequently, our troops have endured the never-ending tensions of combating such tactics—including the nerve-jangling duty of probing for booby traps and mines.

In Sergeant Duncan's review of his combat experience he emphasized the strain of mine and booby trap sweeping, like the time he was with a six-man detail clearing a mined area. Suddenly one man hit a mine—then there were only five men in the detail.

"When you see a thing like that happen right in front of you, everybody is really shook," Sergeant Duncan said. "But we went back to sweeping. It was not more physical work, yet it took more *effort*— we really sweated it out. Nobody said much, but we *endured*!"

Captain Nathan Jones—with sixteen years' service, his first thirteen years in the enlisted ranks—brought up a point also mentioned by Sergeant Duncan. "Officers should be alert to avoid unnecessary physical demands on their men, with particular reference to loss of sleep. Any time regular sleeping hours are disrupted, a carefully thought out 'sleeping plan' is just as important as feeding and ammunition plans."

Nothing makes it harder for men to bear the great pressures of the battlefield than loss of sleep. Over the years, I not only experienced the vicious effects of sleep loss, but saw lack of sleep literally destroy the careers of some fine officers. The importance of this vital need for sleep is too often overlooked.

From Capt. William Cole, I received some broad philosophical comments, taking into account not only service in Vietnam, but an officer's career in general. He breaks down *endurance* into these segments:

(1) sustaining without impairment,
(2) perseverance,
(3) patience, and
(4) steadiness in the face of adverse force or influences of any kind.

His first point is fundamental to military service. A soldier is on duty twenty-four hours a day, seven days a week. Further, individuals of intelligence and order find it hard to accept what they consider inefficiency, undue laxness of discipline, and apparent indifference to responsibilities. Some officers, lacking the steel resiliency to stay in there and pitch, feel it's "more than they can endure." They leave the service.

The requirement is not to "endure low standards"—far from it. It is to recognize that in a tremendous organization like the military services, with constant turnover in personnel and many in uniform against their wishes, standards will always be varied. It is the test of a real pro to endure such frustrations as part of his job. He does everything within his power to bring his segment to the highest level of efficiency. To paraphrase Gen. Douglas MacArthur: "The true professional does not take counsel of his frustrations." In effect, he does not become indifferent, intolerant, or inferior. He endures and strives.

Not all intangible pressures on military men, fighting battles for others, come from the enemy or the home front. Sometimes these come from allies in the theatre of operations. Captain Cole cites his experience:

In Vietnam, I served as advisor to a Vietnamese Ranger battalion and later with a similar unit. I experienced a situation with both these battalions which was hard to overcome. Aside from combat, there was another type of pressure: the "silent treatment." The Vietnamese were always wanting things. Often their requests were legal and reasonable, but sometimes they were not.

When it became necessary to say "No," they would give you the "silent treatment" and become hostile in a passive way. It would wear you down. If you gave in, they would be happy and treat you like nothing had happened—but, deep inside, you knew you had failed, in your eyes as well as in theirs.

If you endured long enough they would understand you meant to stand by your decision, and eventually revert to normal behavior. It was a struggle of opposing wills in which endurance was essential.

Colonel P. A. Downward, from the Officer's Wing of the British School of Infantry, was an official visitor to the Florida Ranger Camp during part of my stay there. This distinguished officer was interested in our discussion about the will and capacity to endure.

He pointed out that geography and climate can place critical demands on soldiers—varying from sultry heat and diseases of tropical jungles to blistering sand and thirst in deserts to paralyzing cold in arctic or winter weather. He recommended reading "Defeat Into Victory" by Field Marshal Sir William Joseph Slim, the famed British soldier who rose from the ranks to become chief of the Imperial General Staff.

Not only have our soldiers endured all these soul-searing tests in modern times, but history is replete with examples of the heroic will to endure nature's tests: Washington at Valley Forge; Hannibal's almost unbelievable crossing of the Swiss Alps in the dead of winter; Napoleon's disastrous invasion of Russia—where pitiless winter weather, combined with broad reaches of barren space, was more than even his veteran army could endure.

Each man has his personal and emotional crosses to bear, which he alone knows—too varied and numerous to even touch on here. Sometimes men allow private problems to upset their will to endure duty demands; unfortunate news from home has resulted in more than one soldier yielding in battle, robbed of his inner strength. The diversity of things that must be endured can never be categorized completely, but these comments seem pertinent:

- As Col. Jim Tucker says, it's not physical stamina, but the inner will to endure that is the ultimate test for military men.
- No one belittles the blazing valor that inspires soldiers who win decorations for gallantry, for extraordinary heroism, and for "above and beyond the call of duty." Without this type of flaming courage, no army can succeed. But the quiet, silent, endless will to endure must also exist; bursts of heroism, alone, are not enough.
- Every officer should keep in mind that his men are human and should never be called upon to endure needless physical or mental stresses. There are limits to human endurance; Napoleon realized this on the road to Moscow.
- As we seek within ourselves the strength and will to endure, let us respect the way our enemy in Vietnam has survived through this tenacious quality, both on the battlefield and by their people at home. It is an incontestable demonstration of the will to endure.
- Every man must build into his own character the quality that says to himself, "Keep on!" Many men have tried to put into words their way of thinking about this. The quote that best summarizes it for me comes from the Roman thinker and poet Persius Flaccus. More than 1,900 years ago he said, *"He conquers who endures."*

49

Reunion for Peace: Military Policy in Practice

SOMEWHERE IN THE dim past, I saw a cartoon about the Pentagon with a multistarred general pounding a fist on his desk and glaring angrily at the subordinate standing in front of him. The caption read: "There is no reason for it I tell you—it is just our policy!"

Sometimes Murphy's law does invade policy-making along these lines: "If a policy can be written without rhyme or reason, somebody will write it that way." On the other hand, we may see the results of a sound policy and not recognize what we see, which happened to me on a trip I took to the Philippines.

The Philippine government announced a "Reunion for Peace" program in the year 1977. Veterans of World War II, on both sides, were invited to return to the scene of their battles in mutual friendship— now and for the future.

A highlight of this Reunion for Peace year was dedication of the Gen. Douglas MacArthur Memorial at Red Beach on Leyte, 20 October 1977—the thirty-third anniversary of his famous landing there. That occasion had a special meaning for me, so I joined a group of General MacArthur's former Southwest Pacific Area (SWPA) commanders and staff officers who made the trip.

Our plane was met in Manila with music and enthusiasm by civilian dignitaries, representatives from veterans organizations, news media, and active military—including the chief of the Philippine Army Nurse

Corps, as two members of our group were Army nurses who served on Bataan and Corregidor in 1942. A memorable feature of that greeting was a certain excitement and happiness in their welcome that one can feel but not describe.

Our first visit was to the beautiful U.S. military cemetery and marble war memorial near Manila. Like other overseas cemeteries, it was meticulously landscaped, with crosses carefully aligned in every direction—not just hundreds, but thousands.

An immaculately uniformed Philippine honor guard was drawn up for a brief but impressive ceremony, including a prayer by a member of our veterans group, Father Edward M. Flannery, of Chicago. His words included:

"It matters not how well or how little educated each was, nor how well blessed with earthly health and social standing, for life is precious to all men everywhere. . . .

"It is well that we single out no individual, for none gave more than the others. . . ."

The quavering notes of Taps rolled out their peculiarly sad and penetrating sound across those fields of crosses, and remembered words came back to me: "Greater love hath no man than this, that a man lay down his life for his friends." In one sense the principle was the same here, though it involved thousands of lives and the relationship was between peoples—yet there was something else involved, too, that I could not quite put my finger on.

Next stop was Leyte, for dedication of the MacArthur Memorial on 20 October. Since I commanded the regiment that cleared the way for his dramatic "return" to the Philippines on Red Beach, I decided to fly down a day early. This allowed me to follow the route of my 34th Infantry (24th Infantry Division) as we fought our way across Leyte— until a piece of Japanese steel relieved me of command.

When my wife and I stepped off the plane, we were met by an unexpected crowd and a band, again with that aura of excited happiness and enthusiasm that cannot be counterfeited.

How could this be, just for a regimental commander from thirty-three years ago? My name had been associated with an action on Red Beach before General MacArthur's arrival, but there was more to it than that. Well over a hundred veterans returned to Leyte for this occasion, and every one of them was received with *joy*—there is no other word for it.

Dedication ceremonies by the Philippine government for the Mac-Arthur Memorial were inspiring—accenting the Reunion for Peace idea. In a great parade of colorful floats, the Philippine, American, and Japanese flags waved in the breeze from Leyte Gulf. Also, countless hands on the floats and in the crowd held aloft three small replicas of those flags. Nothing could have pleased General MacArthur more than those flags waving side by side—especially since a contingent of Japanese veterans, headed by Maj. Gen. Eiichi Hirose, was there to participate.

The impressive memorial is hard to describe. Its central feature is on a raised earth mound on the beach where General MacArthur made his landing and historic broadcast to the Philippine people: "I have returned!"

At the highest point, there is a square reflecting pool of shallow water. In its center is a larger than life-size bronze statuary group, designed in the postures shown in the famous picture of General MacArthur as he waded ashore.

When the ceremony ended, we were surrounded by an indescribably friendly crowd of smiling people. I was vaguely aware there was a pattern to what I was seeing on this trip but did not realize what it was.

We next visited two more impressive memorials. As on Red Beach, each was designed to commemorate uniquely different battle actions.

On the peak of Mt. Samat, highest point on Bataan, stands a great cross visible for miles in all directions. Just below that is a fine marble memorial, the Altar of Valor. Contiguous to the marble structures is an underground museum originally dug as part of that great defensive line once anchored on Mt. Samat.

Around another fine memorial on Corregidor, unlike those on Leyte and on Mt. Samat, we found grim evidence of furious battle everywhere. One large-caliber mortar battery, deep in a protective pit, was reduced to rubble and tortured shards of steel.

Among many shattered concrete and steel buildings was the famous "mile-long barracks," now an immense roofless hulk of battle-blasted walls. The famous Malinta Tunnel, its many branches blown shut, staggers the mind with its miles of underground corridors. Our taxpayers got their money's worth from that great structure and the years of labor it took to build—because without Malinta, Bataan and Corregidor could not have held out as they did.

As we left Corregidor by boat, there was again that elusive "Why?"

Not only had we fought here so far from home, but we had planned to do so for years. What was the big picture that both explained and justified it?

We met Ferdinand Marcos, who emphasized the importance of the Reunion for Peace in which we were participating. He pointed out that he had lost his own father in the war but that the war was over now and we must all work together—the Philippines, the United States, and Japan—for a peaceful, secure future.

Reflecting on his words, I realize he was stating a basic element of Philippine military policy and that the principle was taken, consciously or otherwise, from our own military policy. In fact, as our group of World War II veterans moved from Manila to Leyte to Bataan and Corregidor, the nebulous pattern that I sensed connecting them was simply our longtime military policy in action. When that is understood, it explains clearly why this happened and why it happened here.

I did not realize the United States had any well-defined military policy until 1947, twenty-two years after receiving my commission. As director of instruction at the Armed Forces Information School, I attended several lectures on the subject by the commandant, Brig. Gen. (later General and Vice-Chief of Staff) Williston B. Palmer. Unfortunately, I do not have a copy of those lectures, but here are some comments, based on what I recall, which place in clearer focus what we saw, heard, and felt in the Philippines:

General Palmer's reference to *The Military Policy of the United States,* by Bvt. Maj. Gen. Emory Upton, first made me aware of that great historical document. It is based on the premise that our military policy is revealed by a study of precedents. His assembly of facts in support of this premise is exceptionally detailed, beginning with the Revolutionary War and extending through the Civil War, and is brilliantly illuminated by General Upton's perceptive comments.

The lectures did not cover all angles and facets of our military policy (wise and unwise), as documented by General Upton, but accented some fundamental elements. Among those relevant to what I witnessed in the Philippines were:

- We have, as a policy, always wanted to fight with allies.
- We have always been slow to get into wars, but once in them (he was talking in 1947), we fought them to a victorious conclusion—thus our allies could depend on us.

- We always recognized a threat to us before it reached our shores, so we have fought our wars outside of the continental United States.
- We have been magnanimous in victory, thus paving the way to turn our former enemies into friends and potential allies (as with Japan and West Germany).

Looking backward now, I can see clearly that what I experienced in the Philippines was the fruition of the successful military policy features summarized above.

50
Reunions: Times to Recall

IT IS A GREAT privilege to know Junior Harris and Spike O'Donnell, to have served with them and others during World War II in the 24th Infantry Division—and to have shared the special friendships, for many years, at our annual reunions. Along with some two hundred other "Taro Leafers," we registered at the Marriott Inn in Pittsburgh for our 1980 reunion.

That explains how a baker's dozen (ranging in rank from former teenage private Junior Harris to our former two-star division commander) happened to congregate in a room Saturday afternoon, under the active management of Vic Backer—a former first sergeant, naturally. As a time-proved organizational procedure Vic directed distribution of liquid conversational lubricants, then initiated one of the reasons for being at reunions, *reminiscences*.

"Spike," Vic said, "what is the story about you and Junior drawing fire in that banana grove in Mindanao?"

"Yeah, I know the time you mean," and Spike tilted his glass to improve his memory. "That was after we got this new lieutenant, fresh from the states—but I forget his name."

"Hell, his name don't matter," Junior said. "We can call him Sledge."

"Yeah," Spike agreed. "Anyway, Sledge crawls over to me and says, 'You and Harris move toward that banana grove and draw fire.'

247

"Well, I wasn't a sergeant any more—because of that misunderstanding when I redistributed some Coca-Colas from our Army commander's plane. But I was still senior to Junior here, so I said, 'Junior, go out there and draw fire.' "

"Yeah, that's what Spike said," added Junior. He took a good gulp from his can, then continued the after-action report. "So I said, 'We been drawing too damn much fire already, Spike. Besides, my mother wrote that she wanted to see me again, and if I go out and draw fire in that banana grove she won't ever see me again.' "

There was a contemplative pause as we sipped our liquids, knowing Sledge would reevaluate his strategic plan in the light of that logic. Then Junior looked at his beer, shook it, and said, "Hell, Vic, this can is empty."

Of course, some reminiscences included more action—like during an enemy night attack when Spike saw this big Jap loom up in the moonlight, and shot him; only thing was the Jap was only wounded when he fell on top of Junior in the next foxhole. For more details, come to one of our reunions so Spike and Junior can brief you personally.

Unfortunately, most veterans have never attended their unit reunions, thus have missed this experience in patriotism and friendship. In "A Brotherhood That Binds the Brave" (*ARMY,* March 1969) I discussed attending my first reunion, more than ten years after the war. For uncounted thousands of veterans who have not attended unit reunions, here are some observations, gleaned from subsequent Taro Leaf reunions.

Most of those who attend our reunions are not career soldiers, but veterans who served in war then returned to civilian life. Many come back year after year, taking their annual vacation at that time, and truly share this "friendship like no other."

Our 24th Infantry Division Association has, over the years, been sparked by these civilian-soldier veterans. Junior Harris and Spike O'Donnell are both past presidents. Others include two sergeants from my wartime regiment, and a soldier from one company I commanded before the war, all later successful in business.

Officers are not discriminated against, however, as our past presidents also include officers of assorted ranks from our war years. While respect for rank remains, there is no "pulling rank"—except former Sgt. Spike O'Donnell lines up and counts off everybody—although Spike sometimes encounters lèse-majesté from Junior and Vic.

One facet of such reunions is that you never know who will remind you of some shared combat experience. A tantalizing mystery for me was the memory of regaining consciousness as I was dragged down a ditch on a shelter half, en route to the battalion aid station, and saw briefly (before losing consciousness again) the head of a man on the edge of the ditch, who was bleeding from an ear. For thirty-three years I wondered who he was and if he lived or died, until he attended the Norfolk reunion in 1977.

That was the first reunion for Charles Craw. We met again in Pittsburgh, sharing the unique friendship of two soldiers who, in a split second, had their lives radically altered by fragments of steel from the same enemy shell.

Variations in contacts are unlimited—like a conversation at Pittsburgh with Lester Wheeler. Les was assistant G3 on the division staff at Hollandia in 1944 when I was chief of staff. We shared an early breakfast in the Marriott and he lifted the veil from a little happening in the New Guinea jungle.

"Chief," Les said, "I remember bringing you an action paper before breakfast in Hollandia, at your tent in our jungle command post. You sat on your folding canvas cot and I on the folding chair, facing where your field jacket hung on a nail in the tall stake just outside the tent, when a two-and-a-half- to three-foot snake crawled out of your field jacket pocket and flopped down on the ground. Remember, chief?"

"Sure," I said, "and I still wonder why you didn't kill it before it got away."

After a pause and quiet smile Les countered, "Well, what I wonder is who put it there—because it seems unlikely the snake could have climbed that stake and found the pocket and got in there without help."

From 1944 to 1980 that idea had never occurred to me. But now— well, some ten years ago Ed Henry told me my code name around division headquarters at the time was "that redheaded SOB" (except Ed did not use the abbreviation). Also, that *was* a tall stake and—well, like Les said . . .

So much for personal contacts and reminiscences. The high point and climax of our annual reunions is the banquet (sit-down dinner) on Saturday evening, especially the memorial service for members of the 24th Infantry Division (and attached units) who died in battle or from wounds.

When all are seated, our president announces, "Bring in the colors!" to initiate the memorial service. A uniformed color guard then marches in with our national and division colors and halts opposite a kind of improvised altar, which stands next to and opposite the center of the head table and our president. On this altar there is a large closed book, and on each side of the book a row of three tall unlighted candles.

Last year our newly elected chaplain, Joseph I. Peyton, conducted the memorial service (written by our late, much-loved Father Christopher Berlo), which includes these extracts:

> . . . The friendship engendered among those who fight together on the field of battle, risking their lives not only for the cause for which they fight but also for one another, is different from every other kind of friendship; different from the ties of flesh and blood, different from the ties of business association, different from the ties of social acquaintance. Once cemented, the military and combat friendship lasts forever. Our gathering here today is proof that it lasts beyond the grave.

> . . . We now light the tapers as symbols of their living memory . . . upon this shrine we place the Honor Roll in which their names are inscribed. As each taper is lighted for the various combat units, members present from that unit or group rise and stand in reverence to the memory of their fallen comrades.

> . . . And grant, O God, inspiration to those in whose hands lie today the destinies of nations, that they may never make a decision . . . which might be inimical to those God-given rights of life, liberty, and the pursuit of happiness for which we have fought and for which so many of our comrades laid down their lives.

Finally, these comments:

• As each of us stands during the memorial service, we are enveloped in memories of familiar names inscribed in that closed book, and of sprawled silent figures whose names we never knew. And this year (with the draft in mind) an added thought arrived unbidden: Any man who refuses to answer the call to duty, to stand ready to fight for his country when summoned, has no right to breathe the free air over America that these men and others fought and died for.

- Do not be misled by the reminisced byplay involving Junior, Spike, and Sledge. There is a different and closer soldier-to-soldier relationship in combat from that on the peacetime drill field, and it varies with situations and individuals. You must have shared it to understand, and reunions provide the opportunity to again live together your experiences, and maybe gild the lily a little in retrospect.

  Among ways to find out where and when your old unit will hold its reunion next summer, look for notices published in military-related journals and bulletins.

- All reunions do not follow the same program, but all are based on the same fundamental foundation: patriotism, friendships, and that special martial pride that George L. Skypeck had in mind when he penned these (extracted) words: "I was that which others did not want to be . . . I went where others feared to go . . . and am proud of what I was . . . a soldier."

51

Inculcating Martial Pride

WE BELONG TO the proudest profession on earth, the profession of arms in defense of our country. Looking back now, I have always had that special pride—the pride of being a soldier. Yet my book of familiar quotations denigrates the word "pride": from "Pride is the vice of fools," to "There was pride on Casey's face . . ."—that famous day in Mudville when the mighty Casey struck out.

My dictionary adds to the confusion with various definitions:

1. An undue sense of our own superiority; an inordinate self-esteem; arrogance; conceit. 2. A proper sense of personal dignity and worth; honorable self-respect. 3. That of which one is justly proud; a cause of exultation. 4. The best or most excellent part of anything; the nation's pride. 5. The best time or flowering of something; the pride of summer.

Neither the quotations nor the definitions mention "martial pride," that special intangible the Army strives to inculcate in every soldier and in all military units. While martial pride includes "that of which one is justly proud" in a personal sense, it goes beyond that to include pride in professionalism and military heritage.

More specifically, the martial pride of each soldier is based on four elements: pride in self, pride in unit, pride in service branch, and pride in the nation. To isolate some realities that are the foundation of martial pride, I have reviewed my case in retrospect, a method we octogenarians favor as the simplest and most direct form of research.

Further, since my branch was infantry, this "reverie research" will have a doughboy focus. Much that is written about the Army concerns the close combat of infantry: the fury and flame of battle; mud, sweat, and grinding fatigue; foxhole fear; and the valor of hand-to-hand assault. These are generously apportioned to infantrymen on the battlefield and should be accorded them in the record.

Other branches and services play their vital roles on the battleground and in support operations, but we take nothing from them by recognizing the unique nature of the infantry.

To those unfamiliar with battlefields, the infantry is a vague mass of soldiers in mud-smeared uniforms and is usually found where explosions, flame, and violent death characterize the action—it is something heroic, impersonal, and remote. To the battlewise infantryman, that moving mass of "smoke-begrimed men" includes vital supply and supporting troops, as well as those who fight with long-range weapons and machines. But it is not crowded where he is: the cutting edge in contact.

History reveals the dramatic place of infantry in wars since antiquity. Here are some extracts from the record.

A description of the Assyrian Army, seventh century B.C., reads: "There is an average of 100 foot soldiers to every ten cavalry and every single chariot; the infantry is really the Queen of Assyrian battles."

The great Napoleon Bonaparte said, "Let nothing obscure the fact that good infantry is the sinews of an army."

A summary published at The Infantry School in 1923 put it this way:

Not in one battle nor in one campaign, not in one war nor in one century, did the infantry win the crown Queen of Battles. Enthroned 2,500 years ago, the infantryman's royal place through the succeeding ages has become fixed.

In our own War of Independence, the infantry played its historic primary role—the first armed conflicts at Concord and Bunker Hill were infantry actions. Our infantry heritage is graphically illustrated by the battle of Trenton in New Jersey, which turned an apparently lost cause into triumph and independence.

The brilliantly conceived attack on Trenton stemmed from the genius and courage of Gen. George Washington, whose early experience was in infantry fighting against the French and Indians. The Trenton attack was launched by an infantry-artillery task force, with twenty-four hundred men and nineteen cannon—beginning with the famous night crossing of the ice-clogged Delaware River on 25 December 1776.

This entry from General Washington's diary tells its own stark story:

> Christmas, 6:00 P.M. It is fearful cold and raw and a snow storm is setting in. . . . It will be a terrible night for the soldiers who have no shoes. Some of them have rags tied around their feet, but I have not heard a single man complain.

The victorious result of that daring attack stands out in history; then began the tortuous countermarch back. Before reaching their huts, General Washington's men had marched and fought for as long as fifty hours, some marching as much as fifty miles in the cold. The English historian Sir George O. Trevelyan said of that battle:

> This was a long and severe ordeal, and yet it may be doubted whether so small a number of men ever were employed in so short a space of time with greater or more lasting results upon the history of the world.

This heritage has been amplified in all of our wars since. The bright legacy of infantry was given added gloss by two legendary World War I Medal of Honor winners—Sgt. Alvin York and 1st Lt. Samuel Woodfill.

In World War II, Korea, and Vietnam, infantrymen continued to make the reign of the Queen of Battle illustrious. The old Queen of Battle, with her outdated weapons, was history, but a new Queen, with new weapons and equipment, commanded those battlefields.

General Paul Freeman (infantry), when commandant of The Infantry School, said:

> While a ship may symbolize the Navy and an airplane or long-range missile the Air Force . . . the only adequate symbol of our

Army is man—the frontline soldier. He is not superman, but he must be a little better than most men, a little tougher in character, with stamina, guts, determination, and discipline. . . .

General Bruce C. Clarke (armor) said:

Plain for all to read is a battle record which marks the American infantryman as a man in the eyes of other men. He has stamped his valor on the pages of U.S. history from the slopes of Bunker Hill to the crest of Heartbreak Ridge . . . that he has borne the brunt of sacrifice for his country's sake is told in the casualty figures of all our wars. Respect for the fighting doughboy is shared by . . . all other ground soldiers, particularly those who have known and seen war. . . .

General Maxwell D. Taylor (artillery) said:

As I describe the Army mission, I describe the infantry mission because the infantry will always be the core of the fighting capability of the Army. . . . I often reflected in Korea that we had complete control of the air and sea. We had tremendous destructive power in all the weapons of the Air Force and Navy, and we had a great artillery. Yet . . . victory was measured by . . . terrain objectives. . . . The last 200 yards still had to be taken by a determined man on the ground with his rifle and grenade. . . . There will always be an infantryman in the final act of battle—the man who closes with the enemy on the ground.

These quotations and the last lines of "I Am the Infantry" surpass any words of mine:

Wherever brave men fight . . . and die for freedom, you will find me. I am the bulwark of our Nation's defense. I am always ready . . . now and forever. I am the Infantry—Queen of Battle! Follow Me!

The great pride of my life is this: that under the reigning Queen of my day, I was a combat infantryman. That is how martial pride can be summed up for me, as an infantryman. Each soldier will have his own source of martial pride—from artillery to engineers, armor to aviation, signal corps to quartermaster, from airborne to general staff.

Some comments, with other branch slants:

- Artillerymen will point to (among countless others) Napoleon's fame, beginning with the decisive actions of his batteries at the siege of Toulon (December 1793), and the brilliant young Confederate Maj. John Pelham's spectacular combat artillery actions in the Civil War.
- Armor did not begin with Gen. George S. Patton, Jr., and World War I, but traces its ancestry back through cavalry to chariots, including the climactic cavalry coup de grace in Hannibal's masterpiece battle at Cannae.
- Engineers, signal corps, and other branches have their special sources of martial pride, which are there to be researched and chronicled. Examine the history of your branch, review your own experience, and it will be the same for you as it has been for me. You will feel a renewed and greater martial pride as a soldier in the armed forces of the United States.

APPENDICES

Appendix A

Medal of Honor Citation for Sgt. Charles E. Mower

*MOWER, CHARLES E.

Rank and organization: Sergeant, Company A, 34th Infantry, 24th Infantry Division. *Place and date:* Near Capoocan, Leyte, Philippine Islands, 3 November 1944. *Entered service at:* Chippewa Falls, Wis. *Birth*: Chippewa Falls, Wis. *G.O. No.:* 17, 11 February 1946. *Citation:* He was an assistant squad leader in an attack against strongly defended enemy positions on both sides of a stream running through a wooded gulch. As the squad advanced through concentrated fire, the leader was killed and Sergeant Mower assumed command. In order to bring direct fire upon the enemy, he had started to lead his men across the stream, which by this time was churned by machine-gun and rifle fire, but he was severely wounded before reaching the opposite bank. After signaling his unit to halt, he realized his own exposed position was the most advantageous point from which to direct the attack, and stood fast. Half submerged, gravely wounded, but refusing to seek shelter or accept aid of any kind, he continued to shout and signal to his squad as he directed it in the destruction of two enemy machine guns and numerous riflemen. Discovering that the intrepid man in the stream was largely responsible for the successful action being taken against them, the remaining Japanese concentrated the full force of their firepower upon him, and he was killed while still urging his men on. Sergeant Mower's gallant initiative and heroic determination aided materially in the successful completion of his squad's mission. His magnificent leadership was an inspiration to those with whom he served.

*Posthumous

Appendix B

To the Ultimate Weapon
By Col. Anthony L. P. Wermuth

First in, last out . . .
Fidelio,
The angel Gabriel in a muddy
　helmet,
A flame-charred devil on the
　ninth level of *Inferno*—
The Infantryman!
The fighter's fighter.
The soldier's soldier.
He travels not along the super-
　highways
But along the faint trails of the
　world,
High along the ridges and down
　the defiles,
Tracing the veins and capillaries
On the skin of the earth,
To thrust his bayonet
Personally
Into the incandescent heart of
　battle.
The cost of this trip
Is the highest
Exacted in war.
Not for him the three-
Or ten-hours-a-day war.
Sheltered by a parasol of planes,
Served by men and machines of
　infinite variety,
Reassured by mortars and ships
Prowling the nearby meadows and
　seas,
He is,
Nonetheless,

In light and darkness,
Perpetually
Shadowed
By death.
Until, at last,
On some strange promontory,
In the midst of comrades fallen,
Suddenly,
He stands alone.
The only powers of body and
　spirit
Available
To be summoned
Are such as he happened to bring
To the battle—
To the personal battle
No other man
Is called upon
To undergo.
Sooner or later,
Struggling in the vortex of the
　whirlwind,
Tested over and over again,
With the scarred body,
The bloody fist,
The indomitable heart,
The blistered feet, and
The fighting hands,
He stands alone,
Where the danger is.
The Infantryman
Volunteers for nothing,
But every lethal device in war
Volunteers for him.

When they come after him,
They've tried and failed
With everything else
To reach
The point of power,
The focus of freedom,
The pivot of decision,
And the hottest spot in the war.
Sprawler during every
    opportunity,
Plodder, racer,
Stalker, raider,
Waiter,
Walker over mountains, glaciers,
    and swamps,
Outwitting the machine he witted,
He does what no one else can
    do—
He storms the parapets yet
    untaken
By all the machines
And munitions of war.
He lays his manhood,
Sometimes not yet reached,
On the line,
And sometimes stays forever
    there,
Reformed to a grotesque
Memorial,
Having given a massive
    transfusion
To hills like home
Or desert sands.
If there is blood on his hands,
It is a stain he carries
For every man,
Woman, and child
In friendly lands.
The rifleman lives,
If he does,
On what is left after lending time;
The beloved people
Of his country
Live afterward on borrowed
    time—
His.
Decorated with a flower
Flushed from a field bathed in
deadliness,
Dressed in dirt,
With dusty lungs,
He hardly suggests
The beau ideal
Of every other fighting man.
Too numerous to be distinguished;
Too full of the memory of fear
To swagger;
Too tired to boast;
Too well aware of the luck
Of his own survival
To pontificate;
Too mindful of a platoon
Of missing heroes
To be a hero;
Too grateful to demean any other
    fighter—
If he is unimpressed with others,
It is the natural result of being
    unimpressed
With himself.
He is the personal fighter,
The champion,
The first in and the last out,
The irreplaceable,
The ultimate weapon! . . .
The Infantryman!

Appendix C

An After-Action Report*

There are still memories, ideas, and lessons learned from experience that ask for the light of print, but it is time for this scribe to blow "Recall." More than twenty-seven years have "gone aglimmering" since retirement, and my eighty-fourth birthday is history. While *the human element in uniform has not changed,* the situation has—with new technologies, weapons, fighting vehicles, and all-volunteer Army concepts that are strange to me.

Editor in chief L. James Binder was kind enough to give me this chance for a backward look at how "The Forward Edge" was born and nurtured, because "The Edge" did not spring into being full blown. So this is my aloha in the Hawaiian sense of greetings and farewell.

The physical production of "The Edge" started in the summer of 1966 with a phone call from then-editor John Spore. I had been a periodic contributor to *ARMY* (and its predecessors) since early 1932, and two of my manuscripts were on his desk when he asked if they could be used to begin a monthly column.

So the column began in the September 1966 issue of *ARMY* with "Hell-for-Leather Years," an article about my tribulations as an infantry lieutenant in the troop officers' equitation course (as a riding student only) at the Cavalry School. That was my sixtieth appearance in *ARMY* and its predecessors, including articles under pen names, such as Company Commander, Colonel Riposte, Lieutenant Learning, and Stone Borealis. My second column, "Don't Dim The Glitter," appeared as a new department called "The Forward Edge," which continued regularly, now completing its twenty-first year.

Writing for publication enriched my life in retirement beyond measure with new friends and a new mission. Some readers have written letters to the editor and others have written me personally, from privates

---

*This article, General Newman's farewell to readers of his "The Forward Edge" column, appeared in *ARMY* in January 1988.

to four-star generals, from wives of military men to civilians in various categories. My file of these letters is a private treasure.

My writings also resulted in invitations to speak to varied audiences, ranging from active-duty units (in which I once served) to a couple of graduating second lieutenant classes at The Infantry School. I also spoke at the Command and General Staff College at Fort Leavenworth, Kan., and a combat arms ball at Fort Leonard Wood, Mo., an ROTC graduation at Syracuse University, and to Rangers at Fort Benning, Ga., and Eglin Air Force Base, Fla. All this has not only kept me in touch with the active Army but has aroused my admiration for soldiers in our Army today who are meeting far greater and more complex problems than those in my era.

Finally, "The Forward Edge" brought me the signal honor of the 1983 Distinguished Doughboy Award, an award that is "presented annually on behalf of all infantry officers to a man or woman who has made outstanding contributions to the morale and effectiveness of infantrymen throughout the years."

I am often asked if I have a particular approach or method that formed the foundation for how and why I wrote as I did. The answer is yes. From the beginning, my approach was based on these simple ideas (though I did not write them out; it was more a *feeling*): First, to write what would be helpful to others, because when I was a young lieutenant, nobody lost much effort helping me, and, second, to provide readability, I would write in a simple talking-to-a-soldier style, use illustrative anecdotes, and work in some humor, as opposed to the arid nature of training memoranda.

Another logical question is, "Since you were afflicted with rejection slips before receiving consistent acceptances, what made the difference?"

The answer to that finally seeped through my skull when I wrote a 500-word article—and received several rejection slips. The idea was good, so I revised and condensed it. Then, at 250 words, I received more rejection slips. When I polished it down to 92 words, however, *True* magazine paid twenty-five dollars for it.

The lesson was clear: Revise and revise again to get the fat out of your manuscript. So I began selling "Cerebrations" regularly to the *Infantry Journal,* writing the first draft in about 1,500 words, then revising to 600 to 800 words . . . and received fifteen consecutive acceptances.

This may seem a tiresome method, but for me, multiple drafts and meticulous revisions were necessary for magazine articles.

For "The Edge," my initial draft was around 2,000 or more words, ending with the published article from 1,500 to not more than 1,600 words. This was laborious, but it beats writing several articles and getting them back unpublished. Besides, revising is interesting—constantly seeking just the right words that fit.

Since *ARMY* readers are potential contributors, it may be of interest to backtrack the road I traveled that made "The Edge" possible. At the outset, it is well to recognize the validity of Mortimer Snerd's answer to Charlie McCarthy's question, "Mortimer, how can you be so stupid?"

Mortimer's timeless reply, "It ain't easy!" applies to most successful endeavors, which include writing for publication.

After graduating from the U.S. Military Academy in 1925, I was back there in 1931—this time as an Army lieutenant on an athletic detail trying (unsuccessfully) to repeat my 1928 membership on the American Olympic Team in the modern pentathlon. It was my athletic swan song, bringing with it the realization that, athletically speaking, I would increasingly resemble the "old gray mare." I was not what I used to be.

It was then that I understood that competitive athletics had been my hobby for years; so, while I would continue recreational sports, I needed a lifetime hobby.

I made an estimate of the hobby situation, listing the requirements this hobby must have:

- One to follow the rest of my life.
- One that was independent of geographical location and climate.
- One I could exercise in sickness and old age.
- One that involved no excessive impedimenta or cost, but which had some potential for revenue.
- One that would be of value professionally while on active duty, if possible.
- One I could work at as little or as much as I wanted.

Next, I listed possible hobby interests and studied the value of each hobby against the requirements. This was easy, because free-lance writing answered all my requirements.

I bought a portable typewriter, subscribed to *Writer's Digest,* and taught myself touch-typing. My first article, "Carpentry on Commutation," illustrated with photographs and sketches of furniture I had made from packing boxes, was published in the *Infantry Journal* in early 1932. Then the rejection slips started coming.

My first overseas tour was in Hawaii (1933–35) at Schofield Barracks. Serendipity soon made me a local moonlighting reporter for the evening newspaper the Honolulu *Star-Bulletin,* which was an invaluable experience and a welcome addition to my paycheck.

Concurrently, I continued to receive rejection slips from various magazines, took correspondence courses with the *Writer's Digest*— and became a company commander in the 26th Infantry at Plattsburgh Barracks, N.Y. It was there that I began writing "Cerebrations" (under pen names) for the *Infantry Journal.*

In addition to learning the value of revisions and condensing, I also found what I wanted to write about: *the interaction of the human element in military service with the professional requirements of the Army, based on my experience and presented in a readable fashion to be helpful to others.* World War II interrupted this program while I was on my second tour in Hawaii, but the pattern was clearly established.

After the war, in the spring of 1948, I recorded my wartime experience as a regimental commander in combat in a two-part article on the theme "Planned Leadership." This was published under the title "Command Performance" in the July and August 1948 issues of the *Infantry Journal.*

Other articles published before my retirement were based on service with airborne troops (command and staff) and in various high-level staff assignments in joint and theater-level commands and also as chief of staff of a unified command. This varied service provided experience for later use in "The Edge."

After retirement in 1960 (after nearly thirty-five years of commissioned service), the general pattern of my writing continued, but its scope broadened. In addition to military-related themes, there were sales to minor civilian publications. This included a dozen fiction stories— to *Alfred Hitchcock's Mystery Magazine* and *Mike Shayne Mystery Magazine,* and one to *Zane Grey Western Magazine* (to see if I could)— but my heart was not in fiction, so I began an autobiography with the focus on the human element in military service.

Then that call came from editor John Spore; thus, the nature of my writing changed and so did my whole purpose and outlook. It was as if I were going back and reliving my experience in the Army.

As I wrote in "The Edge" about happenings when I commanded Company G, 26th Infantry, names, faces, and events became clear. I served again in retrospect with 1st Sgt. James S. Redding and the other eight sergeants there when I assumed command. To write about them and the lessons learned there gave new purpose to my life in retirement. Each manuscript was written and rewritten in an effort to get it just right, in the hope that how it was for me yesterday would be of some interest and value to soldiers and young officers today.

Now, it may be clear why I have summarized my learning pains in writing for publication. Without that training and experience, I would not have been ready to write "The Forward Edge" when the opportunity came. My shoe box file of notes collected over the years on active duty now proved useful. Also, it was fortunate that I understood how 92 words could be worth twenty-five dollars, but that the same idea in 500 words was worthless, so every article went through multiple drafts.

Few readers would believe (if I had kept count) the number of hours I spent on what, as you read them, seem simple little narratives from memory, but writing "The Edge" was not really work; each was a fine visit to the past with so many wonderful soldiers. It was a pleasure and privilege to strive to bring each memory to life.

One last question could be asked: "Did you originate any technique, method, or procedure in writing The Edge?" The answer is, "Yes, the use of *Comments* as an ending."

The basic form for a story or an article is a beginning, a middle, and an end. The old country preacher said it best: "First, I tell them what I'm going to tell them; next, I tell them; then I tell them what I done told them."

Of course, that presumes you have something to say; therefore, the first requirement is an idea or a theme—as illustrated in my February 1987 "Forward Edge," which can be outlined along these lines:

Title: The Commander's Proper Place in Battle.

Opening narrative hook: To catch the reader's attention and introduce the subject—incident of the Ranger captain who informed me I was not in the proper place in the action when my regiment landed on Leyte in the Philippines (20 October 1944).

Body of the article: List personal-knowledge incidents and anec-dotes bearing on the theme; also relevant case history anecdotes from World War II in Europe.

Ending, some comments: Not conclusions, not recommendations, not a summary—just *comments* that reflect my views or points to remember. If I had not stumbled on the comments-ending technique, it would have been far more difficult to continue "The Edge" so long.

The number of comments varies with their strength, length, and relevance to the theme, and may include facts or anecdotes not previously mentioned. All are listed independently with no connecting wording.

But enough about the genesis of "The Forward Edge."

Of my 230-odd articles appearing in *ARMY* (and its predecessors), some 185 were written after retirement, and 172 of them were "Forward Edge" columns. Upon reflection, it is clear that I have had the unique experience and special privilege of living my active-duty life *twice*.

The first time was with actual members of the organizations in which I served—and I am still in contact with many of them, especially members of the 24th Infantry Division in which I served during World War II.

The second time around was with members of our present Army who shared my experiences from the actual first time around through reading "The Forward Edge," and they have written uncounted let-ters to me.

It is just as hard to retire this time as it was to end my active-duty years; but in each case, it has been a simple recognition that the time has come. There are no regrets, just heartfelt thanks for my years on active duty in the U.S. Army with the wonderful soldiers of all ranks with whom it was my great privilege to share service.

As I remember the Old Army and admire the far more complicated Army of today, I will continue assembling my next book. If a good article subject coalesces in my mind along with supporting informa-tion, however, I will submit it for consideration elsewhere in *ARMY*.

Finally, as I wait for my last bugle call, I like the way Alfred Lord Tennyson said it: "Moonlight and Evening Star, and one clear call for me . . ."